COGNATION AND SOCIAL ORGANIZATION
IN SOUTHEAST ASIA

Cover design: Hans Borkent

VERHANDELINGEN
VAN HET KONINKLIJK INSTITUUT
VOOR TAAL-, LAND- EN VOLKENKUNDE

145

COGNATION
AND SOCIAL ORGANIZATION
IN SOUTHEAST ASIA

Edited by

Frans Hüsken and Jeremy Kemp

1991

KITLV Press

Leiden

Published by:

KITLV Press
Koninklijk Instituut voor Taal-, Land- en Volkenkunde
(Royal Institute of Linguistics and Anthropology)
P.O. Box 9515
2300 RA Leiden
The Netherlands

CIP-GEGEVENS KONINKLIJKE BIBIOTHEEK, DEN HAAG

Cognation

Cognation and social organization in Southeast Asia / ed. by Frans Hüsken and Jeremy
Kemp. - Leiden : KITLV Press. - (Verhandelingen van het Koninklijk Instituut voor
Taal-, Land- en Volkenkunde ; 145)
Met bibliogr., index.
ISBN 90-6718-030-0
Trefw.: relatievormen ; Zuidoost-Azië / sociaal milieu ; Zuidoost-Azië.

ISBN 90 6718 030 0

Printed in the Netherlands

Contents

MAP OF SOUTHEAST ASIA

Figures refer to the locations discussed in the chapters of this volume:
(1) Borneo (Victor King), (2) Bali (Mark Hobart), (3) Kerinci (C.W. Watson), (4) Negeri Sembilan (Maila Stivens), (5) North Central Thailand (Jeremy Kemp), (6) Langkawi Island (Janet Carsten), (7) Pahang (Bill Wilder), (8) Pahang (Josiane Massard), (9) Central Java (Frans Hüsken), (10a) Central Java (Willem Wolters), (10b) Central Luzon (Willem Wolters), (11) Negros Occidental (Rosanne Rutten), (12) Kedah (Diana Wong).

Cognatic Kinship in Southeast Asia

Jeremy Kemp and Frans Hüsken

'Southeast Asia' as a popularly recognized distinctive cultural and social entity is of comparatively recent origin and the significance of external rather than local, internal, factors in determining the general currency and boundaries of its present designation must still be recognized.[1] For anthropologists there are no superficially simple universals to distinguish the region and identify its would-be interpreters as have existed for historians, among whom the concept of 'Indianization' has been a major focus in the analysis of state societies 'East of India and South of China'.

That said, in the field of social and cultural studies two important themes in the contributions of anthropologists working on Southeast Asia have been in the realm of kinship, with the interpretation of what came to be known as *prescriptive marriage alliance* and *cognatic systems*. The former, which achieved early prominence, was at the heart of what J.P.B. de Josselin de Jong first elucidated in 1935 as the so-called Field of Ethnological Study (FES) (1977:169). This approach, to the extent that it almost became a sub-discipline in its own right, left a clear imprint on Indonesian ethnology for many years.

In contrast, cognatic systems were for a long time neglected if not totally ignored, and even today do not receive the attention that one might legitimately assume to be their due given their demographic preponderance (the majority of Southeast Asia's population living in cognatic social environments) and association with both simple and complex societies. This neglect was not, we argue, the result of any intrinsic characteristics of Southeast Asian social organization but rather an outcome of the history of ethnographic research and the predominant theoretical concerns determining the development of anthropological analysis.

While pioneering anthropologists did field-research in Southeast Asia, the area was by no means a major arena for field-workers and this was especially so as far as the emerging discipline of social anthropology was concerned. Hence, among the early studies of the *'adat* law school' (Van Vollenhoven 1918), of

---

1. See Emerson (1984) for an outline and discussion of the emergence of Southeast Asia as a distinct field of study.

village organizations and the state (e.g. Van Leur 1955 [1934]; Gourou 1936), just as in much later classics such as Cora Du Bois' social-psychological study *The People of Alor* (1960 [1944]), Rosemary Firth's *Housekeeping Among Malay Peasants* (1966 [1943]) and H.N.C. Stevenson's analysis of Chin economics (1968 [1943]) the focus was other than kinship.

Where kinship did appear as a primary element in the literature it was mainly, as indicated above, in the Dutch ethnological tradition, being concerned mainly with Indonesian societies with lineages. There, the specific ethnological concern with original forms and the structuralist interpretation of the dualism and 'asymmetrical connubium' of what Geertz called the 'ur-society' (1961:500–1) resulted in concentration on the lineal systems of eastern and western Indonesia. The 'deviant' patterns of the central part of the archipelago, Borneo, and of course Java, where there was a general absence of lineal organization, were consequently largely ignored as far as the analysis of kinship was concerned.[2]

Southeast Asian ethnography was not the only field where cognation received very little attention. More generally, this neglect of non-lineal forms was associated with the fact that in anthropology as a whole the dominant focus of ethnographic research lay elsewhere. Thus it was that in 1950, with kinship studies still very much at the heart of the discipline, it remained possible for an eminent social anthropologist like Radcliffe-Brown to write confidently of the rarity of cognatic systems.[3] This was no peculiar prejudice of his as at that time there was relatively little material available to contradict such a view. The lack was due not just to the geographical bias of the day with its emphasis, for British anthropologists in particular, on Africa, but to the contemporary theoretical concern with corporate groups as elements of social structure. With rare exceptions such as the work by R.F. Barton in Luzon (1919; 1949), the potentially rich Southeast Asian ethnography of cognatic organization remained unrealized until well after the Second World War.

When in the 1950s anthropologists did at last turn their attention to cognatic systems their early articles were primarily concerned with societies in which some form of kin-linked corporate but non-unilinear organization existed, as exemplified in the case of papers by Goodenough on the Gilbert Islands (1955), Firth on the Maori (1957, 1963), and Davenport (1959). Still, however, at that stage the ethnographic focus of this type of research remained outside Southeast Asia.

The publication in 1960 of the collection of essays *Social Structure in Southeast Asia* focusing largely on cognatic forms of social organization could therefore be

---

2. The one apparent exception is primarily a reinterpretation of Javanese historical texts seeking to subsume Java within the dualist model of eastern and western Indonesia (Rassers 1922).

3. 'Cognatic systems are rare, not only in Africa but in the world at large. The reasons have already been indicated: it is difficult to establish and maintain a wide-range system on a purely cognatic basis; it is only a unilineal system that will permit the division of a society into separate organized kin-groups.' (Radcliffe-Brown 1950:82.)

considered an important landmark in the study of the region. However, looking back at it a quarter of a century later it is difficult to assess its contemporary impact and, for various reasons, the volume now appears quite odd and in some respects unduly dated. Despite the fact that several contributions have been frequently quoted the collection as such failed to stimulate new research and its subsequent influence on later work has been curiously limited. This was primarily due to the framework imposed by the editor, G. P. Murdock, and the rather programmatic introduction in which he attempted to point out new directions for further research on theoretical classification and general concept definition. In fact, with only a few exceptions no subsequent research was conducted along any of the suggested lines.[4] Nevertheless it is important to note that the collection was one of the first major academic publications to specify the region by its now recognized appellation. Yet even in this respect the inclusion of Ceylon (Sri Lanka) and Formosa (Taiwan) would nowadays elicit surprise and probable repudiation (cf. Emerson 1984).

A more telling criticism though, which lies at the heart of the limited long-term impact of the book as a whole as well as of the individual essays, is that made by a reviewer (Goody 1965:61–2) concerning the manner in which social structure is made to equal kinship. This was a perspective already elaborated by Murdock in an earlier work (*Social Structure*, 1949) in which kinship patterns constituted the framework for the discussion of social structure and the basis upon which societies were to be classified and ordered for comparative analysis.[5] Hence the Sinhalese and Javanese were described and analysed in much the same way as the Iban and 'Aboriginal People of Formosa', an extraordinarily cavalier treatment given the enormous variations in scale and complexity.

In many respects then the collection was an example of being 'too little and too late', it represented the end of an era rather than, as it professes to be, a foray into the future. Even so, Murdock's opening essay 'Cognatic forms of social organization' remains a convenient starting point for a discussion of the vicissitudes of Southeast Asian kinship studies in the post-war period. This is because of what it reveals of immediately preceding developments in kinship analysis and the very marked character of the change since 1960 as established 'truths' came under attack.[6] Although Murdock comments that others have defined cognatic systems negatively, he begins the same way with a discussion of unilineal descent and corporate groups. Noting that 'at least one third of the societies of the world

4. Research instigated by Murdock includes a paper on the kindred by Koentjaraningrat in *Ethnology* (1968), and the discussions by Louis Berthe of state versus lineage structure in Java (1970).

5. The chapter headings are revealing in themselves: the nuclear family, composite forms of the family; consanguineal kin groups; the clan; the community; analysis of kinship; determinants of kinship terminology; evolution of social organization; the regulation of sex; incest taboos and their extensions; social law of sexual choice.

6. As exemplified, for instance, by *Rethinking Kinship and Marriage* (Needham ed. 1971).

are not unilineal' (1960:2) he then refers to the considerable variation in terms used to designate such systems and proceeds to draw up a general classificatory framework by no means restricted to the region.

This turns out to be based on the assumed association between a system of kin-term classification and other patterns of social organization. That enables Murdock to engage in some typology building. Claiming that five of the systems described in the volume have many features in common, he 'aligns' them with the 'Eskimo' subtype, for which he offers eight definitive criteria consisting of a mixture of broad empirical generalization and linguistic distinctions. A detailed critical analysis of these criteria and the validity of their assignment to the actual societies listed as fulfilling them is beyond the scope of this chapter as well as historically irrelevant to the issues discussed in this volume. Nevertheless, it is appropriate to note the structural determinism of such an approach, which by now has been abandoned by most anthropologists.

Nowadays, there is a reluctance to classify societies according to their descent system or even to see the classification of descent as consisting of mutually exclusive categories. Furthermore, many anthropologists refuse to discuss kinship as a discrete area of study which can be described and discussed without reference to social context. It is also arguable that anthropologists who, since the early 1960s, turned to the study of complex peasant societies perceived the kind of framework presented by Murdock to be irrelevant. On the other hand, where Murdock's framework was influential its effects were negative. His crude generalizations, to the effect that the household was a corporate group and the largest significant kin unit, legitimized the little attention given to kinship matters in subsequent anthropological field-work in the state societies of the region with their bilateral organization.

Of course, Murdock is not the only one responsible for this trend in Southeast Asian kinship research. The same period of the 1960s saw another shift in focus on the part of the growing numbers of anthropologists working in Southeast Asia. The most lively fields of study and debate shifted away from the classic domains of cultural and social anthropology, the study of 'primitive social organization' and, in particular, the idea of kinship as its major structuring principle.[7] Instead, research focused far more on peasant societies and especially upon the problems of social and cultural transformation. In Southeast Asia that involved a turn towards the densely populated and generally cognatic heartlands: the Thai Central Plain, Central Luzon, Java and the Malay peninsula, which proved to be a fertile breeding ground for a new type of anthropology. In the words of Hans-Dieter Evers:

> social scientists had to develop new concepts and new theories to tackle the empirical problems posed by their objects of research. Thus Boeke used the term of 'dual

---

7. See for example *The Social Anthropology of Complex Societies* edited by Banton (1966) based on the ASA conference held in 1963 entitled 'New Approaches in Social Anthropology'.

organization' for his analysis of colonial Indonesia, Furnivall, dealing with Burma and Indonesia invented the concept of 'plural society', Embree coined the term 'loosely structured social system' by contrasting Japanese with Thai rural society, and Geertz brought out his theory of 'agricultural involution' after comparing Javanese development with that of Japan. (Evers 1980:2.)

One might, of course, add to this list the discussions about the character of the Southeast Asian village community, social stratification and patron-clientage, the problems of ethnicity, and state formation. Conspicuously lacking were any comparable theoretical developments or even descriptive ethnographic interest in the cognatic systems of major regions of Southeast Asia where most anthropological research was now being carried out. One was left with Geertz's reference to the 'so-called bilateral systems – a highly unsatisfactory residual sort of category' (1962:23). Overall then, Murdock's conclusion that kin ties outside the small circle of the nuclear family were of minimal importance were supported by new anthropological research in the 1960s and the subject largely disappeared from view in the study of complex societies.

Another, very different, though contemporary theoretical landmark in the study of cognatic systems, and one which is still of interest, was Freeman's essay 'On the concept of the kindred', published in 1961. Whereas this paper has certainly not been ignored, the issues it raised have generated most response with respect to simpler societies. There, the assumption that kinship was of primary structural importance became an issue of lively debate, as exemplified by the work of Jerôme Rousseau on the significance of rank (cf. King this volume). Furthermore, it is now clear just how selective these responses to Freeman were, in that the discussion of the concept of 'stock' which potentially brings together the discussion on kinship and stratification was not taken up for many years despite Freeman's very pertinent comments on the consolidation of linkages.[8] For a long time, then, the implications of genealogical connection and systematic in-marriage for the study of at least some sectors of the complex societies of the region were misunderstood or overlooked.[9]

Freeman's first aim was a critique of the considerable inconsistencies in the use of the word kindred and their deviation from the original Early Middle English. After re-establishing its usage for the recognition of linkages through both males and females, he proceeded to emphasize that the unit so designed was a 'category'

8. A stock consists of all those descended in both lines from a common ancestor. As Freeman noted, where 'the marriage of cousins is continued generation by generation, this results in a continuing consolidation of stocks and produces a closer cognatic network than in societies in which the marriage of close cognates does not occur. This, I would suggest, is a most significant feature of some bilateral societies, for while they lack the large-scale descent groups of unilineal societies, their cognatic networks are close and cohesive and so of great importance in the multiplex relations of social life.' (Freeman 1961:207.)

9. See, for example, the discussion of marriage rules and stratification among Thai and Malay elites in Kemp (1978).

and not a group.[10] This essentially simple point is one which many still fail to grasp, no doubt due in part to Murdock's persistent use of the latter word, though one must also note the historical role of group-centred concepts and theories in so much of social anthropology. The result has been a sometimes tediously convoluted discussion, most obviously among Borneo specialists, of the definition of kindreds and their significance, which arguably misses the whole point of what Freeman was trying to do.

Perhaps one reason for this is that while Freeman carefully spells out why the kindred is a category or 'set' without group characteristics he nonetheless writes of 'membership' and indeed his prose understandably reflects the especially predominant group-oriented perceptions of the period. It was still to be some time before the discussion of social networks and 'non-groups' really began to make its mark. Even so, he specifically contends that:

> for the proper understanding of societies in which bilateral kindreds occur that a distinction must be made between (1) the kindred as a cognatic category, and (2) the kindred-based action groups formed from time to time for specific purposes, which ordinarily contain only a proportion of the total kindred, and also, on occasion, non-kindred in the shape of affines and friends. (Freeman 1961:203.)

In retrospect it is evident that in elucidating the concept Freeman was at pains to avoid the 'sin' of reification and treat kindred as concrete forms of social organization. Yet this is exactly what many have committed with confused and confusing results, especially when they made attempts at comparative analysis.

There is no need here to rehearse the discussion about the irreducibility of kinship (Needham 1971; Schneider 1972); the debate has passed well beyond that. What remains necessary is further consideration of the interplay between ideas, ideology, categories, and the circumstances and situations in which they play a part in structuring social activities. It was precisely these issues and questions which lay at the basis of the seminar on 'Cognatic Forms of Social Organization in Southeast Asia' held in Amsterdam in 1983 and which were the pivot of the discussions held there. The seminar was a gathering of anthropologists with a strong interest and field-work experience in the empirical analysis of social organizations in the region.[11]

The present volume is the outcome of these and subsequent discussions and addresses some of the major fields of debate on Southeast Asian cognation. These may be broadly defined as:

10. '[B]y the very nature of its composition, the members of a kindred have no collective perception of unity, no persisting common objective and no leader or organization. A kindred, therefore, is not a group in the sociological sense of the term, but rather a category of cognates, a set of persons who have in common the characteristic that they are all related cognatically in varying degrees to the same person.' (Freeman 1961:202.)

11. The region's countries covered by the participants at the seminar include Thailand, Malaysia, Indonesia and the Philippines. Given the restricted research opportunities in the other parts of Southeast Asia, viz. Burma and Indochina, we were not able to achieve as complete a regional coverage as we had wished.

1. the distinction between cognatic and unilineal systems and the extent to which such classifications are mutually exclusive;
2. the relation between kinship and that other important domain of social organization generally designated 'community'; and
3. the part played by kinship in political and economic affairs.

Nevertheless, what is readily obvious from perusal of the present collection is that for most contributors 'kinship' does not represent a distinct class of phenomena: domestic relations and kin linkages are intimately connected to the domains of production, politics, religion, or whatever.[12] Indeed, much of the material discussed here arises not from some specific project to study kinship per se, but rather from the experience, while in the pursuit of other topics, of 'discovering' at the local level the importance of kin ties exceeding the boundaries of the family or household. Seen from that perspective, this collection reflects an attempt at bringing kinship back into the anthropological study of Southeast Asia's peasant societies.

Reconstituting cognation:
The dynamics and dimensions of cognatic kinship

In introducing the present collection, it seems obvious to do so according to the three themes mentioned above. In fact, that is the way in which the Amsterdam seminar was organized. This, of course, poses a problem as several contributors do not confine themselves to one of these thematic boundaries; even in Southeast Asia 'reality' is rarely one-dimensional. Nevertheless, allowing for some overlap, all authors address themselves predominantly to one of the three themes of the seminar. We will therefore discuss them in that order.

Given the place of the Borneo ethnography of cognatic organization, King's contribution is a timely review and assessment of the longstanding debate on the association of kin and rank. He documents the way in which 'classical' approaches to kinship with their clear essentialist positivism set up a major dichotomy in the analysis of Borneo societies, placing 'kin-based' in opposition to ranked systems. A root cause of this seems to have been the difficulty many, including Freeman, had in accepting the implications and consequences of recognizing that the kindred is, by definition, a category. In practice, many anthropologists made more of the kindred as a concrete social entity than either the concept or the ethnographic data could sustain. A result was that where societies were egalitarian and what some would term 'kin-based', the kindred was often isolated as a significant structural feature, but where the society was hierarchically stratified its importance or even existence was denied. Thus King

---

12. This is, of course, a perspective already familiar in classical functionalist approaches which is, however, all too often abandoned in accounts dealing with the subject.

himself abandoned any reference to the kindred in his own work on the Maloh of Kalimantan.

King's conclusions may seem unduly negative, but they have to be seen more within the positivist character of the debate and are concerned with repudiating the falsely ambitious attempt to make the kindred or even bilateral kinship itself general structural features which could serve as frameworks for the comparative analysis of Borneo societies. He thus echoes Godelier in affirming that whereas in ranked societies kinship relations undoubtedly exist, they have lost 'their capacity to be the general form of social relations'. That the debate should have proceeded as it did is itself interesting. It reflects not so much Freeman's work but Murdock's, who explicitly rejected the interpretation of the kindred 'merely as a "category"' as this would 'deprive it of all utility as an analytic tool' (1964:134).[13]

Just how much things have changed since Murdock's time with the repudiation of descent systems as being a means of objectively classifying and analysing social systems is revealed in all three sections of the present volume. It is documented not just in discussions of political economy and community organization, but in the basic classifications anthropologists make and the implications they have for theory and methodology. The shift is apparent in the three articles following King's, most especially in that of Hobart. Such classifications are ways of looking at things and Hobart provocatively indicates this by examining Balinese social organization from both a patrilineal and a cognatic perspective. His contribution, moreover, is part of an epistemological critique of anthropological praxis in general, and as such it is an explicit repudiation of '[c]lassical approaches, such as the Aristotelian, [which] organize particulars by reference to essential, or definitive, properties possessed by proper class members'. For him, category terms and, for that matter, classifications such as agnation or cognation 'do not denote unambiguous classes of person any more than those who turned up can easily be pigeon-holed', and are, basically, anthropological constructions or 'self-confirming hypotheses'.

Watson does not go so far as Hobart in his rejection of categories and deconstruction of received anthropological wisdom. Nonetheless he too is aware of the extent to which a conceptual framework determines how social relations are perceived by demonstrating how a shift in that framework can result in a very different impression. In the case of the North Sumatran Kerinci both cognatic and matrilineal perspectives 'work' in their respective places: classifications like 'matrilineal' and 'cognatic' are not mutually exclusive global designations. The point here is not that within a society with unilineal descent we also find kinship, which is *per se* cognatic, but rather that different elements of the politico-jural domain are handled quite distinctly in different ways.

13. Murdock did so in his magisterial dismissal of Mitchell's article (1963) on the kindred. This article, partly because it was published independently and nearly at the same time as Freeman's, did not receive the attention it deserved.

From a somewhat different perspective Maila Stivens also attacks an established 'truth', namely the idea that matriliny is associated with a weak state
organization. She tries to show the converse, how matrifocality can be seen to
be increasing with the progressive penetration of capitalism. Underlying this
thought is the realization that to classify a society such as Rembau in Negeri
Sembilan as matrilineal on account of its *adat perpatih* is a crass simplification.
Further, the balance changes over time as well as receives a different emphasis
from individuals depending on their age: *adat* is by no means a unitary phenomenon. One must recognize the existence of both matrilineal and cognatic
elements as well as the distinction between ideology and practice.

Following these contributions discussing basic theoretical and epistemological
problems by contrasting cognation with unilineal systems, the next sections are
concerned with the dynamics of cognation, community and political economy.

The second section focuses on the territorial domain, on what might be
broadly described as the relationship between kinship and community. Three
of the chapters, those of Kemp, Massard and Carsten, are concerned with the
empirical analysis of social organization in villages and examine the interplay
of 'kin-based' and 'community-based' behaviours. Kin categories are used by
participants in ordering social relations within the village or local 'community'.

Kemp demonstrates how these concepts of kin and kin relations play an important part in maintaining cultural and social continuity in a changing context
in North-Central Thailand. What should be borne in mind is that the relationship also works the other way round, it is a two-way process. Kinship is a set of
symbolic relations; it cannot be reduced to neighbourhood nor may neighbourhood be simply rendered in terms of kinship. Instead the two dovetail together
to create a new set of meanings. As Kemp states it, 'kinship and locality create
a degree of stability and a means of integrating and structuring the relations of
individuals with the result that for them and other people from the surrounding
area [the settlement of] Hua Kok is far more than a physical locale'.

In Langkawi, the island where Carsten did her field-work, some of the key
communal values are expressed not by kinship as such but by the *bisan* relationship between pairs of in-laws. A kin terminology is, of course, a means of
expressing a universal hierarchy whereas the special quality of the *bisan* tie in
the Langkawi context is its expression of an ideal of equality. Carsten links this
with the social isolation of the island and stress on egalitarianism. *Bisan* stands
for the idea of villagers claiming to be on the same footing as one another and
bound by mutual obligations. The case is an instructive one, as the *bisan* concept
is by no means limited to Langkawi. It can be found elsewhere in Southeast Asia
as well, but its special, possibly unique, significance in Langkawi can only be
understood in the context of that particular social situation.

Elsewhere this emphasis on equality is less pronounced and other elements
come to the fore. Wilder's discussion of the various levels of kin categories among

the Pahang Malays is another repudiation of the conventional anthropological desire to render things unambiguous. What one sees is that these various levels utilizing a variety of different cultural categories constitute a series of principles of association, resort to which has be analysed in terms of social context. As he observes, Malay kinship is many things, not one.

Massard, writing also on the Pahang Malays, considers the interconnection between kinship and exchange. In the demonstration that kinship is used in both 'equal' and 'hierarchical' exchange her contribution is again a warning against the simplistic association between, for example, kinship and generalized reciprocity. The linkage between kinship and commensality is, of course, well recognized but Massard also depicts a still frequently overlooked aspect: the issue of gender, and she places special emphasis on both the extent to which women prepare food and then are the donors and recipients of such items. Given the interconnection between kinship, neighbourhood, religious values and hierarchy, people do develop various strategies which emphasize very different dimensions of existing patterns of social relations. Depending on the particular context kinship is an important element, but to claim some simple 'primacy' for it even at the level of values is, as Massard shows, far too superficial.

The third and final section of the volume is concerned with kinship and access to resources, particularly in relation to social differentiation and stratification. Some of these aspects are also relevant to the preceding sections but here the emphasis is much more explicitly on what one may term the issues of political economy.

Hüsken's contribution challenges the received view of the insignificance of kinship and marriage in Java beyond the confines of the household. He also links this challenge with a recognition of the considerable extent to which social differentiation may exist within the village. His own research revealed that wider networks of kinship can be particularly important in the realm of village politics and the control of land. He documents the role of a particular family who have managed to exercise control over a considerable amount of land and other key local resources for more than a century.

In his comparison of a Javanese with a Philippine village Wolters analyses the extent to which marriage strategies are the means by which local and regional elites try to maintain control of land, economic and political resources. Especially interesting are the circumstances in which systematic choices with respect to in- or out-marriage appear to be made. It is strikingly apparent that these patterns cannot be explained just in terms of norms but have to be analysed with reference to the types of resources controlled.

The Javanese material in particular demonstrates the frequently asserted truism that those with no resources have fewer kin and that it matters less with whom and where they marry. Of course, it is dangerous to assume the universal validity of such a generalization. On occasion the situation can be different, as

Rosanne Rutten illustrates with data from Negros in the Philippines. There, among the landless, kin ties can be an important factor in attempts to gain access to work. This chapter is also interesting for its discussion of the problems arising out of the conflict between kinship and 'class solidarity' with respect to the actions of trade unions and attempts to mobilize support.

In the last contribution to the volume, Diana Wong discusses the relationship between kinship and economic resources in a village on the North Kedah Plains. She refers to the proposition associated with Chayanov that in peasant societies 'access to resources depends mainly on control over family labour and that this control is intimately connected with the demographic composition of the house-hold'. In contrast, Wong indicates the reverse and shows how the existence and specific nature of these resources affect household membership by analysing the way in which the inter-generational transfer of resources is managed.

Taken together, the collection provides ample evidence of the extent to which cognation remains a valuable avenue both for exploring and for analysing social organization in Southeast Asia. If not definable as a separate field of study it is nonetheless clearly a major dimension of social relations which has received far too little attention. Unlike Murdock's forerunner this introduction is in no way definitive or programmatic in intention. However, it does reintegrate the subject into the wider discourse on the region and calls for a renewed perusal of the issues raised by the individual authors. These open up a series of hitherto largely neglected aspects of social relations, an omission which has occurred much to the detriment of our understanding of the area and the dynamics of its social organization.

Part I

Cognation and Unilineal Descent:
Theoretical Considerations

Cognation and Rank in Borneo

Victor T. King

Any discussion of the central issues and controversies surrounding the study of the problematical notion of 'cognatic kinship' would be incomplete without some reference to the anthropological literature on the indigenous societies of Borneo. Indeed, anthropological investigations of certain Borneo societies have played an important part in formulating various concepts and in shaping particular debates within the study of cognatic social organization. In this context some of the penetrating work of Freeman on the Iban and Appell's wide-ranging edited volume *The Societies of Borneo* (1976) immediately spring to mind.

This essay draws together and comments on some of the writings on Bornean social organization insofar as these relate to my main focus of interest, which is the relation between cognation and rank. Before launching into my theme, I should say something about the concept of the kindred, since it has usually connected in one way or another with cognation in Borneo. For example, Murdock pointed to the kindred (along with the 'small family') as a key structural element in societies like those in Borneo. These he labelled 'bilateral' societies and categorized them as a definite sub-type of his general category of 'cognatic' societies (1960:2–7). Furthermore, in his survey of Sarawak peoples, Leach isolated the 'personal kindred' as one principle, among others, of a 'Bornean type of pattern of organisation' (1950:61–2), initially defining the kindred as comprising 'the whole body of an individual's [recognized] relatives'. The three studies of indigenous Borneo societies, which arose from Leach's recommendations in his *Social Science Research in Sarawak* (1950), all deal in varying degrees with the kindred. Freeman's Iban (1970) and Geddes' Bidayuh Land Dayaks (1954) are relatively egalitarian societies, while Morris' Coastal Melanau (1953) were, at least traditionally, noticeably stratified. Subsequently Freeman went beyond his specific examination of the Iban kindred to write a general theoretical paper entitled 'On the Concept of the Kindred' (1961). Freeman defined it as 'that cognatic category which embraces all of an individual's father's kin, and all of his (or her) mother's kin' (1970:67 and 1960:70 ff). Freeman further conceptualized it as 'spreading upwards and outwards from an individual standing at its centre, or base' and as an 'uncircumscribed grouping, extending indefinitely outwards' (1970:67). Finally he held that 'it is usual for kindred to admit a special obligation toward one another: an obligation to give help and support in culturally determined ways' (1961:209).

Even in the studies by Freeman, Geddes and Morris various aspects of the concept of the kindred posed certain logical and descriptive problems, but looking at this early literature one could be forgiven for assuming that the kindred was a characteristic feature of Borneo societies. This assumption might in turn entail the view that 'cognatic kinship' operated in much the same sort of way and exhibited much the same sorts of characteristics, despite some differences in detail, in a range of Borneo societies, and that therefore 'cognation' and its structural attributes were positive defining criteria of a distinct type of society. I shall shortly want to question this orientation, and rather than focus on assumed similarities between Borneo societies, I shall be concerned with certain significant social differences.

I have taken up some of the conceptual and analytical problems in relation to the kindred elsewhere in a critical survey of the relevant literature on Borneo (King 1976). There I addressed some of my remarks to Freeman's work, and I do not want to revive that discussion. I would still maintain that there are problems which remain unresolved in kindred analysis, viz. ego-centredness, the status of affinal kin, and the relationship between obligation and choice. However, though I would hold to various of my statements in that article, I would now see some of my conclusions as rather wide of the mark. Consequently I have since abandoned the use of the concept of the kindred in analysing my own ethnographic data on the stratified Maloh of West Kalimantan. Moreover, in my earlier critique of Freeman's writings, it was not so much my intention to cast doubt on the kindred-based nature of Iban society, nor to question the importance of kinship relations in Iban social organization, but rather to seek clarification of the Iban conceptions of kinship (and kindred) relations and their connections to both Freeman's conceptualizations and to Iban social action. In a recent reflective paper on Iban society Freeman has reaffirmed the fact that Iban have a 'social organization based on the kindred' (1981:50; see also pp. 7, 9, 20, 23, 36, 55, and 63).

Following the pioneering studies of Freeman, Geddes and Morris, the status of the kindred in particular and kinship in general in the analysis of Bornean social organization became increasingly problematical. Two authors stand out. Appell stated that in his investigation of the relatively egalitarian Rungus Dusun of Sabah he did not discover a 'social isolate' which could justifiably be called a kindred, and therefore he did not propose to use the concept in his work (e.g. 1967:192–207). Then Rousseau, in his analysis of the stratified Baluy Kayan of Sarawak, argued that there was little point in using a kindred concept, and furthermore that '[k]inship plays only a residual role among the Kayan, as it does in Western society' and that 'beyond the family it is not the basis of any grouping having an economic or political role' (1978:87). For Rousseau the crucial principle of Kayan society is that '[b]ehaviour is determined on the basis of stratum ascription' (1978:88).

Rousseau's comments on kinship and rank among the Kayan serve as my present point of departure. The import of his remarks, I think, is that we may well have a marked difference in the operation and importance of kinship (and the kindred) between the hierarchical and egalitarian societies of Borneo. This observation might also suggest that it is problematical whether we can formulate, even in the context of Borneo, precise cross-cultural concepts of the 'personal kindred' and 'cognatic kinship' for use in analysis. Rousseau's quotation of a statement by Maurice Godelier should cast further light on the problem which concerns me here. Godelier wrote that 'the appearance of real social classes implies precisely the disappearance not of kinship relations, but of their capacity to be the general form of social relations' (1973:116; quoted in Rousseau 1978: 88). Interestingly Freeman, in his recent consideration of aspects of Iban and Kayan social organization, refers approvingly to Godelier's remark above (1981: 63).[1] Freeman also apparently has in mind an important difference in terms of kinship between the egalitarian Iban and the stratified Kayan (see also 1981:25–30, 42–50). He appends Godelier's dictum with his own comment that '[in] the classless society of the pagan Iban, kindred relationships were pervasive' (1981:63).

Some preliminary problems

I am assuming that it is worthwhile pursuing Godelier's assertion in relation to Borneo societies; but there is a difficulty. I have already hinted that in certain analyses of stratified societies in Borneo a kindred concept has been used (and the importance of kinship recognized), while in others it has not; similarly in some studies of egalitarian systems kindred analysis has been found to be appropriate, while in others its utility has been questioned (and the role of kinship de-emphasized).

In an attempt to resolve this apparent impasse, three preliminary points need to be made. First, because of the unimportance of any unilineal descent principle among indigenous Borneo societies, and in the absence of corporate unilineal descent groups, anthropologists have almost of necessity paid some attention to

---

1. Freeman took the quotation from a paper which Rousseau wrote in 1974, and in which the translation of Godelier from the French differs slightly from Rousseau's 1978 translation reproduced in my text. I should also add that Godelier's remark makes no mention of the organizational principle of residence, and this element has also figured importantly in analyses of both egalitarian and stratified societies in Borneo.

relations stemming from a given Ego. This is in turn a logical outcome of the need to ask informants about the categories of 'relatives' which they recognize and the linguistic terms appropriate to them. But, of course, the examination of ego-centred relationship categories and terms does not necessarily mean that a kindred concept is generally useful in analysing patterns of social interaction, nor that there is an indigenous equivalent of the kindred concept (however defined), nor that kinship is an all-important organizational principle in a given society. Unfortunately confusions have emerged among anthropologists, myself included, in applying a kindred concept to a variety of ego-focused relations, whatever their status. These relations are usually located in the familiar conceptual frameworks of 'social networks', 'dyadic ties', 'action groups' or 'sets' and so on.

Secondly, the confusions are often compounded because the apparent variations in types of kindred in different Borneo societies, or reports of their presence or absence in particular societies, may sometimes be the result of differences in anthropologists' emphases and perceptions. They may differ in their stress on various orders of data and levels of analysis (for example, observations by the analyst of actual social activities and events; informants' interpretations of the phenomenal order; indigenous statements about ideal relations between 'kin' and/or distinctions in relationship terms). These variations are themselves related to the choice and use of differently received anthropological models.

Thirdly, analyses of Borneo societies are further complicated by the fact that the obligations attached to kinship are generally not supported by strong jural sanctions (see Harrison 1971:152–3; Miles 1970:309 and 1971:216–17; Needham 1966:28–9); instead of isolating jural rules we are in the more nebulous realm of expectation and 'moral' obligation in which there is *considerable choice* in co-operating with kinsmen and others, and in affiliation to social groupings (see Crain 1978:123–42; Sather 1971 and 1978:172–92); and finally other principles of organization like residence are particularly important in group formation (see Appell 1967:196; Hudson 1972:104–6). I leave aside considerations of rank for the moment. Yet, despite all of this, diverse social relations are frequently comprehended by natives in a cognatic kinship idiom. In these circumstances, I maintain, the personal judgements of the anthropologist about which concepts and modes of analysis to use may intrude very significantly (see Appell 1967:204 and 1978:151–4; and Freeman 1961:201).

Much of the above echoes part of Leach's discussion of the distinction between 'descent' and 'filiation', which he said is a 'special case' of the 'distinction between representative action (where choice is minimal) and individual action (where choice is maximal)' (1962:131). This leads him to the conclusion that 'the analysis of any kind of cognatic kinship structure invariably ends by throwing the emphasis upon mechanisms of individual choice' (1962:132).

Egalitarian Borneo societies

Before commenting briefly on various studies of the relatively egalitarian societies in the context of Godelier's statement, I had better say something about the differences between stratified and non-stratified Borneo societies, remembering that these are broad, relative categories and that there is no absolute boundary between them.[2] In practice, there must be degrees of equality and hierarchy in Borneo (see Freeman 1981:48). However, those societies which are usually classified as stratified are, among others, the Kayan, Kenyah, Melanau-Kajang and Maloh. They have, or had in the past, named hereditary strata, which have commonly been glossed by anthropologists as 'ranks' or 'classes' of 'aristocrats', 'commoners' or 'freemen', and 'slaves'. Attached to these strata are different privileges, functions and cultural characteristics. In contrast, egalitarian societies like the Iban, Bidayuh Land Dayaks, and the Ranau and Rungus Dusun have no hereditary strata, though they certainly recognize differences in personal prestige.

It is readily apparent that a number of anthropologists who have studied egalitarian social systems in Borneo have either concentrated on kinship as an organizational principle, or on kinship in conjunction with residence or 'community'. A few have emphasized physical propinquity in determining patterns of social interaction and affiliation to groups rather than kinship or genealogical relatedness. Nevertheless, in general, kinship does play a preponderant role. As we have already seen, Freeman has placed great stress on interlocking kindred relations among the egalitarian Iban. For him, in societies like the Iban which lack large-scale corporate descent groups (and one might add ranks), kindred ties are an important means of social recruitment. Residence also plays a significant part, along with kinship, in generating such social units as the Iban *bilek*-family, the long-house and the tribe.

Schneider too, in his analysis of the egalitarian Selako Dayak of Sarawak, has argued that kinship is one of the 'principal strands intertwined in the system of Selako social organization' (1978:61, 75). He used a kindred concept, but also examined the importance of descent in giving rise to Selako 'ambilineal descent groups', and residence in giving form to 'corporate' households, long-houses and hamlets (1974:57–172). Furthermore, Crain's study of the Lun Dayeh of Southwestern Sabah (who in earlier literature are usually classified misleadingly as Murut), revealed the importance of the family and marriage — 'the essential features of Lun Dayeh society'. For Crain, it is 'in the contexts of these institutions

---

2. For example, the Berawan of Sarawak may be just such a borderline case (Metcalf 1976a, 1976b), as may the Bisaya of the Limbang river in Sarawak (Peranio 1977). The latter, in particular, have a Brunei Malay-derived title system, but Peranio states that the Bisaya 'never developed social classes' (1977:4) and that the Bisaya differ both from the egalitarian Bidayuh and the more highly stratified Melanau.

that kinship [...] can best be understood' (1970:115), and while he has referred
to the kindred (1970:110f), and paid some attention to kinship and kinship terms
(1970:78 ff), his main concern has been the domestic family (1970:189 ff) and
systems of social exchange, especially in the context of marriage (1970:116 ff;
1978:126–38). Incidentally, Lun Dayeh apparently had a 'class system' in the
past, but this had little importance at the time Crain conducted his field-work
(1970:183–6; 1978:136–7).[3]

Hudson, in his work on the Paju Epat Ma'anyan of Southeastern Kalimantan,
has phrased the bulk of his analysis in terms of 'kin-based groups', viz. the *dangau*
family, *lewu'* family, *tambak* group ('a descent-based kin group that has as its locus
a *tambak*, the carved ironwood box into which the ash residue of its members
is placed at the conclusion of the *ijambe* cremation ceremony'), the *bumuh* ('a
bilineal descent group') and the kindred (analytically distinguished into several
elements — 'core kindred', 'kindred pool', 'active kindred' and 'extended kindred' (1967:245–451; 1972:61–112; and Hudson and Hudson 1978:220–5). For
Hudson kinship, along with residence, is a vital principle of social organization
governing interpersonal relations among the non-stratified Paju Epat (1967:245).
As with the Lun Dayeh, Hudson has pointed to a former 'class' system among the
Paju Epat, but it is 'no longer formally operative' and at the present time plays
only 'a minor role in mediating social relationships' (1978:223).

Sather has forcefully demonstrated, in his examination of the Semporna Bajau Laut of Sabah, that the 'principal social groupings are typically those that
combine kinship and local ties in their organization' (1976:40). He has paid
close attention to the form and function of Bajau Laut conjugal families, village
households, household clusters, local communities and kindreds (1976:43–65;
1978:174–90). On balance, I would place the Bajau Laut in the category of non-
stratified Borneo societies, though I accept that this decision may meet with
objections. I do so for two reasons. First, to my knowledge Sather's work on
these boat-people is pitched very much in terms of cognatic social groupings, and
relatively little attention is paid to stratification. This suggests that rank is not
an important principle of organization in Bajau Laut society. Secondly, although
Bajau were incorporated in a ranked social system along with the Illanun of the
Lanao coast of Mindanao, the system of rank categories was brought to Sabah
by the ethnically different Illanun, who intermarried with the more numerous
Bajau there (Sather 1967:98). Sather noted that the Bajau Laut 'as a group
were incorporated into the bottom of the rank scale [...] [and] as a rule, were
able to advance the status of their children up the hierarchy only by their own

---

3. Deegan in his study of the related Lun Bawang has noted that kinship is one of the primary
means of organizing social relations in that society. He also used the kindred concept (1973:82–6).
Furthermore, he has managed to provide rather more material on the traditional ranking system
than has Crain, but Deegan noted that this system was not as elaborate as that of the Kayan (1973:
86–111).

marriages into Illanun families' (1967:100). Thus the *dato* or aristocratic rank mainly comprised Illanun, while the Bajau were principally *pitu* or freemen (1967: 99). One could then presumably claim that as an ethnic grouping Bajau were relatively egalitarian amongst themselves, but were integrated into a stratified system dominated by the Illanun and organized in terms of ethnic strata.

We have already seen that Geddes' investigation of the egalitarian Bidayuh utilized a concept of the kindred, though this does differ in important particulars from Freeman's formulation. Geddes did examine Bidayuh kinship relations, the household and the family, but these are located in his analysis of the 'community', a residence-based concept (1954:9–56). It would seem that for Geddes the tenor of Bidayuh social life hinges on the twin features of their 'individualism' and 'equality' (1954:48).

Among egalitarian societies Appell's study of the Rungus might seem to pose certain difficulties. Appell has claimed that in his personal opinion, Rungus Dusun have no kindreds, or to put it another way, Rungus do not recognize for purposes of social interaction an ego-centred cognatic category which is under-pinned by special social obligations (1967:192–207).[4] Appell's decision not to use a kindred concept is a little problematical when he noted that Rungus ac-knowledge 'a generalized prescription that cognates should help one another' (1967:200). But the key to Appell's orientation to the role of Rungus kinship in group formation is contained in his statement that 'cognates form the basis of many groups not because they are supposed to or are obligated to but because kinsmen live together' (1967:196). Here Appell is arguing decisively for the primary role of residence in social action and group recruitment. Nevertheless, despite this difference in emphasis, he, like the other anthropologists referred to above, devoted considerable attention to such social units as the domestic family (1965:26–248), the long-house (249–90) and the village (291–350). The domestic family, in particular, is subjected to close examination, and we are provided with details of its internal social relations, religious orientations and practices, and property ownership. Incidentally, I do feel that Appell is more demanding in his 'operational procedures for identifying kindreds' than Freeman, and that despite apparent differences in terms of kinship (and the relevance of the kindred concept) the egalitarian Rungus may be less different from the egalitarian Iban that at first appears. Finally Harrison, in support of Appell, has concluded that in Ranau Dusun society 'family' and 'community' are the basic social units. He, too, argued that the kindred is not present among the egalitarian Ranau, and that again residence or location is the formative influence in Dusun social life (1971:139–219).[5]

4. Appell followed Freeman's conceptualization of the kindred in the main.
5. Rhys Williams, in his study of the Tambunan Dusun, has placed some emphasis on kinship (and kindred) relations, though his study is problematical in several aspects (1965:46–57). Harrison has also noted the importance of the principles of gender and age in orienting behaviour in these kinds of society.

In summary, my reading of a substantial part of the anthropological literature on the non-stratified societies of Borneo suggests the important role attributed by anthropologists to cognatic kinship and residence in analysing social organization. In the majority of cases the utility of the kindred concept is acknowledged though definitions of the concept may vary. Furthermore, although these anthropologists may differ in the relative weight that they assign to residence and kinship (in its narrow sense referring to cognation, and in its widest encompassing consanguinity, marriage/affinity and descent), the same sorts of units for investigation tend to be isolated — small families and/or households, household clusters and/or hamlets, long-houses and/or villages, and in some cases ambilineal descent lines/categories/groups; the analysis of internal coherence of units and external linkages is also often, explicitly or implicitly, pitched in terms of dyads and networks associated with cognation.

Stratified Borneo societies

In relation to the stratified societies I would similarly argue that Godelier's remarks are in large part sustained. What is more, rank in these societies determines the form and content of a number of social features which we lump together for convenience as kinship. We must begin with Rousseau who has maintained that in Kayan society the role of kinship is 'residual'.[6] Furthermore, he pointed out that the only native term which might be translated as kindred is *panak* (literally, 'descendants of a common ancestor' or 'cognates') but Kayan use the term to refer to both cognates and affines, and in Freeman's sense it cannot qualify as an indigenous equivalent of the consanguineal kindred (1978:88, 90). Rousseau noted that Kayan have very few reference terms for kin. There are only six basic terms for cognates and '[t]erminology for affines is similarly minimal, and in part identical to that for cognates' (1978:88). Thus, there is 'a definite tendency in the kinship terminology towards the identification of cognates and affines' (1974:283). Finally, Rousseau has argued persuasively that kinship relations are not the basis for membership in a Kayan village or farmhouse, nor for participation in agricultural work teams, nor for the location of farm sites (1978: 88).

Whittier in his doctoral thesis on the stratified Lepo Tau Kenyah of Kalimantan did not utilize the kindred concept, and provided only a cursory survey of kinship, relationship terms and marriage (1973:77–88). Following additional work among Kenyah in Sarawak he has stated that they 'do not have a special term for the grouping of kinsmen that anthropologists call "the kindred" although

6. Rousseau seems to confine the notion of kinship to ego-centred cognatic relations. He has, however, recorded the importance of marriage in Kayan society in relation to the maintenance of rank boundaries (for example, 1978:84–9).

the term *chenganek* (sibling) may be extended to the sense of "relatives"' (1978: 113).[7] The phenomenon of merging cognatic and affinal kin is also found among the Kenyah. Whittier states 'I was unable to elicit specific kin terms for affines other than *laki* (husband/male) and *leto* (wife/female)' and further that 'There is a kin term, *sabai*, which means in-laws in general, but it is very rarely used' (1973:79). If one checks Whittier's list of reference terms for Kenyah, they are few in number. Finally, rank exerts an influence on kinship (and descent) because Kenyah aristocrats recognize a larger number of individuals as kinsmen than do commoners and they have 'greater genealogical knowledge' (1973: 77).[8]

In contrast to the above two studies, Morris' analysis of the stratified Melanau does assign a more important role to kinship, and he does accept the utility of the kindred concept, as defined by Freeman. He has stated that traditionally Melanau 'made use of three overlapping criteria in organizing social life' (1978: 40–1), viz. locality, kinship and rank (see 1953:51 ff and 1976:114). Two points are relevant here. First, Morris' analytical orientation may have been partly suggested by changes in Melanau society, especially in the context of the Brooke Raj in Sarawak and alterations in the mode of Melanau sago production and its marketing. Hereditary rank, even by the late 1940s, was being undermined and increasingly confined to the arena of bridewealth, symbolic display and the regulation of marriage. Traditionally Melanau aristocrats monopolized political power and economic resources (especially slaves and sago land), but in his analysis of rank, Morris concentrated conceptually on status and not on class structures or political power. These circumstances of change may well have enhanced the organizational role of kinship in contemporary Melanau society, and also influenced Morris' perception of its role in traditional Melanau social life. In other words, though important today, was kinship as important in the past when hereditary rank was clearly more decisive in structuring Melanau social life? Secondly, although Morris has referred to a Melanau kindred, he has made little use of the concept in his examination of social interaction. Perhaps this last point might be clarified by a few remarks that Morris made in his detailed report of 1953. For example, in his discussion of the giving of assistance to close cognates, he noted that Melanau regard help provided 'as a favour and not a right' (1953:65); that in relations between adult siblings 'there is no expressed norm that siblings ought to co-operate and help one another, though in fact they usually do' (1953:114); and that the rights and duties in relation to the category of close cognatic relatives of a given Ego 'are not onerous or rigidly

---

7. He has also remarked that '[n]evertheless principles generally associated with the concept of the kindred are important organizational features within Kenyah society' (1978:113). But the concept is not used as an analytical device by Whittier, and it seems that all Whittier is saying is that Kenyah recognize ego-centred cognatic relations.

8. Note Geddes' observation that genealogies might have been more fully remembered by Bidayuh if they had had a strong rank system (1954:59).

defined', rather they are mainly 'rights and duties connected with sexual relations and marriage' (1953:105). Morris has indicated more recently that kindred
members do share a 'wide range of social and economic interests' (1978:40),
but this is somewhat different from saying that they acknowledge defined rights,
duties and norms. Given the fact that comparison is made difficult because of
the facts of social change, the statements above lead me to suggest tentatively
that Melanau kinship, in most respects, is neither in ideal nor in practice very
different from that of the Kayan and Kenyah.[9] Indeed, in Appell's conceptualization of the kindred, I do not think that the Melanau category of cognates
isolated by Morris would qualify as a kindred (see Appell 1967:204). What is
more, to my knowledge Morris has made no recourse to Freeman's notion of
'kindred-based action groups' (i.e. temporary social groupings formed on the basis
of cognatic kindred membership). In Morris' early discussion of the Melanau
'kinship system in practice' attention is confined to dyadic relations between
categories of kinsmen (1953:98 ff). For the rest there is a detailed examination
of relationship terms and the stages of the individual life cycle (1953:108 ff). On
the few occasions when there is a reference to what might be called 'action
groups' Morris mentioned only that an individual can recruit certain kinsmen
for particular tasks. However, he has provided some interesting titbits on how
individual Melanau conceived of certain action groups. He said, at one point,
that traditionally an aristocrat 'could expect to mobilize a group of villagers for
a war-party or a trading expedition, and that the core of the group might well
be a selection of relatives from his kindred, but he was unlikely to regard the
group as kinsmen even if in fact they were. He was more likely to think of them
as neighbours, clients, or slaves' (1978:45). In another passage which links the
status of Melanau kinship with other stratified Borneo societies, Morris remarked
that most members of a village were kinsmen 'but membership of the village was
with the consent of the ruling aristocrats and not by virtue of a kinship link'
(1978:42).[10]

9. For example, Morris indicated that though affines are terminologically differentiated from
cognates, affinal terms are limited to four in number, and 'wherever possible' one's spouse's relatives
(outside spouse's parents and possibly parents' siblings, spouse's siblings and one's own children-
in-law) are 'placed in a category of blood relative' (1978:57). Furthermore, unlike Rousseau, at
times Morris adopts a broad concept of kinship to include cognation, marriage/affinity and descent. Rousseau distinguishes kinship and marriage, and, as we shall see later, marriage does play
a more important role in ranked Borneo societies. Perhaps this difference in the perception of the
significance of kinship might in part be explained in terms of the variations in the definition of
kinship.
10. I have to accept the fact that Morris and I may still differ on the question of the utility of
concepts such as the kindred in cross-cultural comparison. I assume that he would grant certain
concepts associated with cognation general comparative validity, whereas I would not.

The stratified Maloh

As a final example of a stratified society I would like to give more detailed attention to the Maloh of interior West Kalimantan, whom I studied in 1972–73. In
my initial analyses of Maloh social organization I, like Morris, paid some attention
to kinship, and I decided to employ the concept of the kindred (1974:201–11;
1976:139–42). However, I departed from Freeman by extending the concept to
include both cognatic and affinal kin, because my data suggested that Freeman's
construct did not coincide with 'native categories' and was of limited utility in
analysing the dynamics of Maloh social interaction. Despite my worries about the
concept and its formulation and application in Borneo studies, I believed then
that cross-cultural comparisons of Borneo kinship were desirable and possible.
Therefore, I used the kindred in a broad, flexible way to try and bring Maloh
society into relation with such societies as the Iban, Bidayuh, Paju Epat and so
on. By the time I had to write a general introduction to a volume of essays on
Borneo societies, I began to have serious doubts about my formulation and use
of the concept, and about the possibility of broad cross-cultural comparisons in
Borneo in terms of the categories 'cognatic/bilateral kinship' and the 'personal
kindred' (King 1978:6–12, 205–6). I decided, rightly or wrongly, that my flexible
kindred concept tended to confuse rather than clarify some aspects of Maloh
social organization and to overemphasize the importance of cognatic kinship
relations in Maloh society.[11] I therefore abandoned kindred analysis, though
I would not go as far as Rousseau did in his Kayan study to claim that kinship
plays only a residual role among Maloh. I would, however, be prepared to argue
that the key to an understanding of Maloh society is the principle of rank (and
changes in it) and not kinship, and that rank significantly influences the form
and content of cognatic kinship, affinity and descent.[12]

As with other Borneo stratified societies Maloh ranks have been undermined
by changes set in motion during the colonial period. Nevertheless, considerations of rank still played an important part in contemporary Maloh society. Traditionally (and to some extent in the early 1970s) the range of collateral kinsmen
recognized and the extent of genealogical knowledge generally differed according
to an individual's rank membership. Levels of bridewealth, marriage regulations,
choice of spouse and post-marital residence also varied according to rank. In
addition, a number of Maloh social units were not primarily based on kinship.
The village and long-house,[13] like those of Kayan, Kenyah and Melanau, were
not kinship units. Village membership required the consent of the aristocrats
and it was not sufficient simply to claim a kinship link with residents of a village
if one wanted to affiliate to it. Nor could individuals leave a village without

11. See Appell's critique of my early position on the kindred concept (1976:146–51).
12. See also Whittier on the Kenyah (1973:85–6 and 1978:113–16).
13. Traditionally Maloh villages comprised one or more long-houses.

aristocratic permission. Kinship was not the basis of membership in swidden field-houses; residence in these and the location of farm sites were based on a range of considerations such as rank, physical proximity, economic factors, as well as kinship. What is more, the composition of agricultural work-teams could not be explained in terms of kinship since these co-operative labour groups were based on a principle of strictly reciprocal labour exchange, and kinsmen were treated like anyone else. Finally, traditional raiding parties and travelling bands were usually led and mobilized by aristocrats; their raison d'être was not kinship.

Kinship was, however, one of a number of factors which was taken into account for purposes of social interaction. Kinship also partly defined sexual access between various categories of individuals and certain close relatives could call on one another for the supply of goods and services, especially in such matters as birth, marriage and death, though close relatives were also commonly members of the same rank. Maloh also frequently talked about different kinds of relationship in cognatic kinship terms.

Maloh recognized a category of cognatic kin called *saparanak* (literally 'related children' or 'cognates'). An individual reckoned relatives on both the mother's and father's sides and ideally gave maternal and paternal kinsmen equal social weight. This cognatic category was seen by some people to extend outwards beyond one's immediate family (*kaiyan*), to fifth cousins and in ascending and descending generations from there. It was usually aristocrats who recognized relatives as comprising fifth cousins, while commoners more frequently limited the range to fourth or even third cousins. The aristocratic practice of maintaining long ambilineal genealogies (*tutulan*), in contrast to most commoners, and their preoccupation with marrying individuals of the same rank and 'blood' (*dara*), meant that kinship knowledge was more comprehensive and exact for aristocrats than for commoners. Aristocratic genealogies, usually traced to illustrious ancestors possessing magical powers or linked to important deities, legitimized aristocratic status by providing it with a quality of sacredness.

At first sight the cognatic category *saparanak* seems to be equivalent to Freeman's kindred concept. But Maloh extended the term to include all categories of affinal kin as well. Maloh agreed that terminologically they distinguished certain categories of close affinal kin from cognates, but generally in terms of behaviour and obligations affines were treated like consanguines and addressed as such. Moreover, it was only close affinal kin (parents-in-law and their spouses, siblings-in-law and their spouses, children-in-law) who were referred to by affinal terms as distinct from cognatic ones. There were no reference terms for affines beyond these. Thus affinal reference categories were lineally and laterally less extensive than those of cognates.

The tendency to merge cognates and affines can be explained in at least two ways. First, Maloh conceptualized a conjugal pair as 'becoming one' after marriage. This entailed that on marriage a man entered his wife's kinship circle and vice versa. Secondly, the perception of consanguines and affines as in some sense equivalent is partly the product of relations of rank and their associated ideology. In other words, the principle of rank endogamy, which has resulted in the majority of marriages taking place between close cognates, leads to the conceptualization of the members of one's own rank as undifferentiated relatives. The distinction between consanguinity and affinity is played down, but not totally eliminated.[14] This latter fact finds expression in Maloh terminology. The Maloh word for rank is *ranakan* and is etymologically related to *saparanak* through the root word *anak* (cognates). Both terms, in the idiom of cognatic kinship, nevertheless merge 'blood' and affinity, so that for Maloh the important distinction was not so much that between consanguines and affines, but that between members of different ranks. It may well be that as traditional rank continues to decline in importance, differentiation between cognates and affines may emerge more prominently, but I was not aware of this during fieldwork.

Affines such as siblings- and parents-in-law might be called on for assistance and might co-operate with a given Ego in various tasks. They might also contribute to a fine which Ego had to meet, or offer financial help or labour in ceremonies which Ego has sponsored and organized. This is hardly surprising given my comments above, and the added fact that obligations were usually met not by individuals but by households as units; in relation to a given Ego a household normally contained both cognates and affines. Furthermore, intermarriage between close consanguines meant that the new affinal ties reinforced the already existing cognatic ones. In any given task grouping one could usually find both consanguines and affines of a given Ego, and some of these were both a cognate and an affine of Ego. Members of a co-operative grouping might also have been offering assistance or working together for any number of reasons, not necessarily stemming from kinship obligations. For all these reasons it makes little sense to me to use Freeman's concept of the kindred to analyse Maloh action groups. I do not see much value in examining these groups in terms of ego-centred cognatic networks, and demarcating sub-sets of consanguines and affines. This would tend to assign an anonymity or, at the very least, a markedly subsidiary role to affinal relationships.

As I have indicated, certain obligations among Maloh stemmed from relations between both cognates and affines, who usually happened to be members of the same rank. Moreover, outside the immediate circle of grandparents, parents, siblings, children, and close in-laws, there were no defined jural norms or strong sanctions underlying kinship obligations. An individual did not have the right to demand help from a kinsman outside his immediate family. Furthermore, the

14. See Maurice Bloch's analysis of the Merina of Madagascar (1975). More attention is needed to the cognatic-affinal problem in the context of such phenomena as 'kindred' endogamy, marriage between a given Ego's affines and the process of turning affinity into cognation.

refusal to co-operate with a kinsman was not automatically greeted with social opprobrium.

Given the ideal rule of rank endogamy in Maloh society, which was adhered to in the majority of marriages,[15] most members of one rank may well not have been closely related to members of another. Nevertheless, inter-rank relations were still expressed in kinship terms. Most aristocrats, even in the early 1970s, were likened to cognatic kinsmen of the senior genealogical levels who should be respected. They were addressed by terms which I have translated as 'grandfather'/'grandmother' and 'father'/'mother'. Aristocrats frequently talked of other villagers as 'our children' (*anakka banua*) or 'grandchildren' (*ampuka*). In myths three different ranks were conceived of as having been created by three brothers, each being the founding ancestor of a rank. What is important is that we should not confuse the basis of rank relations (i.e. social inequality and differential access to and control over resources and privileges) with the idiom or ideology in which these relations were sometimes expressed or talked about (i.e. kinship).

Apart from variations in the extent of lineal and lateral recognition of relatives according to rank, there were also differences in relation to the principle of descent. Traditionally Maloh possessed ambilineal descent categories (*kapulungan*) based on undivided rights to key resources such as land, productive trees (e.g. fruit trees) and heirloom property. With the increasing extension of more permanent cultivation of rubber and irrigated rice, and the selling off of heirlooms such as gongs and the introduction of the concept of private property, these descent categories have subsequently declined in importance. But in the early 1970s they still operated in certain parts of Maloh country in relation to swidden fields and trees. The institution of descent categories was formerly especially marked among aristocrats. Maloh aristocrats also tended to act together in a range of activities and had a common interest in maintaining their superior political and economic position. In comparison with commoners, aristocrats were fewer in number and tended to intermarry with close cognatic kin to reconsolidate rights to *kapulungan* property. In practice, therefore, aristocrats in a village would appear to have taken on the characteristics of a localized corporate descent group. However, particularly in the past, I would argue that common interests and co-operation stemmed much more from shared rank affiliation and the need to sustain ranks than from common descent. Descent like cognatic kinship was, in part, an expression and a way of talking about relations of rank and property ownership. I would question the utility of descent ideology in analysing Maloh social relations, especially when this ideology was part of, or more exactly subordinated to, an overall ideology of rank and social inequality. Furthermore, while ranks incorporated every Maloh individual into an all-embracing system of social units, descent did not. Slaves did not recognize *kapulungan* because they

15. Although inter-rank marriages did occur and have increased in frequency over the past forty years or so.

had no rights in property which they could pass on. Some poor commoners were in a similar position. I also noted that certain commoner households and those of former slaves, who had been given their freedom after the Dutch abolished slavery, did not keep their rights in property undivided, but divided them equally between children. Even where commoners had *kapulungan*, their genealogical depth was usually less than those of aristocrats who kept lengthy genealogies.

Finally, let us consider the institution of marriage, which has a significant role in ranked Borneo societies. In a small-scale society an important means of maintaining the ideological and practical exclusiveness of ranks is by means of a rule of rank endogamy.[16] But marriage served the requirements of the ranking system, and this in turn explains four main features of aristocratic marriage practices, which differed from those of other ranks. First, aristocrats, unlike other villagers, tended to marry partners from outside their own village. In the interests of rank endogamy this was necessary because of the small number of potential marriage partners within the village. Usually there were only two to three aristocratic households per long-house. It was also a means of political alliance. Aristocratic genealogies revealed a ramifying network covering many villages, and, on occasion, extending to some of the leading families of neighbouring Malays, Iban, Kayan, and Punun. Secondly, the importance of succession to office meant that aristocrats favoured post-marital virilocal residence. Commoners more often adopted uxorilocal residence. An aristocrat was more likely to occupy office, or at least exercise influence in his own village.[17] An important indication of a gradual fall from grace of aristocratic households was their willingness to contract uxorilocal marriages for their males. Thirdly, given the small number of potential partners and the rule of rank endogamy, first-cousin marriages were more frequent among aristocrats.[18] Ordinary villagers disliked first-cousin marriage and rarely contracted it. Fourthly, there were sometimes large age differences among aristocratic spouses as a consequence of the difficulty of finding partners of roughly the same age.

There was also variation in the quantity, type, and quality of bridewealth according to rank.[19] The importance of rank was made very apparent in pre-marriage negotiations between representatives of the prospective bride and groom. The main concern was the suitability of the prospective partners in terms of their relative rank positions and other factors which might affect their status. The outcome of these deliberations resolved the amount and kind of bridewealth due to the bride's side, though there was an ideal graded scale of bridewealth for the different ranks which served as a framework for negotiations.

16. See also the Kayan (Rousseau 1978:36 and 1979:220–1), the Kenyah (Whittier 1978:113) and the Melanau (Morris 1978:48–9).
17. See also the Kayan (Rousseau 1978:86) and the Kenyah (Whittier 1978:113–16).
18. See also the Kenyah (Whittier 1978:113–14).
19. See also the Kenyah (Whittier 1973:86) and the Melanau (Morris 1953:54–64).

In addition, despite the ideal of rank endogamy there was always some movement between ranks. The only means to initiate a change in rank position was through marriage. Again an ideal graded system of marriage payments covered inter-strata unions. It is clear that marriage between ranks complicated the ranking system and led, in practice, to gradations within ranks and to a blurring of rank boundaries, which were theoretically rigid. But it was a necessary mechanism to bring rank levels into line with the changing economic and political fortunes of individuals. Traditionally it also served to maintain the dominant position of aristocrats by allowing enterprising people from lower ranks to channel their energies into acquiring higher rank for their descendants rather than challenging the existing system. It also provided a means of demoting 'failed' aristocrats (see Rousseau 1979:230).

Conclusions

I have briefly examined the importance, form and function of kinship in a range of Borneo societies. Using a detailed case study of a stratified society I have also looked at the relation between rank on the one hand and cognatic kinship, descent and marriage/affinity on the other hand. I hope to have demonstrated that there are significant differences in terms of kinship between the egalitarian and hierarchical societies of Borneo. Moreover, it cannot be assumed that in a stratified society cognation, descent and marriage/affinity are in some sense autonomous, homogeneous and uniform in operation. Differences in rank generated variations in the form and function of kinship and other related institutions.

Perhaps then we have to agree with Rodney Needham that 'it is probably not useful to assume that cognatic societies must characteristically have some special forms or principles of social organization in common. It is at least arguable that cognatic societies are classed together primarily because of what they *lack* [...]. In other words cognatic societies constitute a negatively defined class' (Needham 1966:28). Needham continued: 'The cognatic recognition of relatives is common to all societies and characteristic of none' (1966:29). Interestingly, Marshall Sahlins, in an early review article of Murdock's *Social Structure in Southeast Asia*, came to the same conclusion when he remarked that the majority of societies in that book 'do have something in common: they lack unilineal descent groups' (1963:39). Furthermore, Sahlins argued that Murdock commits a serious error '[b]y taking as decisive the superficial resemblance of bilateral reckoning' (1963: 40).

What I suggest, in line with the reasoning above, is that in the context of Borneo it is debatable whether we could or should formulate a concept of 'cognatic' or 'bilateral kinship' and other related concepts such as the 'personal kindred' to indulge in broad cross-cultural comparison. It is even more problematical to isolate cognation and features usually associated with it to establish a positively defined type of society. However, this is not to suggest that more limited comparisons of, say, ranking systems among a carefully selected sample of Borneo societies are not possible nor desirable. We have to attempt generalizations in our subject but I doubt whether we shall do it by concentrating on the cross-cultural comparison of cognation, cognatic kinship and the personal kindred.

The Art of Measuring Mirages,
Or Is There Kinship in Bali?

Mark Hobart

The inter-bubular groove is a vital statistic. Its possibilities were first exposed by Dr. Eberhard Fleischer (1881), an ethnologist and mathematician, who was greatly attracted to its firm digital properties. His views met with resistance and languished neglected until they were revamped by Hsien and Weiss in their seminal contribution (1954), which held that Fleischer had indeed had a sound grasp of the salient issues. Its advocates have embraced it warmly, holding it to have vast scope. So the inter-bubular groove (the earlier spelling with 'oo' is no longer preferred) has been connected statistically with I.Q. (Zderzaki 1969), with variation in linguistic performance (Gabel 1970), and some have even sought a quantitative ideal (given as 18 cm., Rein-Dreque 1976). Recently, in a vitriolic attack, however, the whole approach has been dismissed as inflated out of proportion and a typical positivist obsession with manifest superstructures (Little and Moe 1977). Whether there is any case left after this rough handling is a moot point.

Perilous presuppositions

What has all this to do with kinship? The answer is simple. Stipulating a cross-cultural reality to kinship and then classifying its forms is about as useful as postulating the inter-bubular groove and then measuring it.[1] What is commonly called kinship is a chimaera, a mythical monster (whose eponym was fittingly fathered by hot air!) with a face of folk categories, a body of received anthropological wisdom and a tail of Western metaphysical assumptions. A few

1. I make no apology for trying the reader's patience with an imaginary idea — it is hardly less far-fetched than much scientism in anthropology and serves to make the point. In writing this paper, I am grateful to Mischa Penn for his help and criticism, especially about the dangers of what might be called *Luftmetaphysik* as a purported explanation. Field-work in Bali was carried out between 1970 and 1972 with grants from the Leverhulme Trust Fund, the London-Cornell Project and a Horniman Anthropological Scholarship; and from 1979–80 with a research grant from the School of Oriental and African Studies.

Bellerophons have tried to put paid to the monster. Needham has challenged the validity of prevailing principles and modes of classification (1971, 1975). Schneider has sought to sever the cultural constructs from a heterogeneous social conglomerate (1968, 1972); while Inden has tweaked its metaphysical tail by pointing out that other cultures may have quite different assumptions about how humans are related (1976). Yet the monster staggers on, largely I suspect because anthropology is heir to a strongly essentialist intellectual tradition. Unless we are quite clear about what kind of 'thing' kinship is, we may find we have been wasting our time talking about it.

There are three grounds on which I wish to argue that kinship does not have the kind of reality usually attributed to it. First, there is a problem of translation and comparison. How do we know that what we call kinship denotes something comparable in another culture? Second, there is the question of what statements about kinship are about. Are we dealing with descriptions about the world? Or is it more a matter of what various classifications of relationships may be used, for particular purposes, to assert, claim, challenge or deny? Finally, there is the metaphysical issue of what the members of different cultures recognize, explicitly or implicitly, as existing in their world. How does the classification of relationships relate to what is held to exist? In other words, how are events, states and agents or whatever understood in different cultural theories of being, identity, nature, causation and so forth? I would suggest that using the notion of kinship, even as 'an odd-job word', tends to cover up the difficulty in knowing how we translate; what uses of language may exist; and whether the entities classified by other cultures are remotely comparable. Our cultural heritage has yielded a particular jural, moral and ontological package we call kinship. It would be a startling example of what someone once delightfully called 'RUP' — Residual Unresolved Positivism — were we to fail to see that our ideas about kinship are no simple truths about the world but affected by our changing assumptions. It is not an issue of how to compare facts but of how, using one cognitive model, to talk about others.

As the issues are complex, let me spell out some of the points most relevant to a discussion of kinship. In its easiest formulation the problem of radical translation (between unrelated languages where there has been little, or no, cultural contact, see Quine 1960:28 ff) is an extreme example of the hermeneutic issue of how to interpret texts or statements within one culture. For 'the special problem of interpretation is that it very often *appears* to be necessary and inevitable when in fact it never is. This appearance of inevitability is a phantasm raised by the circularity of the interpretive process' (Hirsch 1967: 164). The reason is that one is dealing with a system of signs which 'must be construed before it furnishes confirmation of an interpretation. Furthermore, the manner in which the signs are construed is partly predetermined by the interpretation itself' (Hirsch 1967:165). In radical translation the ethnographer faces the trap of self-confirmability of interpretations with metaphysical knobs on.

Why can one not simply translate by finding out what native words or expressions correspond with the facts? In order to understand the difficulty, it is useful to look at the theory of truth, and meaning, which is required for such an approach. This is the classical 'Correspondence Theory' in which truth, and so true meaning, consists in some form of correspondence between facts and ideas (Hobart 1985a:33–7). Significantly this was the view espoused by Aristotle. For, as we shall see, the kinds of schemes used to classify kin relations rely on Aristotelian metaphysical assumptions of particular things or people having essential properties, by virtue of which they may be definitively classified.

There are serious problems in any 'Correspondence Theory'. Three are relevant here. First, many of the words critical to a translation, such as logical connectives, do not correspond to any facts. Second, as Gellner (1970:25) has observed trenchantly, in effect introducing 'reality' as a stage in translating one language into another merely adds a further language and compounds the difficulties. Why this should be so is clear in the light of my last objection, namely that there is an indeterminacy in translation, such that more than one scheme may make sense of the linguistic data. There is no simple way of climbing out of one's translational scheme to ask even the best-informed native informant whether one is correct without having to translate him or her. The catch, as Quine (1960:72) remarked, is that 'there can be no doubt that rival systems of analytical hypotheses can fit the totality of speech behaviour to perfection, and can fit the totality of dispositions to speech behaviour as well, and still specify mutually incompatible translations of countless sentences insusceptible of independent control'. In other words there is no way of knowing whether the ethnographer's translation of concepts like kinship, family, or father are in fact what the members of another culture intend in their speech behaviour, or not. Once the ethnographer gets going on his or her scheme, however shot-through with one's own cultural presuppositions, it tends to become self-confirming because many of the key notions are mutually defined and sufficiently far away from statements for which there is empirical evidence (see Quine 1953). How do we know that the comfortable seeming similarity of ideas about kinship round the world is not a result of the observers sharing similar preconceptions which they invest in their translational systems? Consider, for instance, how radical would be the difference were common notions like 'soul' or 'spirit' to be rendered as 'identity' instead, and how hard it would be to invalidate either. I have a suspicion that the wee ghosties and goblins which seem to pervade other cultures are a product of our Victorian imagination of the 'Other'.

Leaving aside the difficulties in translation, what in fact are we comparing anyway? The problem is that, whatever their purported basis in biology, kinship relations are not natural facts as such. What the anthropologist traditionally goes by are native statements held to describe the social relationships of a particular kind in which humans are engaged, so to speak. Now statements differ from 'facts' by being asserted by people on particular occasions, rather than, in some sense, being 'out there'. 'Being someone's brother' is construed from the 'facts', whatever they might be in any instance, in terms of cultural categories, which include ideas of taxonomy, logical operations and much else besides. Statements about kinship are therefore, among other things, applications of classificatory principles to the actions, events and so forth from which relationships are inferred.

There are other grounds too on which to question whether statements about kinship could ever be neutral propositions about the world. Austin's point about language was that words do not just say things, but do things at the same time (1962). In speaking one does not simply make propositions but also presents that proposition, if such it be, in different ways or with differing (illocutionary) force, which may further have effects in the world (perlocutionary force in speech act terminology).[2] I shall try to show later quite how dangerous it is to think of statements about kinship as descriptions.[3] It fits better with ethnographic evidence to treat these as prescriptions, assertions, denials, questions or any other way in which people may use language on different occasions for particular purposes. The confusion created by mistaking claims for descriptions, in the words of an American cynic, makes Harlem on Father's Day look quite orderly!

These difficulties seem to pale in the face of the hurdles involved in comparing ideas from different cultures. Evans-Pritchard (1963) has made the point that comparison easily leads to a circularity. To compare things one requires criteria, but how does one establish the criteria in the first place without comparison? Our notions of comparison are highly conventional and subsume learning 'similarity relations' (Kuhn 1977:307–19, on 'finitism'). Matters are worse still when dealing with the classification of jural or moral relations which are widely argued to be key aspects of kinship (e.g. Fortes 1970a). For a start, on what grounds could we assume that ideas of 'law' are similar across cultures, or that jural notions such as person, obligation, or prohibition are comparable when they have changed so much within our own culture? The assumption that the moral dimension of kinship is important does tend to presuppose that ideas of morality have equivalents in different cultures, which rather flies in the face of the evidence (Hobart 1985b). A great deal of anthropology consists in closing one's eyes and hoping the world will go away.

2. See especially Searle (1971) on a celebrated version of the relationship of illocutionary force to propositions.
3. The 'insight' that kinship is just an idiom for other kinds of relationships depends, I suspect, on the kinds of argument discussed above. This is not to my mind however a very helpful way of formulating the problem. There is often a covert implication that native statements about relationships are merely an idiom for something more 'real' — presumably the trusty old war horses of power and production. Unless such an argument is handled with care, it smacks of positivism and essentialism at its worst.

More serious still, just how inadequate are the kinds of taxonomic principle invoked by anthropologists has become increasingly obvious (Conklin 1964; Tambiah 1973; Needham 1975, 1979). It is bad enough when considering the ways in which nature may be classified, but matters become worse when one is considering kinship classifications, which are relational, and raise awkward questions about what kinds of attribute are at stake. Classical approaches, such as the Aristotelian, organize particulars by reference to essential, or definitive, properties possessed by proper class members. This does not always work comfortably for relations like 'being taller than' or 'being younger than'. Nor is it universally accepted, or uncontentious, that objects and people need be defined in terms of 'properties'. As Goodman (1978:97) has noted, our present predicament can be traced back to the pre-Socratics who 'made almost all the important advances and mistakes in the history of philosophy'. In particular they left us with the metaphysical assumption that what distinguishes the substance of which all things are constituted is the set of properties which somehow inhere in each and upon which the distinctions of classification are based. What gives kinship classifications a semblance of universality is the tendency for members of different cultures to divide the world up in various ways for convenience and this generally extends to include the important field of other people. It may be a truism that cultures include various linguistic modes of differentiating 'reality', but this does not mean that all cultures need share the ways in which they do this and certainly does not entail that what is classified is comparable.[4] The healthy empiricism many anthropologists claim is often a polite way of saying that they admit not just to frighteningly naive philosophical ignorance but rank ethnocentrism as well.

Why though should kinship be the focus of so much anthropological attention? The reason, I suspect, is that it seems to refer to basic ways of classifying natural facts found in all cultures by virtue of having living, breeding species' members of *homo sapiens*. Now, while it is generally recognized that kin classifications differ from those of nature — hence the attention given to the difference between social fathers (*patres*) and genitors — this part recognition covers up a far more serious assumption. This is the presupposition that, whatever the classifications, they refer to the same nature. Nature is, however, not a natural category but a cultural construct. Worse, it is one which differs between cultures and even within our own has been subject to massive reformulation in the course of history (Collingwood 1945). It does not really help to argue that recent discoveries of the genetic determination of phenotypes solves the problem. To paraphrase Voltaire, if genes had not existed, it would have been necessary for essentialism to invent them. In fact, of course, if one allows a measure of validity to Kuhn's stress on the constitutive nature of scientific paradigms, then genes are the product of a

---

4. As I understand it, this is why Needham combines an interest in formal classification with a sceptical awareness of metaphysical problems (Needham 1979 as against 1976).

particular paradigm and the one reasonable certainty is that further research will
show all the problems of indeterminacy and alternative models which have beset
apparently definitive discoveries.

The natural facts to which observations about kinship ultimately correspond
may then vary between cultures. Are the similarities upon which biological
relationship is inductively established in fact self-evident? We can, out of
amusement, apply Wittgenstein's famous argument (1969:17) about 'family resemblances' to see what is assumed in searching for common properties among
family members. For what exists is

> a *family* the members of which have family likenesses. Some of them have the same
> nose, others the same eyebrows and others again the same way of walking; and these
> likenesses overlap. The idea of a concept being a common property of its particular
> instances connects up with other primitive, too simple, ideas of the structure of lan-
> guage. It is comparable to the idea that *properties* are *ingredients* of the things which
> have the properties e.g. that beauty is an ingredient of all beautiful things as alcohol
> is of beer and wine, and that we therefore could have pure beauty, unadulterated by
> anything that is beautiful.

If there is no simple method of induction to determine membership by resemblance, perhaps we need to consider the kinds of assumptions about what, if
anything, different cultures hold to be common between family members.

If the principles upon which taxonomies are organized raise problems, how do
such classifications correspond to the world? There are no grounds a priori for
assuming isomorphism between taxonomy and cultural notions of how the world
is constituted. The question of how the two are related involves metaphysical
ideas about reality. For instance, among the Balinese there is little idea of eternal
natural law set against custom. Regularity, such as it is, is imposed by the will
of a supreme, but remote, Divinity. Just as custom changes according to place,
time and circumstance (*désa, kala, patra*), so it is assumed (but unknowable) that
Divinity directly, or through a Hindu pantheon of gods, may alter arrangements
and what stability there is may stem from human attempts to propitiate the
agents which control nature. An important guide, at once moral and objective,
is the idea that action has determinate effects upon the actor, according to the
doctrine of *karma pala* (the fruits of action). Not only does this affect humans
throughout their lives, or across incarnations, but it directly influences their
constitutions, characters and the circumstances of birth. To assume that ideas
about kinship in Bali rest on some bedrock of natural fact underwritten by the
observer's knowledge of how the world truly is, would be crass ethnocentrism.

If there is no universal, shared view of nature, what are the Balinese ideas
about the material base of kin relations? Curiously, the Balinese tend to be vague,
not only about theories of conception, which reflect differing social claims as
much as anything, but also about the notion of matter (Hobart 1983). They
stress the transformation of appearance or the causation of events instead. The

elite, in suitably essentialist spirit, tends to put more weight than peasants on pedigree, for purposes of political legitimacy. This is expressed in an ideology of ritual purity, held partly to be transmitted by conception. Quite what purity is is a complex and debated issue; and the ostensible evidence of procreation may be overridden where other factors intervene — as when a low-born man attains power or the attributes of princes. As I discuss below, the realm of 'kinship' may well, for the Balinese, be largely to do with what makes men similar or different in which many considerations combine. Nor do Balinese handle family resemblances just by referring to inherited traits. Besides the doctrine of *karma pala*, villagers recognize the disparities between 'kin' as much as the congruences. Part of the inquiry about new-born children is finding out from a spirit-medium which ancestral identity has manifested itself. Quite different kinds of contextual factor come into play too. In Balinese theories of causation personal identity is partly determined by the circumstances of birth, including time and space, and it further remains inextricably linked with the fate of a child's four mystical siblings (the *kanda 'mpat*, the ejecta at birth). So there is no mechanical theory of the natural basis of kinship. Rather, personal identity and domestic relations are decided by various factors operating within a causal field.

A final point should be made about my reference to metaphysics. By this I mean the kinds of idea, category, logical operation, ontological commitment or whatever, which Balinese appeal to, explicitly in speech, or implicitly by inference or reflection on discourse. Such a metaphysics-in-the-buff, as I have called it (1983), is more common than anthropologists often allow (cf. Evans-Pritchard 1937, 1956; Lienhardt 1961; Inden 1976; Vitebsky 1982). Certainly in a literate civilization like Bali, texts and traditions of philosophical speculation abound and are used with enthusiasm and aplomb in daily life to explain actions and account for the nature of the world. It is one thing for the Balinese to interpret matters this way, but to what extent does my approach claim to explain why men do what they do? The short answer is that it does not claim to do so. My concern is simply to look at the empirical conditions — which include native statements about metaphysics — under which action takes place and, given the particular sets of circumstances, piece together the ways in which the Balinese interpret what is happening in different contexts. There is no way, I suggest, in which we could ever know which of the possible sets of constructs, if any, is the one *in fact* responsible for the events. This modest constraint on my aims follows directly from arguments such as Quine's, noted above, about the underdetermination of theory by experience. If such a caution has any validity it is the death-knell for anyone who purports that any scheme can, in principle, *explain* events. There is an unstated step in many cultural analyses. After positing a theoretical framework which bears some relation to the ethnographic evidence, there is a surreptitious assumption that, given the best and richest conceptual scheme, a causal account could be read off on demand. My aim is less ambitious, but I suspect more realistic.

These general remarks about the questionably substantive status of 'kinship' need to be argued from the ethnography. In what follows I try to show, in the light of my strictures on explanation, that we can not only talk usefully about the Balinese, but possibly come closer to appreciating the richness of other cultures, once we let go of notions like 'kinship'. I start by looking at the language of 'kinship' and the institutions which might seem associated with it. Then I consider why statements about relationships of this kind are in the register of assertion rather than the description of facts. Finally I outline various models used by the Balinese to explain the 'facts' in any instance. The conclusion is that reading any particular classification (let alone defining the 'system' as patrilineal, matrilineal or cognatic) into Balinese 'kinship' is like looking for the definitive reading of an ink blob or the inter-bubular groove. We are dealing with native models of terminology, action, metaphysical ideas or whatever, and to try to read through them to the essence of the system is akin to rubbing the print off a page in order to see what it really says behind the words.

The vocabulary of Balinese 'kinship'

Among many kinds of temple congregation in Bali are those known as *pemaksaan*, *dadiya* or, more specifically, as *soroh* followed by the name of the worship group. The terms are found in different parts of the island with slightly different usage. The folk etymology is interesting. *Pemaksaan* is usually held to derive from the root *paksa*, force; and refers to those who are expected to worship at (*maturan*, to give offerings, and *muspa*, to pray), or who are obliged to support (*nyungsung*), a temple. *Dadiya* is commonly linked to *dadi*, to grow or become, but also allow.[5] So it may be read either as those who have grown from one origin, *kawitan*, or those between whom certain acts or exchanges are permitted. *Soroh* is the general word for class or kind. So it denotes a class of people linked to a temple. In common with almost all temple associations in Bali, the main function of its members is to perform calendrical rituals to the incumbent deity (usually known by a title, *Batara*, which indicates divine status, followed by the name of the temple or worship group — most Balinese taxonomy stresses terminal classes in nominalist fashion). The principles of incorporation of different groups vary little except in the range of functions and the criteria of eligibility. The ones under discussion do little but worship. The grounds for membership are what we must look into.

---

5. *Pace* Lansing (1974:28), where the unlikely derivation is given as from *daja*, in the north, towards the (pure) mountains.

The criteria for inclusion in such worship groups may be expressed in several ways. A key, but complicated, term is *purusa*. In Sanskrit it is often translated as 'male' (Gonda 1952:73; Inden 1976:13), but also as 'seed-man' (Inden and Nicholas 1977:30) or as part of the 'cosmic manifestation of the primal Superman (*purusa*)' (Long 1980:58). The notion of *purusa* is variously interpreted in different Hindu philosophical traditions: as an aspect of deity (Gonda 1970:16ff), as self opposed to substance (Potter 1980:263), as consciousness beyond matter, 'sheer contentless presence' as against 'awareness [which] is active, intentional, engaged' (Larson 1980:308). It is not an easy concept.

At first sight matters are much simpler in Bali. *Sakèng purusa* belongs to a contrast set with *sakèng pradana*, 'from the male (side)' and 'from the female (side)' respectively (see Gonda 1952:173). Here *sakèng purusa* designates those related to a male ancestor. In this sense the worship groups mentioned above may be read as having their membership defined by descent — the Balinese use the same metaphor, *turun*, as in English — here agnation. *Purus(a)* also means 'penis': so does *sakèng purusa* refer to socially recognized, or biologically conceived, connections? This is not a quibble. Such ambiguities are critical to how the Balinese interpret group membership and explain action.

There is a subtlety here. After all why not define 'kin groups' straightforwardly by who joins, and dismiss folk semantics as incidental? This is an easy way out, but it imports Western ideas of the relation of word and object. Defining *purusa* by denotation is woefully inadequate.[6] Granted the range of implications, the Balinese suffer from the dilemma of what the key concept of *purusa* is all about. Is *sakèng purusa* about conventional association or about acts of procreation? Is the stress on transmission or substantive qualities? Or is it about something else? Is it, for instance, sharing something with a given (ancestral) deity? Or worse, is it some shared attribute, or perhaps outlook, separate from the individual interests of those concerned? Such issues tend to arise when the ambiguous grounds of incorporation are highlighted inevitably in disputes or changing circumstances.

It will be obvious that the interpretations Balinese may place upon the notion of *purusa* stem in part from some of its many senses noted by Sanskrit scholars. This is equally true of the other terms noted so far. For instance, my villagers treated *dadiya* on occasions as deriving from *dadi*, as 'to allow'. Sharing a *dadiya* had the sense of being allowed to share things like food, so those who did not in fact do so were not of the same *dadiya*. By varying the defining attributes Balinese can, and do, give quite different slants to what terms should refer to, whom to include and exclude, and what such moves might imply. Whether we like it or not, interpretation is not easily removed from the Balinese stage of action, nor translation from the task of the ethnographer.

6. Balinese theories of reference incidentally seem to differ significantly from our folk and philosophical accounts.

Should it be thought I am splitting hairs, let us look at the other terms Balinese use to classify people with whom they live and worship. A common way of speaking about whom one regards as related is as *semeton*, the etymology of which is given as *se-metu-an*, or roughly 'one exit' or 'from one source' (but also 'see the light', 'break through'), so on one reading the exit may be the mother's womb, as *metu* is a synonym in high Balinese for being born. As divorce is common, coming from one mother does not entail having the same father. So perhaps the two most used words to refer to criteria of membership in 'descent groups' are complementarily linked to male and female sexual roles in a rather loose way.

Metaphor plays an interesting part in how relationships are portrayed. So far the possible images are of a procreative penis and coming from a mother's womb. The other terms used for 'kin ties' have, significantly, equally strong metaphorical associations. To refer to ties traced strictly through males (jurally?) the term is *seturunan*, of one descent, from *turun*: to descend, drop or fall. To cloud matters, however, there is another word, *keturunan*, the abstract noun from the same root, which designates all who can trace descent (filiation would be the less metaphorical anthropological expression) through males, females or any mix of the two. Under what circumstances, and with what care, Balinese distinguish between the two terms in actual use is a tricky question.

So far the images refer to sequence expressed spatially (descent), or perhaps better to causal juxtaposition (penis or womb → child, a relation sometimes described as 'metonymy'). Other words conjure up different associations. *Lingse-han*, from *lingseh*: a stalk of rice, refers to a bilaterally reckoned grouping.[7] Perhaps the most widely used term in the region of Bali where I worked is *nyama*. As the noun denoting persons, *penyamaan*, its range is similar to *semeton*, if not broader still. When coupled with *beraya* (a word hard to translate, see Boon 1977:122 where he remarks on its 'egalitarian implications'), *nyama beraya* is used for fellow villagers (sometimes set against *penembahan*, those one prays to, or bows before, *sembah*, i.e. persons of high caste) and so suggests having a common bond. In public meetings it attains a sense at times close to 'moral community'. *Nyama*, however, also refers to parents' siblings, genealogically or by age, and sometimes to all senior members of a *dadiya*. Again *penyamaan* and *nyama* are used interchangeably in many contexts. *Nyama* either comes from the root *sama*, or is its perfect homonym. *Sama* normally is used to indicate something like 'same' or 'similar', sharing some aspect of identity, and the connection is not lost on the Balinese. Whether etymologically or metaphorically these terms have precious little to do with 'kinship'. Nor would we be wise to infer that *nyama*, or *semeton*, which is equally used of 'non-kin', *really* denote kin and the other uses are just marginal, or ancillary, extensions. On what grounds can we be sure that the narrower use is not just one of a number of special applications? To argue

7. Perhaps less surprisingly the language of segmentation is starkly spatial: *késah*, leaving; *kisid*, moving; *pekaad*, going away.

the extensionist case is to impute a degree of essentialism to the Balinese which there is no evidence that they have.

Events and interpretations

So far I have argued that there is little ground to assume from Balinese use of certain important, and closely related, concepts that they mark out conveniently the equivalent to a domain which we call 'kinship'. To what extent, however, does such an argument stand up to an examination of what people do, and say they do, in daily life? In this section I would like briefly to present material dealing with the kinds of groups found in practice and articulated in terms of these Balinese notions and also look at inter-personal relations intended to produce children, namely 'marriage'. In so doing I shall provisionally use the familiar language of kinship but go on to suggest that the data may equally be represented in other terms. For any given interpretation, or theoretical scheme, is underdetermined by the evidence which can be construed in terms of several different possible models.

Whether one wishes to regard the Balinese 'kinship system' as patrilineal, cognatic, about putative origins, or dealing with degrees of similarity or difference will depend in part on the theoretical predilections of the anthropologist *de cuius gustibus non est disputandum*. What is foremost in one model is decentered in another; what are prescriptions or proscriptions in one version are preferences or dangers in another; what one stresses as ideal, another treats as usual practice and so on. From this it should be clear that there is no 'kinship system' as such to describe, for we are dealing in assertions made by people in culture about the different ways in which the 'facts' are interpreted. If the Balinese can, and do, represent what is going on in terms of alternative, if not always fully articulated, models, it does not necessarily follow, however, that these are all much of a muchness to an anthropologist. Some models account for the facts with greater elegance, with fewer imported assumptions and so on, than do others. There may also be internal grounds on which one version is preferable to others. In fact I shall suggest that the interpretation which most adequately accounts for the available ethnography has, in fact, nothing to do with kinship per se at all.

As Balinese domestic and kin relations have been fairly fully outlined elsewhere (Boon 1977; Geertz and Geertz 1975; Hobart 1979; Howe 1980), only a few remarks are needed here. Traditionally after marriage a couple sets up its own home, except for the youngest child or designated heir. Usually a male assumes this role but, failing sons, women are quite acceptable. As land has become increasingly short, sons tend to stay in their parents' compound, as may daughters. In the village ward of Pisangkaja, in the settlement of Tengahpadang in central Bali, on which the following account is mainly based, residence arrangements were as follows. In compounds with more than one household, 22% are related by ties other than between males. This excludes female heirs, who may be argued to rank as jural males (see Hobart 1977). If the constituent compound ties are calculated by sex, those not through males are nearly half. In many instances the exceptions, if they can be called that, are where people live with affines. As living with one's wife's family involves a double humiliation — one cannot afford to keep a family in one's own compound, and one's family cannot afford to keep one — perhaps it is surprising that the figure is so high. If one chooses to read *purusa* as a principle defining agnation however, the problems this entails merge with horrible clarity.

The Balinese do not, as we have seen, speak of their relations in simple kin terms. As with temples, local ties are defined commonly in terms of sites of worship, known as *sanggah* (shrines) or *sanggah gedé* (simply: big shrines), according to the perceived remoteness of the ancestors involved. Traditionally inclusion is expressed in terms of *purusa*. Two points should be noted. It is not uncommon for people to be told, when illness is diagnosed by spirit mediums, that they are worshipping at the shrine of the wrong *purusa*. This allows a play both between social and biological paternity and about ideas of wrong association. Also women, if they are not divorced or do not return home, become ancestors (of neutral sex) in their husband's group as defined by *purusa* (and vice versa, of course, for in-marrying males). The work for, and worship at, ancestral shrines is in theory therefore the critical means of distinguishing members of a group claiming shared *purusa* from others. At marriage women publicly inform both their natal and their marital ancestors of the change of residence and the same on divorce or return. When we look, however, at who actually turns up on such occasions, the results are rather unexpected if one regards *purusa* as simply agnation.

In some parts of Bali many people do not know, or choose not to pay attention to, the sites where they may worship their *purusa*. In the settlement of Tengah-padang, however, such knowledge was pretty general (88% of the households). Attendance at temple affairs being compulsory for its members, on pain of fine or expulsion, turnout is high. At domestic shrines matters are different and while everyone claims that it is almost unthinkable for a person with proper *purusa* ties not to turn up, this is far from the mark in accounting for actual attendance in Pisangkaja, on which I have data, and details of which are given in Table 1. Help in preparing the substantial offerings was undertaken largely by the household, however constituted, of the compound heir (69% of the helpers), as this is regarded as the place of origin, *kawitan*, of families which have moved away. What is a little unexpected is that jural agnates accounted for less than half the remaining help. In all, 10% of the work force were affines, and a further 5% just neighbours (from different worship groups), while several other people turned up who had been adopted into other groups and so had no formal link. So far the pattern is interesting but not perhaps very surprising.

Table 1. Recruitment to ancestor worship groups in Pisangkaja

Activity	Househ.	Agnates	Ex-agnates*	Affines	Neighbrs	Clients	Other	Total
Offering preparation	103	18	6	15	5	1	1	149
Worship attendance	–**	38	62	11	–	4	–	115

* Ex-agnates refers to people who have married out of the compound or who have been adopted into other families, and so properly speaking, worship at other shrines.

** As my concern is with links to the shrine, I exclude the households who are obliged to look after it, as their attendance is a sine qua non, punishable by loss of rice land and other sanctions of a mystical nature. So for convenience, they have been excluded.

When it comes to worship at ancestor shrines, however, the picture is curious. Of those who came to worship only 33% were agnates in any jural, or strict, sense. Close on 10% were affines, who properly should not worship at another's shrine at all. There was also a smattering of political clients where even caste category was in doubt. The largest single category were what one might term 'out-marrying agnates', that is men and women who have left the group on marriage or adoption. In the formal language of agnation therefore, those entitled, and indeed required, to worship at the shrine form a minority.[8] Obviously one may allow a measure of idiosyncrasy in personal motivation. But on what grounds, one wonders, at least as far as worship is concerned, is it justified to impose our category of agnation, rather than say cognation, a general sense of shared origin or mutual concern, or other reasons yet to be discerned? It is inelegant to dismiss the exceptions as mere contingencies. The scientific ploy of moving from the nomological to the statistical does not apply in the same way where human intention or reflexivity is involved. It is also a moot point whether one can assume — as almost all anthropological analyses do — that the actors' interpretations are homogeneous; in other words that they all have the same ideas of what worship, *purusa*, and so on are about. Lastly, to claim that what is important is the jural, or ideal, model does not help at all. Words like *purusa*, *seturunan* or *nyama* do not denote unambiguous classes of person any more than those who turned up can easily be pigeon-holed. One suspects that most of the neat analyses of 'kinship systems' are achieved by looking at the evidence through the wrong end of the ethnographic telescope. That way the warts do not show!

Of what value then is the technical language of kinship? To speak of agnates as a fixed jural category suitable for cross-cultural comparison is of questionable worth. On the one hand such categories do not fit easily with indigenous

8. Agnates are still less evident in agricultural labour relations, the milling of rice and other general forms of work exchange or help. Here affinity, neighbourhood and friendship or political clientage predominate (see Hobart 1979:338–44).

principles, on the other they do not even correspond with the 'facts on the ground' (whatever those be). Most of the terms Balinese use are sufficiently open to interpretation that they can encompass almost anyone who feels like turning up: *nyama* (*beraya*) can be used, for instance, of anyone with whom one wishes to declare relations of a certain warmth and equality. So the Balinese can, with clear Wittgensteinian consciences, declare that those who work and worship together are all *nyama*! The significance of *purusa* may now be clearer. While it may be used to give ostensibly jural instructions (as in adoption when the rule tends to read something like: when looking for an heir take the nearest person from the *purusa* — although low castes in fact tend not to), it may equally refer to different categories. It may be those who feel attachment to a place of birth, or to people they grew up with, or those with whom one has something (still to be defined) in common and so forth. Might one however conclude with the trite comment, that patrilineal systems in theory are always bilateral in practice? For reasons which will be discussed shortly, this is not an adequate answer either.

Now let us turn to marriage. It is sensible to look at this in the context of male–female relations generally. Humans are not the only class of beings, or things, which properly are found in complementary pairs. In myth, male deities have female counterparts, sometimes known, as in India, as their *sakti* which is commonly translated from the Balinese as 'mystical power', but might more adequately be rendered as 'manifest potency or potentiality'. Female deities, like Durga or Uma (associated with destruction or witches, and rice, respectively), tend to be more immediately involved in Balinese life than do their male 'consorts'. It makes little sense, however, to treat the relation between aspects of complex principles (which is how they are often understood) as marriage. The rite of *ngantèn*, which is the normal cultural condition for forming an effective functioning human domestic unit, is also required for other recognized pairings as diverse as pigs (Hobart 1974), drums or slit-gongs. The stress in each instance is upon parts forming a functioning whole (see Hobart 1983, on a capacity to function being a criterion of identity). Priests must have female counterparts to undertake a range of ritual activities but these need not be their wives. In just the same way, a man or woman requires a member of the opposite sex to form a viable household unit because of the sexual division of labour, but this need not in fact be a wife/husband; a sister/brother or another unrelated woman/man is acceptable. The Balinese emphasis on complementarity includes recognition that good cannot exist without evil (Hobart 1985b:188–9), kings without peasants, mystic heroes without anti-heroes. It makes at least as much sense to regard the sexual and reproductive union of humans as an aspect of Balinese ideas about the 'dualistic' functioning of wholes as it does to isolate from context one relationship and compare it with others taken out of context. If we wish to focus on marriage as such, should we not include pigs and slit-gongs which pass through the same rite?

Table 2. Distribution of kin marriages in Tihingan and Pisangkaja

	Tihingan No.	Pisangkaja High caste No.	Low caste No.	Total Pisangkaja No.
Father's brother's daughter	18	2	4	6
2nd and 3rd patrilateral parallel cousins*	17	–	1	1
Ward Endogamy	84	31	126	157
Cumulative	119	33	131	164
Total	243	97	321	418

* There is a regrettable difference between the Geertzes' figures (1975:96) and mine as the latter are based on second-cousin patrilateral unions only. The reason is that third-cousin marriages always involved other closer ties, never patrilateral alone. Therefore I have kept them out.

According to traditional accounts the Balinese practise preferential patrilateral parallel cousin marriage (since Bourdieu 1977, this should be a signal of trouble to come), or failing that, at least marriage within the *dadiya* (Geertz and Geertz 1975), that is traced by ties of *purusa*. The frequency with which such unions occur varies greatly. In the village of smiths studied by the Geertzes it was high, in the mixed-caste community of Pisangkaja (and equally in the other parts of the settlement) it was very low. The figures are given in detail in Table 2, and speak largely for themselves. As against actual father's brother's daughter marriage of 7% in Tihingan, the equivalents in Pisangkaja were 2% and 1% for high and low castes respectively, and sank lower still for second patrilateral parallel cousins. In fact more high-caste marriages between kin were contracted with non-agnates than agnates (66% as against 33%). For low castes the comparable figures rose to 87% with non-agnates. This suggests that, whatever the ideals stated in the literature, most cousin marriages tend towards other possibilities (the more so as notionally father's sister's daughter unions are avoided because they involve direct exchange, so the other three possible cousin unions are not equally open in theory). Quite what this implies will become clearer when we look at the overall pattern.

Table 3. Frequency of approved marriages in Pisangkaja

Relation of partners	High caste No.	Low caste No.
A. Descent group ties only	23	26
B. Descent *and* known kin tie	21	29
C. Kin tie but no descent tie	–	54
D. No tie	5	87
Totals	49	196

Not all marriages take place with the agreement of the families involved, or even the assent of the partners themselves. As my concern here is with the evidence that recognition of kinship in some sense affects positive marriage choice, I shall omit all those unions (22% for unions between members of the same high caste, 44% for all other unions — the basis on which all calculations are made can be found in Hobart 1979:354ff) in which extraneous factors like being caught *in flagrante* or elopement in the face of disapproval seemed dominant reasons. What is striking is the high proportion of kin marriages where there is no agnatic tie at all among low castes (28%, see Table 3). In fact, if one contrasts unions where agnatic ties exist (28%, A + B) in Table 3, with those where kin ties of some kind are held to occur (43%, B + C), there is little evidence in favour of a bias towards agnation. The comparable figures for high castes show an equal balance of agnation as against kin ties. So far it is hard to detect from the figures a preference, especially among low castes, for agnatic unions. Were we now to rephrase matters, for the sake of argument, in bilateral terms, the picture is of an even spread with a slight bias, if anything, towards matrilateral kin. On this evidence, the Balinese might appear to qualify through the backdoor of practice for a volume on cognatic organization!

The discussion so far remains seriously incomplete. Almost half the approved marriages of ordinary villagers are between people with no kin tie of any kind in traditional terminology. Need we consider these? The villagers themselves offer an account which is of interest. There is tacit, and not infrequently explicit, agreement on the importance of wealth. Richer families try to avoid their children marrying into poorer families, while often trying to place their own offspring as advantageously as they can. Realistic Balinese remark that one tends to land up marrying those of one's own kind, by that referring not to *purusa*, *dadiya* and so on, but to family capital assets (or rarely, secure salaries). The results of testing this suggestion statistically are spectacular. Marriage is approved significantly more often where the partners come from households of equal wealth.[9] The choice seems to be cash or kin. Or is it kith or kin?

How do wealth and kin connections compare as criteria for approval of marriage? In kin marriages, where unions are agreed to, the parties are closely equal in economic assets.[10] Regrettably the sample of appropriate marriage was too small to give reliable results on other ways of formulating the problem. In any case, for reasons to which I wish to turn, it is not necessarily useful to ask if the villagers of Pisangkaja contract ties with others for wealth or because of putative kin links. Wealth, certainly, seems to play as important a part, if not more, than kin ties in securing the approval of parents. As the data do not suggest a strong

9. By Spearman's Rank Correlation Test it is significant at 5% if only the two households are taken, but significant at 0.1% if allowance is made for a measure of spill-over between households in a compound, which is the basis on which many Balinese said they operated.
10. By Spearman's test significant at 0.5%, see Hobart 1979:348–62 for a detailed analysis.

bias in favour of agnation as against bilateral kin, an intriguing possibility arises. Family fortunes do not, for the most part, change rapidly in one generation. So those who marry people of equal wealth in one generation may find their children in a position to marry the same people, now kin, in the next! Kin endogamy may be just another way of saying: marry people of like means.

'Aha!' might murmur a cavilling critic, 'for all your fancy footwork at the beginning, you see you cannot do without using kin terms yourself. Your argument is based as much on statistics as the rest of us, so you are just measuring your own mirages!' At the risk of disappointing the critic, I must demur and suggest he or she is confused. First, all anthropological, and indeed everyday, talk about other cultures involves translational schemes. The problems start when we confuse these with 'reality'. Second, my point has been just how inadequate the received categories of anthropological wisdom are; for they are self-confirming hypotheses, which can be turned against themselves. Quite what are these translational schemes, or models, though? It is to this problem I turn in the last part of the paper.

Models and mirages

As a start it is useful to undermine my own material. What I have treated as facts are in effect assertions as to what took place, often countered by rival assertions by others. When a *dadiya* is a *dadiya*, or some other kind of worship group, may well be open to disputed claims (for two examples, see Hobart 1979:604–9). Equally, in marriage the Balinese distinguish several kinds of union which include real and mock capture, arranged marriage and so forth. Each has subtly different status implications. So how a marriage is represented is not a neutral matter, but is rephrased according to circumstance. Powerful political figures may go to pains to show their marriages as by capture, while the victims deny it. Similar considerations of presentation of self apply for other forms of marriage. Further, in small communities with much endogamy people tend to be linked by several ties at once, not just of 'kinship', but wealth, neighbourhood, friendship and others. It would be a fool who would try to reduce these all to some 'real' pervading principle of motivation, such as power (in whose terms, one might ask?). With this underdetermination of the evidence by any single interpretation, we might be wiser to concentrate on the conditions under which Balinese assert one view against another. To do otherwise is to measure mirages.

'Surely', it might be countered, 'there is more order than you suggest. After all there is an organized system of prescriptions, preferences and prohibitions. There is an underlying system of rules.' For various reasons this reply is less adequate than might at first appear. For a start the ontological status of rules is unclear: are they constitutive, regulative, ideal, expectations or observations of normal practice? Further, any positive rule in Bali is open to more than one interpretation. The preference for 'real' patrilateral parallel cousin marriage as sacred (Boon 1977:132) is countered by noting that it is dangerous to the welfare of the partners (one reason given is that ties through males are hot, in contrast to those through females), and serves largely to consolidate wealth and ties within the *purusa*. (One might question whether it is sacred at all, for the nearest term in Balinese is *suci*, 'pure', and such unions are not generally regarded as *suci*.) Perhaps the most celebrated proscriptions involve what might be called a reverse in the flow of women, such as father's sister's daughter marriage (Boon 1977:131) or sister exchange (1977:138). Not only do both occur, but they are justified by alternative interpretations of what is desirable (here that ties through women are cool and so good; and that direct exchange avoids nasty overtones of rank difference). In other words, prescriptions, preferences and prohibitions tend to be re-evaluated in different interpretations. Recourse to rules are lures for the unwary.

With these comments in mind, we may turn to models of Balinese 'kinship', with a close eye on how fully they reflect Balinese ideas and what theoretical assumptions they make. As various versions have already appeared, I need not recapitulate them in detail here (Geertz and Geertz 1975; Boon 1977; Hobart 1979). What is interesting in the Geertzes' *Kinship in Bali* is the contrast they draw between the African (in this instance, polysegmentary) lineage and Ba-linese kin groups which stress origin, *kawitan*, represented spatially by shrines. The central Balinese opposition here is between ideas of origin and citizenship. In contrast, say, to American kinship as portrayed by Schneider, where the di-chotomy is between shared substance and legal code, in Bali it is

> a competition between the symbolism of settlement and citizenship and that of filiation and origin-point. The competition [...] is at once religious, stratificatory, aesthetic, and political, and it amounts to a struggle between the principle that the fundamental bond is coresidence, sociality, and the principle that the fundamental bond is sameness of natural kind, genus. (Geertz and Geertz 1975:167.)

At this level, origin-point is opposed to village or state, but a village here is not 'a body of custom but a metaphysical idea [...] an expanse of sacred space within whose bounds the fates of all residents are supernaturally intertwined' (Geertz and Geertz 1975:167). In other words we are dealing with contrasting clusters of symbols, or cultural constructs.

Certain points should be noted. There is a parallel between the Geertzes' work and Schneider's approach to kinship. Whereas villages from one point of view are constituted by their legal codes, *dadiya* are based on ties of natural kind as well as having codes of conduct (see Schneider 1968:25–9). Similarly Clifford Geertz earlier distinguished Balinese institutions into 'planes of social organization' (1959a), which bear an intriguing resemblance to Inden's carefully ethnographic account of the several 'substance-codes' found in Bengal which include those of worship (*puja*), place or country (*désa*) and livelihood (*jivika*; Inden 1976:13–15) as well as that of *jati*, or genus, into which humans are classed. The difference is that the Balinese do not stress substances, nor their being natural — so that Balinese taxonomic classes (*soroh* rather than *jati*, see above) are differently defined, largely by appearance and function I suspect. Finally, it is implied that the cultural constructs are instantiated by means of a spatial metaphor.

In *The Anthropological Romance of Bali*, Boon elaborates this model to distinguish three 'cultural components' or constructs which form ideal marriage types (1977:121–30). These are love, or romantic marriage, typified in elopement and mock capture; political marriage; and sacred endogamous marriage. Behind these ideals lies a conflict of love and true kinship (see 1977:141), to be found in literature and, sometimes, in life. Romance has two senses, but both ways can be predicated of Balinese culture, in contrast to Epic. For

> Epic posits constant, consistently principled, heroic familial aristocracies whose leaders establish the lawful and the just at the expense of the enemies of right. Romance portrays vulnerable, disguised protagonists, partial social misfits who sense surpassing ideals and must prove the ultimate feasibility of actualizing those ideals often against magical odds. (Boon 1977:3.)

So romantic marriage seems to be pitted against the demands of duty.

For all the apparent similarities, Boon's argument heads at times in the opposite direction from the Geertzes'. Where they focus on Balinese social institutions and the play of spatial metaphor, Boon seeks ideals held to be immanent, as part of a cross-cultural classification (see his criteria of Romance, 1977:3 and 225; his typification of societies, 1977:1 and 6; or his taxonomy of motifs and love, 1977:7). The problem of this idea of 'actualizing ideals' is that it smacks of a cheerful essentialism, which is borne out in Boon's enthusiasm for implicit comparison. The difficulty of leaning on literary sources for support is that they beg the problem of translation (romantic lust might be a more apt caricature of Balinese attitudes than love). And I confess I find it hard to tell whether Bali is a Romantic or an Epic culture. It depends a bit on whom you ask and at what time of the day. Where the Geertzes approach the whole notion of kinship with commendable caution, Boon at times seems to assume that it exists in some sense — if not, I would not know why he should ignore questions of translation, comparison and metaphysical assumptions.

As the last model is my own (1979), I shall refrain from commentary as much as I can for fear of what the Balinese call *nyinggihang dèwèk*, speaking highly of myself! I also had the advantage of writing in the light of the other accounts which I tried to incorporate in an empirical model of possible permutations. Rather than try to isolate ideals, as has Boon, I focused on the ways in which terms and concepts were used in practice. For instance in Tihingan the stress is on relative distance from an origin (*kawitan*). In Tengahpadang it seems to be on belonging to one or another *soroh*, often treated as bounded classes. So membership may be regarded by the Balinese either as a matter of degree or as clear alternatives (that is analog or digital functions respectively). In turn, of what one is a member may be phrased in terms of various words suggesting principles of reckoning or recognition, each of which carries a range of conventional associations. The result is a field of possible representations of relationships. There was empirical evidence of an expressed concern with the criteria of sameness, or similarity (one might note the use of the prefix *se-*, indicating that what follows is grouped as a unity), implied in 'kin' metaphors, whether spatial (origin, descent, exit from one source), or processual (grains on a single ear of rice, the growing implied in *dadiya*). Some of the concern was summed up in villagers' play on *nyama* which was held, rightly or not, to be about sameness (*sama*). Now sameness differs from ideas of kinship in that it allows a wide range of criteria. There was confirmatory evidence that this could equally be read as about shared interests, life chances or even physical looks, by virtue of the doctrine of *karma pala*, by which people are similar or different according to their past actions. Instead of treating Balinese actions in terms of models of kinship and marriage, it made good sense to view these as a question and injunction respectively: who is like you? and marry someone like you!

* * *

In conclusion, on what grounds might one prefer one interpretation to another, allowing that the 'facts' will support alternatives? I suggest two considerations. If a model depends upon assumptions for which there is little evidence in the culture under study, or if it makes assumptions which are questionable on internal philosophical grounds, there are reasons for caution. Boon's approach may be questionable on both grounds. Part of the problem goes back to Schneider's thesis that culture has many levels of reality, none being 'any more or less real' than others (1968:2), except that 'the cultural *level* is focused on the *fundamental* system of symbols and meanings which inform and *give shape* to the normative *level* of action' (1972:39; my italics).

Cultural constructs are seen, then, as having an independent reality and structuring action at other levels, such as the normative, psychological and so forth. The difficulties are several. It has not been established for Bali at least that such levels exist or are recognized. The argument is curiously reminiscent of Plato with abstract ideas giving shape to action and, by implication, explaining them. Finally, postulating levels of reality involves an uncomfortable degree of essentialism (the dangers of which have been spelled out well in Gudeman and Penn 1982:92 ff). Almost any problem can be cleared up, as Russell tried to do with his paradox, by proliferating levels but it is at the cost of making an ontologically cluttered world. The solution may also be spurious (see Hobart

1985a:48–9). The difficulty can be highlighted in the difference of Boon's ideals and the idea of metaphor touched on by the Geertzes. It is one thing to suggest the Balinese use a spatial metaphor of a centre and relative distance in terms of which to talk in a certain context. It is another to impute an abstract ideal in terms of which reality on the ground, or in fact, is ordered. The former just asks us to look at how men use ideas in practice; the latter beckons us into Plato's cave where '*Lasciate ogni speranza voi ch'entrate!*'

Let me reflect for a moment on where this leaves us, if my arguments for more sensitive ethnography and greater awareness of the problems of translating and comparison are worth anything. Allowing a place to indigenous metaphysics is not intended as a grand explanation of why people act as they do in other cultures. It gives more, and less ethnocentric, scope for the modest aim of looking at the empirical conditions under which humans act, even if we are steering away from a safe world of generalities and into doubt. For

> Our doubts are traitors,
> And make us lose the good we oft might win,
> By fearing to attempt.
> (*Measure for Measure* 1.iv, 75–7.)

If comfortable anthropological theorizing and the illusion of easy explanation looks more remote, at least it is closer to what every ethnographer knows at heart, and what the man in a Balinese street could tell him, namely that the world is a complicated place with no simple answers. It also returns the world to the kind of people who live in it, with its paradoxes, uncertainties and all. What anthropologists do when they interpret, or reflect on interpretations, can be seen in different ways. Some, as far apart as Radcliffe-Brown (1952) and Geertz (1973), think of it as a stage towards a sophisticated science. Others — myself included — begin to wonder where anthropology shades into the arts and literature. We are in danger of finding what we are looking for. If we wish to go out and measure the world, we can do so, but we may merely create phantasmagoria like the inter-bubular groove. Perhaps the Balinese are right and there is a price to pay for such doings. As someone closer to home once remarked:

> Haste still pays haste, and leisure answers leisure;
> Like doth quit like, and Measure still for Measure.
> (*Measure for Measure* V.i, 410–11.)

Cognatic or Matrilineal:
Kerinci Social Organization
in Escher Perspective

C.W. Watson

Those familiar with the work of the Dutch painter Maurits Escher will know that he achieves remarkable visual effects through illusions brought about by a *trompe d'œil*. By carefully using the laws of optics and deliberately subverting visual assumptions underlying perspective Escher confuses the observer in such a way that the form of the image changes while he is viewing the picture. Adopting one perceptual frame he sees a certain cluster of objects arranged in a specific order, but when the perspective slips out of that frame into another the objects are rearranged in a different pattern of order. The technique is also found in a simple form in children's puzzles, but Escher developed it into an aesthetic phenomenon of interest to adults.

The methodological consequences of definitions

The primacy of one's initial perceptual frame in determining precisely what is seen is the point which we need to recall in considering questions of kinship and social organization in Southeast Asia. In just the same way as we are visually constrained to view things from one particular perspective in an Escher painting, so are we constrained by the intellectual concepts underlying terms such as 'unilineal' and 'cognatic' to observe social organization according to a predetermined perspective. The patterns and arrangements which we discover depend on preliminary cognitive framing, and consequently, what cannot be accommodated within an adopted perspective is unconsciously ignored: it fails to be perceived. Thus to label a society 'unilineal' or 'cognatic' immediately sets in train the construction of patterns and arrangements to which our observations must conform. The implications of this procedure are what I investigate in this paper in relation to the social organization of the Kerinci in Central Sumatra. As we slip between cognatic and matrilineal in attempting to pin down the society we find neither label is satisfactory: seen through one lens Kerinci is cognatic, seen through another it is matrilineal. At the least this example should make us

uneasy about the usefulness of some of the classic anthropological labels in the
Southeast Asian context.

In the introduction to *Social Structure in Southeast Asia* (1960) Murdock appears to take it as axiomatic that there are societies in Southeast Asia which are
best labelled cognatic and these are essentially different from societies which
are unilineal or double unilineal. A corollary of this assumption is that the
different labels not only distinguish between societies in terms of certain formalistic criteria but also indicate fundamental substantive differences in social
organization. Underlying Murdock's attempts at conceptual clarification of this
kind is a desire to provide a framework for cross-cultural comparison. If there can
be some agreement about definitions and categories, then one can investigate to
what extent societies with a given terminology and a given structure of descent
organization share common institutions with other societies of the same type.
Our first task is to identify which institutions are shared and which not, and
hence delineate how true to type the society under investigation is. The pitfalls
of this approach have frequently been pointed out (for a good recent discussion
see Barnes 1980). The reason for referring to this issue here is that distinguishing
cognatic social organization from other types in Southeast Asia affords a beautiful
instance of exactly how misguided this approach is.

The 'taxonomizing' anthropologist is inclined first to determine whether there
are any unilineal descent groups within the society, and then to classify these on
the basis of among other things an analysis of kinship terminology as patrilineal,
matrilineal, or double unilineal. Leaving aside the question of terminology which
is now recognized to be a less precise indicator than Murdock imagined, and
simplifying for the purposes of argument, we might label a society 'cognatic'
if there are no corporate unilineal descent groups. Using this criterion alone,
there are one or two anomalies, as for instance quasi-unilineal Sinhalese society
(see Leach 1960), but leaving these aside, the negative criterion of absence is
considered usually sufficient for analytical purposes.

The next step in this approach is to search for evidence of those characteristics
which the ethnographic atlas indicates are usually associated with cognatic organization: particular marriage rules, patterns of residence, and so forth. Finally,
the ethnographer's task is to describe as fully as possible the way in which the
society conforms to type, and, more importantly perhaps, to describe deviations
from that type and account for them.

Of course I am simplifying wildly but the general point is, I feel, valid. Once we
commence with a typological model then the path we have to follow is already
predetermined. In practice the manner in which a society is described as con-
forming to type can be extremely sophisticated, and this sophistication is not only
revealed in the very thorough and meticulous way in which patterns of deviation
are identified, but also in new conceptual ideas which emerge from the analysis
of the data. Nevertheless, the principal weakness of such an approach remains,

namely the exclusion from investigation of all those phenomena relating to social structure which do not fit easily within the frame of our taxonomic category. Thus, for example, to put it crudely, in looking at societies with obvious unilineal descent groups we tend to ignore or neglect groupings and associations outside these groups, and conversely in our studies of societies with 'cognatic forms of social organization' we often miss features of those societies which are best linked with unilinearity.

As a consequence of the frequent reference to Minangkabau society in text-books and courses, anthropologists studying the Minangkabau are very conscious of the fact that they are investigating a matrilineal society, and indeed in many cases the reason why they have chosen the Minangkabau is precisely because they are concerned with a problem relating to theories of matriliny. Inevitably, then, the investigator begins by posing questions like: how does matriliny manifest itself; how corporate is the descent group; how is property transmitted; what is the pattern of post-marital residence; what is the kinship terminology; are there any prescriptive marriage rules; is there any affiliation of the children with their father or their father's group; what is the nature of that relationship between mother's brother and sister's son which is often considered the hallmark of matrilineal societies? A sub-set of questions which might be asked is of particular concern to those who are primarily interested in social change, and can be indicated by the general question: to what extent have matrilineal institutions been eroded by modernization over the past one hundred and fifty years, an essay title which I dutifully set my students every year. These questions bear a striking resemblance to the definitions and analysis of matriliny found in Schneider and Gough's classic *Matrilineal Kinship* (1962) and this is no coincidence. That book directly or, perhaps more often, indirectly, has exerted a major influence on all recent studies of Minangkabau society, especially in relation to its emphasis on what has become known as the matrilineal puzzle. Even De Josselin de Jong whose interest in Minangkabau studies antedates its publication, recently (1985) chose to reassess the current state of Minangkabau studies in the light of propositions put forward in Gough and Schneider's book.

Looking at the work published in the last thirty years about the Minangkabau we find that it is indeed questions of the kind formulated above which have been uppermost in the mind of scholars in the course of their research.[1] The initial focus of several studies is the question of inheritance, in particular as this relates to landed property. In a matrilineal society we expect that the transmission of land over generations will descend through the female line, and if this does not occur we are faced with problems in the definition of matriliny. Scholars have, however, long been aware that there are two distinct forms of

---

1. A comprehensive discussion of the extensive literature on this subject is far beyond the scope of this paper and I hope that non-Minangkabau specialists will take it on trust that I am giving a balanced view.

landed property in Minangkabau, *harta pusaka* (ancestral property) and *harta pencarian* (acquired property) and that the rules governing their transmission differ. This has recently sparked off research in the various ways property rights are allocated and consequently on the impacts of social change on matriliny, specifically the extent to which changes in practice lead to the breakdown of matriliny. Connected with this is the discussion of the complex problem of post-marital residence in Minangkabau society, since again changes in patterns of residence, if they have occurred, seem implicitly to suggest that the traditional character of matriliny in the society is under threat. The implication is that if the trend to neolocal residence is indeed marked then husbands are coming to be in a stronger position to influence developments in the nuclear family. Similar considerations occur in a recent study on Minangkabau migration (*merantau*) which, interestingly, challenges the assumption that the relatively recent trend to *merantau Cina* (migrate semi-permanently *en famille*) undermines matrilineal ethos (Kato 1982).

There have also been attempts to disentangle the complexities of descent group organization at the village level (see K. and F. von Benda-Beckmann 1978). These, however, were usually focused upon the complexities of the historical process of segmentation, and surprisingly little has been done on how the descent group functions as a corporate body. There has been some discussion of the investiture of lineage segment heads (*penghulu*) but not much else. The only other area in which descent group membership has become a matter of investigation is, as we might have expected, in relation to exogamy. Earlier studies referred to marriage prohibitions within a *suku* (maximal lineage segment), but more recently it has become clear that rules relating to exogamy are more complicated and depend on local circumstances. Another offshoot of the preoccupation with marriage rules has been the still unresolved debate on preferred marriage, focusing on a possible shift of preference from matrilateral to patrilateral cross-cousin marriage and whether the evidence for preference itself is statistical or structural.

Even in studies of other aspects of Minangkabau society and culture one has the impression of authors constantly glancing over their shoulders at the problems of matriliny, and being compelled from time to time to make passing comments in relation to mainstream Minangkabau debates.[2]

This focus on a limited range of issues has, however, led to the neglect of other important elements in social organization. Three significant omissions in Minangkabau ethnography which come immediately to mind are: a discussion of the territorial determination of relationships and interaction within the village; an analysis of the affective relationships between kin; and a description

---

2. There have, for example, been some very recent distinguished publications which have looked at matters of dispute settlement (K. von Benda-Beckmann 1981), the development of the indigenous economy (Kahn 1980) and a Minangkabau oral narrative (Phillips 1981).

of political and social control within the village. Although some authors map the residential boundaries of descent groups, no one to my knowledge suggests that geographical proximity is an important determinant of social organization, despite clear indications that this might be a subject worthy of investigation. With the exception of recent feminist studies (Tanner 1974; 1982) it is also striking how little attention has been paid to affective relationships — as opposed to ritual or pragmatic relationships — among kinsmen. A great deal is made of the relationship between mother's brother and sister's son with occasional reference to the relationship between adult brother and sister, but, surprisingly, this is all. Very little is said about a father in relation to his children, for example. What a father's feelings are towards sons and daughters is never mentioned, what role he plays in socialization is rarely considered, nor do we find any reference to fathers working with sons in domestic production units. This is not because these relationships are insignificant in the society, but because they fall outside the range of problems delimited by the concern with matriliny.

Social control, the third blank space, is also unduly neglected notwithstanding the fact that so much has been written about dispute settlement among the Minangkabau in recent years. Upon examination it is noticeable that this literature is taken up largely with a discussion of property and with the mechanisms of disputing. Little attempt is made to set the discussion of dispute within the wider frame of the nature of social control within the society. There is, for example, very little said about social sanctions within the village, very little about the informal arbitration of disputes, very little about the role of religion, either in so far as it manages to mediate in disputes through its institutions, or in so far as it may interfere with traditional modes of social control. Levels of segmentation depth at which disputes may be potentially settled are mentioned, but do not often receive the attention they deserve. The reason why this is so seems to me to be clear. It is taken as axiomatic that in a society with corporate descent groups there is stratification and hierarchy within the society depending on the nature of authority within the group and the particular form which segmentation takes. Given this model of a hierarchic structure it is further assumed that however things may operate in practice, implicit in the social organization of the society is a notion that social control is managed through the descent group. Consequently, the problem of how order is maintained in Minangkabau society does not appear to warrant special consideration.

It is precisely those three omissions in Minangkabau studies — relations among kinsmen, questions of territory, and the problem of social control — which receive most attention in research on cognatic systems in Southeast Asia, and as I shall argue below, given the conceptual preoccupations of students in cognatic societies, this is no coincidence.

Because cognatic societies are defined negatively, as simply the reverse of unilineal societies, it should hardly surprise us that scholars have been preoccupied by the absence of unilineal descent groups. This preoccupation has led, in the first place, to a careful investigation designed to show conclusively that such groups do not exist in the society being studied, and then, as a corollary of this finding, to an analytical description of those kin groups which do exist. This in turn has given rise to debates on the definition of cognatic descent and the kindred, and the question of who constitutes kin continues to be an important feature of the study of cognatic systems. In other words it is precisely because corporate groups are absent or at best peripheral, that the ethnographer has turned his attention to the next best thing, the nuclear family, and the ethnography of close primary relationships is the richer for it.

The other area of investigation by means of which researchers try to come to grips with cognatic systems is through the analysis of inheritance patterns, which show clearly marked differences from the practice commonly found in unilineal systems where transmission is through the children of one sex. Directly related to matters of the transmission of property are questions of residence and territory. Thus we find discussion about who inherits the parental house and what effect marrying out has on the rights to inherit property. Territorial boundaries are of some concern because unlike unilineal societies, where each descent group usually has a clearly demarcated territory, in cognatic societies the relationship of residence to descent is not so straightforward and therefore requires investigation.

Stratification in cognatic societies is also a subject which exercises the analytical ingenuity of scholars.[3] Some societies appear to have a very well developed notion of social stratification, e.g. the Javanese, others do not, e.g. a number of Filipino societies. Since in cognatic societies there are no descent groups where authority can be mediated through the group, this raises the issue of how social control is exercised. One of the ways of investigating this puzzle has been by looking at those individuals within the community who hold official positions or play recognized public roles: the *dukun*, the augur, the Kalinga pact-holder etc. and the manner in which they are able to mobilize support and impose their authority.

The reason why these subjects and not others have claimed the attention of recent anthropological studies is because of a theoretical paradigm stressing the fundamental difference between cognatic and unilineal societies. This leads on the one hand to the study of institutions which are regarded as the counterparts of those in unilineal societies, the obvious example being the kin group, and on the other, to subjects which do not appear to be problematic in unilineal societies, but are problematic for cognatic systems: the association of territory with certain groups or the identification of sources of social control within the society. Such a concern, however, stresses the differences between the two systems and diverts

---

3. See for instance the recent controversies about the Iban (Freeman 1981).

attention away from features which are common to unilineal and non-unilineal systems in Southeast Asia. So, for example, if we looked more closely at the composition of groups on different occasions and the principles of reciprocity which operated among members of the groups we might find that similar structures exist in unilineal societies — always provided of course that one was prepared to look for categories, classes and groupings other than the unilineal descent group. Conversely, if we were prepared to look more closely at patterns of obligation established between two families at marriage within cognatic societies, then again we might find that differences between the two types begin to vanish.

The description of Kerinci society which follows is an attempt to illustrate the advantages of maintaining just such an open view of social organization, and not foreclosing one's options by labelling a particular form either unilineal or cognatic. The intention is not simply to suggest, as others have already done very persuasively, that we have to be more aware of the potential exclusiveness of our categories, but that in the current state of anthropological theory, as in viewing an Escher picture, we should be intellectually agile enough to slip easily and frequently from one perspective to another.

A schematic outline of the kinship system of Lubuk Dalam

I. *From a cognatic perspective*
The population of Lubuk Dalam is now around 10,000 but about half this number comprises Minangkabau immigrants who have settled there since 1922. The native indigenous population, then, consists of about 1,000 families. A sizeable fraction of that number derives their principal means of livelihood from non-agricultural professions. They may be employed in minor civil-service positions in the neighbouring town of Sungai Penuh which is the administrative centre of Kerinci, or may find casual employment as day labourers or petty market traders. Even those who are not full-time farmers, however, retain an interest in agriculture and they often have access to small irrigated rice-field plots in the village. Although the total area of wet-rice land is some 350 hectares, land in the hills behind the village is relatively abundant, and if carefully cultivated by intercropping vegetables and annuals among coffee bushes and cinnamon trees, can yield a modest but secure income, provided that international commodity prices are not too erratic.

Inheritance is bilateral and sons and daughters inherit equally. Occasionally one hears that there is a preference that landed property should devolve on the daughters of a family but in practice we find that land is divided equally. There is, however, an understanding that the parental house should be inherited by one of the daughters, but the way in which this inheritance is hedged round, for example, by allowing brothers relatively free access to it, indicates clearly that such transmissions of property do not imply any preference for matriliny. Although property is not usually formally divided until some time after the death of the original owners, indeed on occasions not until it has passed into the hands of the second descending generation, once formal division has taken place, individuals have the right to dispose of it as they wish. This has meant that in the last sixty years, and especially during the last thirty, there have been numerous sales of land to new settlers in the village as more and more of the agricultural land has been converted into a residential area. Various systems of land-pledging, sharecropping and tenancy arrangements exist but these need not concern us here. Although the incidence of various negotiations and settlements in relation to land has certainly increased in recent times, there is nothing to suggest that arrangements differ in principle from what they were in an earlier period.

Post-marital residence is initially uxorilocal, but it seems that as in the Thai case this is only a temporary arrangement until a couple has found their feet, when they are expected to set up a residence of their own. As among the Aceh-nese the site of the new residence should preferably be on land belonging to the wife which she often acquires through an *inter vivos* gift from her parental estate. Occasionally again one hears of a preference for marriage within the village, but in practice men and women frequently take spouses from neighbouring villages and indeed from among members of other ethnic groups who have settled in Kerinci. Both kinds of cross-cousin marriage are highly regarded and both kinds of parallel-cousin marriage are prohibited.

In everyday social intercourse relations with both patrilateral and matrilateral kin are equally stressed. All other things being equal there may be a slight preference for association with matrilateral kin, but this is hardly noticeable, since all other things are rarely equal. In terms of day-to-day co-operation and or-ganization it is clearly territorial proximity which determines whom one will have most dealings with. Although houses are very densely clustered together in what is approximately a four hundred yard square, and therefore all one's kinsmen are within easy calling distance, in practice one calls first upon one's neighbours for co-operative ventures such as assistance in the cooking of a ceremonial meal. Sometimes one may go further afield to look for help of a special kind, when one is, for example, preparing an upland plot prior to planting, but when one does there is no clear preference for one set of relatives over another and it is usually personal compatibility which is the deciding factor.

Because of this equal stress on both sides Ego in his or her relations with kins-men operates with a notion of a personal kindred. Most people seem acquainted with their degree of kinship with all descendants of their four grandparents. Although this may not appear to be a very extensive range of awareness, if one appreciates that divorce and re-marriage is frequent, and arrangements of residence for the children of divorced parents can be complex, this is in fact no mean feat. Kinship terminology is Dravidian, and one might have expected the terminology to function not only as a system of classification for Ego but also as a first instance mnemonic when it comes to identifying the degree of relationship with someone. In fact this expectation is frustrated because inter-generational marriage is permitted, and Ego often has a range of choice in the kinship term adopted towards the other. There is no space to recount the possibilities which arise in such circumstances. This promiscuity, however, is exactly what one might expect in a cognatic society.

The term for Mother's Brother, *Tuo* (from Malay *Tuan*), distinguishes mother's from father's brothers and at first sight there would appear to be a special relationship between mother's brother and sister's child, of the kind which exists in Minangkabau society. However, we need to note that the term for Father's Sister, *Datua* (perhaps from the Malay *Datuk*), distinguishes that category from Mother's Sister, something not found in Minangkabau, and there is an important relationship between mother's sister and brother's child. Thus we find that there is a symmetry in Ego's relationships with members of the first ascending generation. The terminology and these special relationships (as well as those which exist among cross-cousins of both sides) suggest an as-if pattern similar to that described for the Sinhalese, that is, it is as though the society were divided into two exogamous unilineal moieties.

In terms of ideology or norms I could not distinguish a preference for one set of kin over another. In cases where individuals did express a desire or a tendency to associate with either matrilateral or patrilateral kin this could be explained on the basis of highly idiosyncratic criteria, for example, one set of kin being of higher social standing or wealthier than the other.

If one tried to identify some form of unilineal awareness through perceiving how descent is traced through focal ancestors one finds that here too the analysis confirms that we are dealing with a cognatic system. Most named ancestors of the third generation and above are males. The founder of the village is a man whose name is recorded. There is, however, very little knowledge of discrete individual ancestors above the third ascending generation. One tends to think of such people under the generic term *nenek-moyang*. Where the name of the ancestor is remembered it is usually because he was a man of unusual prominence in the village, and there one notes that his bilateral descendants all claim him as an ancestor. Sometimes this circle of cognatic kinsmen may even combine to form an ad hoc quasi-corporate group for ceremonial purposes.

One good example of this phenomenon occurred when I was in the field. A certain *Haji* Pangeran who had died in 1926 had begotten a son Achmad in 1921 by his last marriage of four. Achmad decided that he would go on the *haj* in 1979. It is customary to hold a ceremonial feast (*kenduri*) prior to the departure of pilgrims, and various groups and associations of people take it in turns to invite the intending pilgrims with whom they have some association to such a feast. On one occasion all the bilateral descendants of *Haji* Pangeran decided that they would hold a feast in honour of Achmad. Even though there had been numerous marriages and births among the descendants, the senior members, particularly the women, seemed to be able to list all the descendants without much difficulty. The feast was a welcome occasion since it provided an opportunity for people who did not meet all that frequently to renew their acquaintance.

The *kenduri* held in honour of *Haji* Achmad seems to be a useful point at which to bring this description of Lubuk Dalam kinship seen from a cognatic perspective to a close. Although it is simply one event, it is representative not only of the way in which bilateral kinship is brought into play in the organization of a ceremony, but also of how the celebration of bilateral descent may itself be the focus of the ceremony.

II. *From a matrilineal perspective*

In the light of the description so far it would be reasonable to conclude that kinship organization in Kerinci is cognatic. There are one or two features, for example the kinship terminology and perhaps the fact of uxorilocal residence, which are slightly at odds with such a categorization, but if we remember Thai and Sinhalese structures these anomalies should not worry us unduly. If now, however, I go on to describe the organization of unilineal descent groups in Lubuk Dalam, it is immediately evident that the classification of Kerinci kinship is not so straightforward as it seemed.

There are in fact four named matrilineal descent groups in Lubuk Dalam, which are to all intents and purposes local descent groups since they exist only in Lubuk Dalam and in no other village in Kerinci. The names of these groups are taken from honorific Javanese titles which must be presumed to have been given to the founders of such groups. They are *Rio Sangaro*, *Rio Mandaro*, *Rio Pati* and *Rio Temenggung*. Each group is known as a *lurah*. Thus in asking a person to which group he or she belongs one asks of which *lurah* he or she is a member. The three *lurah* first mentioned each consist of three sub-lineages or *perut*, the last, *Rio Temenggung*, has only two *perut*. Each *perut* is supposedly headed by a *Depati*, another Javanese title, and hence among neighbouring villages Lubuk Dalam is known as the village of the *Depati Sebelas Perut*, the *Depati* of the Eleven Sub-lineages. Each *perut* is further sub-divided into *pintu*, but the number of these *pintu* appears to be irregularly defined. They are not strictly named: some *pintu* seem to be identified in relation to a geographical area in the village, others are named in relation to an ancestor, sometimes an ancestress. Within *pintu* one finds further sub-divisions known as *sikat* or *tandan* (the metaphor alludes to a comb and bunch of bananas), but these are even more uncertainly defined than *pintu*, and when these terms are used they appear to mean the smallest recognized unit of matrilineally related kinsmen, usually of two or three generation depth which functions corporately in so far as members have rights to a joint estate. (It remains joint only as long as it is undivided, but even when it has been divided, the fact that it was once joint perhaps allows us to view the group as corporate.) As far as I could unravel the complexities of the system, *pintu* seemed to comprise between two and four *sikat* or *tandan*. (The two terms were sometimes used synonymously and sometimes with the implication that *tandan* was an inclusive unit which comprised several *sikat*.) Although these divisions suggest a segmentary model, in fact people did not usually know how their *sikat* were linked through an apical ancestor to other *sikat* in the same *pintu*. They certainly did not know how *pintu* within a *perut* were related through descent. There was, however, a general consensus that in some way the *perut* named *perut panjang* in all the *lurah* was the most senior.

It might have been thought that one of the ways in which descent could have been traced was in relationship to the *Depati* title mentioned above, which is transmitted from Mother's Brother to Sister's Son, but this turns out to be problematic because *Depati* titles although originally restricted to *perut* have now proliferated, so that in most cases we find that *pintu* heads have a *Depati* title, and sometimes even within a *pintu* there may be more than one *Depati* with no agreement among them in relation to seniority. Thus a segmentary conceptualization of the *lurah* structure turns out to be unworkable. Although there is a general recognition in principle of the various levels of inclusiveness reflected by the terms, *lurah*, *perut* and *pintu*, in fact the important operational unit is at the level below *pintu*, as can be seen clearly on the occasion of dispute settlement. One way in which a sense of corporateness can be maintained in a group is through joint possession of landed property, but here again we find that in Lubuk Dalam there is no corporately held landed property to speak of. On the other hand, it should be noted that there is a category of *pusaka* (heirloom) property, consisting of various revered objects, which are the property of the *lurah* as a whole. Furthermore, there are regular occasions on which the members of the *lurah* act as a body under the management of periodically elected *lurah* officials, for example at the annual cleaning of the irrigation channels prior to the commencement of the agricultural cycle. Thus despite one's doubts about whether these are segmentary lineages, it does seem clear that they are matrilineal descent groups.

If we shift our attention for the moment from the organization of the *lurah* to principles of recruitment, then further curious features emerge. In the first place recruitment is automatically through birth. One has the same *lurah*, *perut* and *pintu* as one's mother. However, men also acquire membership of their wife's lineage through marriage. That this is seen as real membership and not just association is evidenced by the fact that when one puts the question to a married man about which *lurah* he is a member of, he almost invariably replies with the *lurah* of his wife. If one wants to know what his natal lineage is one has to rephrase the question. Within the *lurah*, however, one does distinguish male members by birth and male members by marriage. The former are known as the *anak jantan* (the male children) and the latter as the *anak betino* (female children) of the *lurah*. Thus it is possible to become incorporated into a second *lurah* at marriage, although as an *anak betino* one is not entitled to hold any offices in that *lurah*, but is expected to contribute to its welfare. If one is elected to an office in one's natal *lurah*, or through heredity acquires a *Depati* title, then one is, as it were, reincorporated into one's natal *lurah* and has a dual obligation.

In addition to looking at principles of recruitment a further avenue of invest-igation into the nature of descent groups is observation of the marriage rules which obtain in the society. It is often suggested, for example, that exogamy is one of the criterial features of lineage organizations. If that is the case then the matrilineal groups in Lubuk Dalam do not qualify as lineages. Not only is marriage permitted at the *lurah* level between members of the same *lurah*, but marriage is also permitted between members of the same *perut*. I also came across two instances of marriage within the same *pintu*. As far as I could make out these marriages had occasioned no surprise or comment, and indeed the fact that the husband and wife were of the same *pintu* did not appear to have been noticed until I drew attention to the fact in the course of my enquiries. There was, however, a strong awareness in the community of degrees of kin with whom marriage was prohibited. In some cases rules of prohibition were interpreted according to Islamic formulae, but in fact, what were often alleged to be Islamic prohibitions turned out to be non-Islamic, for example the prohibition alleged to be Islamic of patrilateral parallel cousin marriage.

The nearest I came to the formulation of an exogamy rule was that two people who shared the same great-grandmother (*tunggal nunyan*) to whom they were related through maternal grandparents who were same sex siblings could not marry. The interesting feature of this rule is that, although it does not surprise us that there should be such a prohibition when the grandparents concerned were sisters, and hence the couple wishing to marry would be members of the same minimal matrilineage (*sikat*), in the case when the two grandparents were broth-ers there need be no lineage connection at all between the couple. From this it is clear that neither relationships among the various lineages, nor the degree of relationship within the lineage are pertinent considerations in considering mar-riage rules. On the contrary, it is degrees of consanguinity reckoned cognatically which are at issue. Another way of regarding the same phenomenon is to revert to the fiction of there being two exogamous moieties, which as we have seen is a neat way of looking at the kinship terminology. In this perspective one can see at a glance that in the problem case mentioned above the couple wishing to marry would be of the same matrilineage. This fiction, however, cannot be expanded for the society as a whole, since marriage is only prohibited according to this calculation within the limited range of kin (*tunggal nunyan*) mentioned above. Hence seeming anomalies do arise viewed from the perspective of the terminology when classificatory parallel cousins are married or even on occasions when a classificatory parent marries a classificatory child.

Consideration of the marriage rules, then, leads us into difficulties if we try to accommodate them to a description of the society organized around the concept of matriliny. If one had considered them as expressions of a cognatic system the difficulties would have dissolved, although perhaps one would still have been left with the marriage across generations to explain. Taking together the information about the social organization derived from both perspectives we can perhaps conclude that if we leave aside the matter of descent groups then Kerinci falls quite happily into the category of cognatic systems. Unfortunately, it is not possible simply to dismiss the descent groups in this way just so that we can find an appropriate label. However strange they look, regarded either from as far away as Africa or from as close as Minangkabau, they are recognizable matrilineal groups of greater or less corporateness. By way of conclusion, then, I want to suggest an explanation of the social structure with the aid of some historical reconstruction.

Speculative reconstructions

In the literature on South Sumatran societies a lot of space is given to what are known as *ambil anak* marriages (Jaspan 1964), that is marriages where the husband resides uxorilocally and becomes incorporated into his wife's family. It is not altogether clear to what extent he becomes incorporated, nor is it clear whether the patrilineal stress in those societies gives rise to patrilineal descent groups. On the basis of his field-work in the 1960s, however, Jaspan felt confident enough to argue that the increasing statistical preponderance of *ambil anak* marriages over other forms of marriage warranted the conclusion that Rejang society had moved from patriliny to matriliny. Now there are all sorts of difficulties with Jaspan's ethnography, not the least of which is his equation of the attachment of the husband to his wife's family with matriliny. Moreover, there is no description in his work of anything resembling corporate descent group organization. Nevertheless, starting from the institution of uxorilocal marriage in Lubuk Dalam I think we can see that the Kerinci situation offers a much better example than Rejang of the way in which matrilineal descent group organization arises out of that institution.

In Kerinci we find that all marriages are of the *ambil anak* type. The husband resides in his wife's house and becomes incorporated into her descent group as has been described above. How might matriliny thus have arisen in a society which it seems fair to describe as fundamentally cognatic in ideology? To answer this we must look at the way in which villages were founded. What appears to have happened is that individual men and their immediate families moved out from a parent village for one reason or another and set up a settlement in a nearby area. The typical construction was a house to which other houses were added in a terrace as the family expanded, leading to a characteristic longhouse construction. These houses in Lubuk Dalam are known as *larik* and are associated with the various *lurah*. The oldest *larik* is *larik ngoh* and is associated with the *lurah Rio Sangaro*, the *lurah* of the founding father, a certain Sutan Kamat. If an uxorilocal pattern of residence was universal, one would expect that in the early days men would move out of the new settlement and seek their wives from elsewhere, in particular from the parent village. This would mean that in the course of the domestic cycle the able-bodied men in the settlement would consist of men who had married in. When it came to joint co-operative efforts which were periodically needed for communal enterprises, the question of who had the authority to manage the organization of the new community would arise. In the first generation of the settlement the leader of the community would be the founding father, but after his death one was left with the problem of transmission of authority since his sons had moved out.

One solution would be to have authority devolve to the sons-in-law, and in fact that is exactly what one finds in the area of Hiang in central Kerinci. There, titles of office pass through the female line from mother to daughter, but the titles are worn (*dipakai*) by the in-marrying husband. If the wife dies and the husband returns to his natal village, or if there is a divorce, then the title reverts to the wife or her daughters. The other solution is for the title to pass from Mother's Brother to Sister's Son, thus ensuring that it remains in the village. This is the practice in Lubuk Dalam. The objection to this hypothetical account is that when the sister's sons marry out of the village they will temporarily take their title with them, but in fact we find that traditionally there is a stipulation that all men with a title must reside in Lubuk Dalam. Thus one imagines a situation where on the death of a *Depati* the sister's son who replaces him is called back from where he is residing uxorilocally, to his native village in order to assume authority there and assist in leading the community. This would at least explain the matrilineal transmission of titles.

The origin of descent groups is slightly more complex. We can imagine that what existed originally in the way of organization was cognatic in form, that is, all descendants from the founding father were taken to comprise a distinguishable ancestor-oriented kindred. Since, however, residence was uxorilocal, to all intents and purposes this meant that the kin group who remained within the village was matrilineally related. If one wanted to distinguish among families within this group, it would be feasible and pragmatic to distinguish between the descendants of the several in-marrying husbands. This seems to be the case on the *pintu* level. *Pintu*, one should note, refers to a door or a residence. Thus in the past when asking about a family one would enquire about its *pintu* and one would be given an answer, as one still is, in terms of the geographical location of the residence, for example, *pintu dibawah air* ('the house below the water'), or in terms of the woman or the man of the house. Within this fundamentally cognatic society, then, we find that the primary term to designate a group is *pintu*, and it is used to distinguish among the descendants of two sisters.

When we look at the history of the three *lurah* which subsequently moved into the village after the founding *lurah*, what we encounter is that new families were allowed to settle adjacent to the original *larik*, and in assimilating to the existing organization these settlers adopted one of two strategies. Either they joined the structure of the existing *lurah* and became distinguished from the original settlers only in being considered members of a different *perut*, or they established their own families as distinctive groups in their newly acquired territory, thus becoming distinctive *lurah*. In this way one sees the elaboration of a lineage structure through accretion and expansion rather than through segmentary fission. One can next conceive that as the population of the village grew in size, and as the practice of uxorilocal residence became more and more firmly entrenched, matriliny as a mode of classification became increasingly favoured. Since at the same time there is evidence that Minangkabau migrants had settled in neighbouring areas in Kerinci, it is to be expected that their influence gave ideological sanction to the matrilineal institutions which were developing.

How was it, though, that if kinship organization was cognatic there was no transmission of titles from father to son? One cannot imagine all sons residing uxorilocally in different villages, especially when other newcomer families settled in the village and men began to seek their wives from these new families. Here one can only speculate that rules concerning the transmission of titles of office — as opposed to real property — had become so established that the descent rule of transmission from Mother's Brother to Sister's Son was accepted unquestioningly. Alternatively, it might well have been the case that in fact sons originally did have a claim on the title, but this claim was rarely exercised and eventually fell into disuse. This possibility is suggested by the practice in other villages throughout Kerinci, particularly in the south, where Minangkabau influence has been slight. There it is clear that titles such as *Depati* can be inherited through either the patriline or the matriline, and constant stress is put on the classic cognatic mode of reckoning. As the people from south Kerinci put it, they are descended from four grandparents and eight great-grandparents.

* * *

Looking at an Escher picture we see it synchronically and try to organize the images as we regard them at the moment of perception. In the past, British social anthropology was often accused of trying to premise social theory on a similar kind of synchronic perspective. Social organization was conceived as a picture and the task of a theory was to devise a set of analytical terms adequate to interpret the relationship between the elements in that picture. Even though that theoretical approach has long been abandoned, it is perhaps because of the residual legacy of that tradition of anthropology that we continue to be absorbed by questions of definition and typology, still searching for universally acceptable terms of discourse. In any such enterprise which relates to a description of kin-based organizations problems always arise with respect to seeming anomalies, such as described above. Fortunately, however, unlike the viewer of the Escher painting hopelessly trapped into forever having to decide one way or the other how he sees the images, the anthropologist is not condemned to the anarchy of the either/or of synchronic perception. The fact that forms of social organization have a history means that potentially the anthropologist can view them as being in a state of Heracleitan flux. This realization in turn may lead him to discover that categories are not so mutually exclusive as he might have imagined, and consequently it becomes possible to understand how Kerinci society can be seen as simultaneously unilineal and cognatic.

The Evolution of Kinship Relations in Rembau, Negeri Sembilan, Malaysia

Maila Stivens

This paper explores the evolution of kin relations in colonial and post-colonial Rembau,[1] focusing upon two related questions: first, what social forces have created and reproduced matrilineal and cognatic aspects of kin relations, and second, whether — as popular ideology maintains — Malay family structure is moving to a modern elementary form. I argue that while the famous *adat perpatih* is commonly labelled 'matrilineal', this greatly oversimplifies the situation, particularly in the context of modern Malaysia. Many aspects of social and kin organization often seen as special to Negeri Sembilan in fact occur in many other areas of Malay society, especially some degree of female-centredness in household organization and close kin ties. It is a mistake to see *adat perpatih* as a unitary social phenomenon; it is more meaningful to deconstruct the concept and to explore a number of dimensions of kin relations. I suggest that kin relations in present-day Negeri Sembilan encompass a number of historically generated, contradictory dimensions, consisting of 'matrilineal' elements which have been conserved through the colonial and post-colonial social process, together with cognatic elements, always present but recently becoming more important in the reproductive aspects of kinship.

Kinship, cognation and capitalist development

There has been a tendency in discussions of cognation to define it in a negative way, to see the absence of lineality as the problem (see Appell 1976); but patriliny and matriliny are not particularly meaningful constructs, as the debates about lineage theory have pointed out (Kuper 1982). The problems in defining cognatic

1. Research was carried out in three neighbouring villages in Rembau, Negeri Sembilan from July 1975–September 1976 and was supported by a SSRC (UK) Studentship in the Department of Anthropology, London School of Economics. Further visits were made in January–March 1982, funded by the Hayter Travel Fund, and in 1984 and 1985. I am grateful to the participants of the Seminar on Cognatic Social Organization (Amsterdam 1983), and to Maurice Bloch for comments on the paper.

kinship are part of a larger problem of reifying kin relations. An essentialist assumption of kinship as a thing in itself, whether this is identified as an idiom, an affective or cultural core or as a jural mode can be very misleading.[2] My own personal prejudice is to deconstruct kinship into a constituent set of social practices. While the core relations of kinship in specific social contexts often include the social relations of procreation, marriage, socialization and sexuality, to denote any specific set of relations a priori as kinship only produces formalism. Of course, in the formalistic sense of genealogical connection all kinship is cognatic.

Such a deconstruction prevents any simplistic association of kinship with economic forms. Recent empirical work in family history has underlined the need to question the alleged association between the 'nuclear family' and capitalism and its corollary that capitalist development in the periphery also undermines wider kin ties. Much of this debate, however, has foundered on a confusion between household and family and essentialist notions of the elementary family as a basic unit of kinship.[3] I have argued elsewhere that the concrete conditions of capitalist development do not in fact pare kinship down to a basic elementary family form but tend to produce a range of modified extended family forms which, although basically cognatic, are often female-centred.[4] In particular, I argue that in a very general sense kin relations are 'domesticated' by the development process and increasingly centred on the reproductive tasks of maintaining family and household relationships that the sexual division of labour ascribes to women. Some tendency towards female-centredness thus tends to accompany certain stages of capitalist accumulation, especially where male out-migration leaves women in *de facto* control of the household economy. It is easy to interpret such relations as a kin-based welfare system and I explore this issue further below.

I am not arguing here that capitalism directly determines the shape of kin relations. Some recent accounts have come close to arguing that this is the case, and that capitalism *needs* such forms to reproduce its conditions of existence (Meillassoux 1981). Capitalism's conditions of existence may be reproduced partly through such relations in concrete situations, but the relationship should

2. See Geertz and Geertz (1975) for a critique of anthropological approaches to the study of kinship and references to the debates about the definition of kinship. It will be apparent that I disagree with their emphasis on a cultural core of kinship.

3. For example, there has been a noticeable tendency in historical studies of the Euro-American family to read off family structure from economic determinations of the household as a productive unit or from inheritance patterns (see Goody et al. 1976). Household and family structure cannot be reduced to functions of the economy.

4. I suggest that capitalism implicates various sectors and social forms outside the logic of capital–labour relations, including kin relations, into the mechanism of the reproduction of its conditions of existence (Stivens 1984). In the recent past the overall capitalist development process has produced rural backwardness in Rembau and concomitant out-migration to capitalist sectors. While rural social forms in the Third World often retain an outward pre-capitalist appearance and the central significance of kin relations, these relationships are in fact subsumed in the dominant capitalist process.

be seen as contingent. The form kin relations take historically is mediated by a complex of economic, political, juridical, cultural and ideological factors.

The decline and fall of 'matriliny' in Rembau

It is clear that the pre-colonial matrilineal system, as a system, was in decline well before formal colonial rule was imposed,[5] although there is considerable debate in Malaysia today about the characterization of such pre-colonial systems. It is relevant here to refer to the standard anthropological arguments about the decline of 'matriliny'. These assert that matriliny is inherently unstable, because it is assumed either — rather androcentrically — that male authority is inevitable, or that matriliny is demographically unreliable and unworkable. Furthermore, it is claimed that matriliny will automatically dissolve with increasing economic differentiation (see Douglas 1969:110) or, as I would put it, incorporation into world economic systems.

The Negeri Sembilan case defies these simplistic prognoses. The colonial social system politically subsumed *adat perpatih*, the matrilineal 'custom', preserving in somewhat fossilized form some aspects of the kinship system, particularly land tenure and *adat* ideology. Moreover, unlike some other countries where elements in colonial society were very hostile to matriliny, a number of colonial officials' published comments on Negeri Sembilan were in fact favourable. For example: 'If one or other sex had to be favoured as regards general culture and economic stability, it would be well that it should be the female sex' (De Moubray 1931).[6]

Rembau, one of the traditional districts of Negeri Sembilan, was by no means a natural economy before colonial rule.[7] Material on the nineteenth-century Negeri Sembilan village economy suggests that peasants were involved in producing a range of small commodities, including livestock for sale, fruit, sugar, areca and in various experiments with coffee, tapioca, coconuts and gambier, as well as growing rice for consumption (Gullick 1951). Smallholder participation in the rubber boom of the early years of the twentieth century did not in itself create a new petty commodity form of production; such production had existed far earlier although on a much smaller scale and in a relatively uncommoditized form.

There is some debate about the ultimate fate of much smallholder rubber production after the rubber booms. In Rembau, as in many other areas, this

---

5. See De Josselin de Jong (1952) for an account of Negeri Sembilan history.

6. I do not have the space to report here on what is known about colonial policy towards the *adat perpatih*; see Wong (1975) and Hooker (1972).

7. The economic and political development of Malaya has been treated in a large body of historical studies. See Jomo Sundaram (1977) for a theoretical discussion of the history of Malaya and full discussion of this body of historical work, and also Burns (1982) and Lim Teck Ghee (1977). These accounts allow us to trace some aspects of the relationship between the peasant economy and merchant capital invested in Malaya.

has been a sorry tale of continuous crisis with low returns and deterioration of holdings. My own view follows Lee (1973) in suggesting that political controls led to a crisis in reproduction of the means of production; that is, peasants were the low-cost, efficient producers compared to the estates and were hindered from developing by political controls set in motion by various local class factions serving plantation interests. Smallholders were unable to replant efficiently and to extend their holdings because of colonial land controls (Lim Teck Ghee 1977). Although post-colonial development projects have attempted to revitalize petty commodity production, at the time of my field-work rubber holdings in Rembau were very decrepit, with nearly a third of the acreage untapped. The situation has been made worse by the emergence of a severe labour shortage as large numbers of villagers migrate to work in the expanding economic sectors generated by industrial capitalist investment.

Subsistence rice production seems to have maintained fairly constant (lowish) levels of production until the 1960s.[8] Since then it too has been hit by severe labour shortages. There are now large areas of *sawah tinggal*, unused rice land. Fruit production provides some extra income for a minority of peasants. A few people have pensions, and a few earn salaries or wages as teachers, clerks and labourers in nearby small towns. Today, however, few people in my three study villages could survive without remittances from kin.[9]

As noted above, migration from Rembau has risen sharply recently. Malay men in Negeri Sembilan have long been known for leaving their villages to become policemen and soldiers in the colonial area. But today single women and men, as well as younger married men (mainly with their wives and children), are migrating in increasing numbers to the city to seek work in a range of white and blue collar occupations, including clerical, factory and domestic work. Rembau district has something of a reputation for providing schoolteachers, clerks and civil servants for the Malayanized bureaucracy. Thus, in fact, very few people between the ages of twenty-five and forty now live permanently in the villages I studied, apart from some women who are bringing up their children in the rural area while their husbands work away. Many more spend intermittent periods back in the village when laid off work or having babies.

There are growing class differences in Rembau society, but these do not arise out of the structure of village production but from relationships imposed by the growth of the post-colonial capitalist state, and an expanding Malay middle class. There are, of course, some differences in size of land holdings (a very few people

8. The Annual Report of Negeri Sembilan 1892 reports 400 *gantang* of paddy on an average holding, a figure startlingly close to the production figures I obtained nearly ninety years later.

9. On the basis of an investigation of all matrilineal descendants of the oldest female resident in each household or compound (excluding duplication of related households) I derived a figure of approximately 1,400 of whom 950 were non-resident. This figure gives some idea of the importance of migration, although it is itself an underestimation because it did not include migrants who no longer have ascendants living in the village.

in the study villages have ten to twenty acres of rubber land), but these 'concentrations' generally did not arise from the generation of surplus within the village economy but from economic structures outside it.

It is tempting to depict the Rembau rural economy as a subsistence community implicated in capitalist reproduction. Whether its economic forms are generated by the workings of capitalism, or whether they represent the uneven penetration of capitalist forms into pre-capitalist enclaves is another matter (see Kahn 1980; Meillassoux 1981).[10] Whatever the case, Rembau Malay society has only recently formed a sizeable labour reserve; if anything, the remittance economy is reproduced by the subsistence community, rather than supporting it.

The reconstitution of adat perpatih

I now turn to how the colonial incorporation of *adat perpatih* into formal political and juridical relationships tended to conserve and reconstitute a number of dimensions of the matrilineal system, including matrilineal ideology, and the tenure of land.

As numerous writers have noted, *adat perpatih* in the pre-colonial era was a body of oral tradition, imparting customary law and enshrined in a set of sayings (*perbilangan adat*) which governed personal behaviour and kin relations. According to the core concepts of *adat* ideology in Rembau, there are twelve named matrilineal clans (*suku*) in the district, each divided into lineages (or sub-clans, *perut*) which ideally form localized groups.[11] Following the conceptual model of *adat perpatih*, a village consists of a localized lineage core of women living with in-marrying males. Ideally, the mother's brother also plays an important role, *adat* ceremonial marks all important traditional occasions and governs the tenure of ancestral land, with rights passing from mother to daughter. According to the 'experts', lineages form exogamous groups in the clan system, though many villagers actually operate with the notion that one cannot marry someone from the same clan; Parr and Mackray (1910) suggest that this was the practice until the end of the nineteenth century.

Not only villagers and anthropologists, but successive administrations and a range of observers of Negeri Sembilan society have entered into the discourse about *adat perpatih*. *Adat* is still one of the most crucial concepts in Negeri

10. A standard depiction of the subsistence community sees it as reproducing the conditions of existence of capitalism by cheapening the cost of labour power (Meillassoux 1981). As I note in the paper, it is one thing to assert that capitalism implicates other social forms in the reproduction of its conditions of existence, but quite another to suggest that these forms function for capitalism or that their form is accounted for by capitalism. See the critique of functionalist theories in Kahn (1980).

11. See Parr and Mackray (1910) and Hooker (1972) for full accounts of the ideal conceptual model of the system and its political incorporation into the Negeri Sembilan state constitution.

Sembilan Malays' ideology, a core identity setting them apart from other Malays. Nationally, the past history of the state has been incorporated into the myth of the Malay Golden Past, which has a profound significance as a way of asserting Malay ethnic identity. In spite of this, the *adat* does not have entirely positive connotations among some elements, who see it as primitive, matriarchal and non-Islamic (see De Josselin de Jong 1960). Both perspectives see *adat perpatih* as a unitary, unchanging phenomenon; but an adequate analysis would hope to portray it as a structure of meaning, developing new discursive formations through time.

The influence of colonial administration on *adat* discourse was considerable. The recording of *adat* sayings in government reports and the legalistic conceptualization of such documents were central to the development and reproduction of *adat* ideology: at the formal level they have become the basis for the administration of land, at the village level they have played a prominent role in reproducing *adat* knowledge. This is well illustrated by some of my field-work experiences. Villagers told me repeatedly that I should look at some very old *adat* books and brought me to bookshelves where among popular editions on Islam I was shown what turned out to be well-thumbed translations into Malay of the best-known colonial reports, particularly Parr and Mackray (1910). My possession of this and Hooker's book (1972) was seen by villagers who cared about such things as the key to a large body of important knowledge.[12]

This example illustrates the extent to which formal written authority emanating from colonial relationships is accepted by villagers. It is noteworthy how powerful the model of colonial 'experts' has been as an agency to which both informal and legal disputes are referred.

Scholarly discourse has also been greatly influenced by the canonical status of these tracts; even the most thorough accounts are often refinements of *adat* ideology, feeding into the essentialist position that there is a true or correct model of *adat*. They too can act to assert its value at the same time that other ideologies like Islam and modernization threaten to undermine it.

The question of the *adat* expert raises a related problem, that of the extent and distribution of *adat* knowledge. Has this declined? Older Rembau Malays constantly say that the young do not care about *adat* any more and that its demise is very near. In the same breath, they quote the proverb about preferring to let their children die rather than abandon *adat*. It is certainly true that young people know very little about the subject; some cannot name their *buapak* (lineage head), or even their clan. Many men too express an antagonism to *adat*, which I look at more closely below in considering the decline of *adat*. But in terms of knowledge per se the older generation may be overstating its case; it is theoretically possible that *adat* knowledge was hierarchical in previous periods and that only certain

12. See De Josselin de Jong (1960) for a similar research experience.

'experts' knew all the details of the model of the clan system, of marriage rules and ritual observations even then. From all written accounts, the role of *adat* expert or specialist was clearly differentiated by the end of the last century, and, as far as we know, mainly confined to men. How far the populace in general has shared in ritual and ceremonial knowledge is unclear; apparent lack of knowledge of *adat* may thus not be evidence of its decline. Furthermore, the decline of *adat perpatih* cannot be measured in terms of ideology alone, but requires evidence of a decline in *adat* practices and the structural determination of this decline.[13]

How far did colonial land policy recreate and reproduce matrilineal elements in Negeri Sembilan? According to pre-colonial *adat* ideology, all land was owned by the ruling clan, the descendants of the original settlers or by other clans who had acquired it from them by purchase. Customary law distinguished two kinds of land: ancestral property (*harta pusaka*) which was mainly rice land and orchards and which was inherited matrilineally from mother to daughter, and land as acquired property (*harta carian*).

The processes of colonial land registration have been fully discussed elsewhere (Wong 1975). Briefly, the 1909 Negeri Sembilan Customary Tenure Enactment established procedures for the registration of all lands in the administrative parish register. After this, except in a few circumstances, all ancestral land in Rembau could generally be transferred only to a member of one of the twelve clans (see Wong 1975). All vacant land became state property and large areas were bought by British and Chinese entrepreneurs for rubber plantations.

Shortly after this, with the spread of intensive European and Chinese planting throughout the area, legislation was introduced (1913) which prohibited the transfer, charge or lease to a non-Malay of any land held by a Malay within areas designated as Malay reservations. Ostensibly, this was to protect the Malays, who might otherwise be deprived of their means of existence (see Lim 1977) but there is some controversy about the intentions of the colonial state in creating a Malay 'yeomanry' of rice farmers.[14] In practice, attempts to get around these regulations have been one focus of peasant resistance to land legislation.

The registration of land (by Torrens title) was conceived of in terms of individual leasehold titles amounting to ownership, with the administration of land being transferred from *adat* officials to the British (Wong 1975). *Adat*, however,

13. The 'conservation' of matrilineal ideology has occurred at another, very important, political level. I will dwell upon this in the concluding section in which I discuss the history of women's activities to defend *adat* as a way of protecting their property rights and interests.

De Josselin de Jong (1960) gives a full account of one episode of Rembau women's resistance to attempts to alter land tenure. I look at the political significance of Rembau women's ownership of ancestral land in providing some measure of autonomy in a situation where the rural economy is increasingly subsumed in Stivens (1985). Women's resistance can be seen as an explicitly political action as *women* directed at men, and modernist forces in UMNO.

14. This reading of colonial policy has been examined in some depth by Kratoska (1982).

conflicts with such notions of land as a commodity. Although the registration of titles *prima facie* allows the landholder to act on the assumption of freedom of alienation, in theory ancestral property is tied to matrilineal inheritance and cannot be alienated except for certain purposes, like going to Mecca. Such structural contradictions in land rules have led to considerable confusion, particularly in the administration of land at District Office level, where most land disputes are settled.

The status of acquired property (*harta carian*) within these legal structures is also problematical. A holder of acquired land can freely dispose of it without restriction, but has no power to make testamentary disposition. According to customary law experts, on the death of its holder, whether male or female, the acquired land must devolve according to *adat*, although there is much debate about how many times it must descend before it is counted as ancestral property.[15] The formal, logical implication of the system is that acquired land ultimately becomes treated as ancestral in a constant accretion to the 'female' semi-commoditized sector of ownership. The freedom to dispose of this land during the holder's lifetime, however, could place limitations on this process. The constant disposition of rubber land to men, for example, would keep such acquired land out of the 'female' sector. It is interesting to note that, in Rembau ideology, men own rubber land, and women own rice land and orchards. In fact, over half the village rubber land censused is owned by women, although only 2,000 of the 24,622 acres of rubber land held by Malays in the district are inscribed as *customary* (Rembau District Office). This pattern holds elsewhere in Rembau (Norhalim bin Haki Ibrahim, personal communication).

My field data show that the disposition of village rubber land is, if anything, accentuating the move of property to the female sector.[16] Men both inside and outside the village are transferring land to their sisters' names and fathers and mothers are transferring land (sometimes newly purchased) to their daughters. They were doing this, they said, so that the daughters would have 'insurance'. 'The men all have wages! What if she gets divorced or her husband dies?' This cultural recognition of women's vulnerabilities in the present-day economic situation appears to be perpetuating what I have called elsewhere the feminization of property outside of formal matrilineal transmission (Stivens 1985). I think there is a case for seeing these transfers of land relegating village land to its 'traditional' keepers, the women, as integrally linked to the backwardness and decline of the rural economy.

A further point which seems to have been overlooked by other commentators is that women's greater longevity would accentuate this process of land becoming

15. See Taylor (1929, 1948), Hooker (1972), and Wong (1975) for discussion of the difficulties affecting the implementation of the rules for acquired land.
16. See Fett (1983) whose examination of Land Office records supports my contention that land tends to move from male registration to female registration through time.

feminized, as they more often receive a spouse's share in joint acquired property. Of course, this situation is complicated by the former very high rates of divorce in Negeri Sembilan—the average annual rate from 1945 to 1953, for example, was 59% (Djamour 1959), although the rate in 1975 had fallen to around 15% (District Office Rembau). Other kinds of property like houses are also affected by this; many men spend large sums (up to several thousand Malaysian dollars) on houses in their wives' villages, which, for purely practical reasons, they generally have to forfeit on divorce.

Thus, with the formal registration of land, the colonial state was attempting to create juridical structures controlling non-village land as a commodity, and preserving the 'customary' tenure of village land. Although peasants received individual grants, their land was not truly alienable as we saw. It is ironic that these individual grants probably strengthened women's rights to land, replacing ancestral usufruct with titles transmitted in the female line. Thus, the feminization of acquired land, the incorporation of *adat perpatih* into the Negeri Sembilan state constitution, and the preservation of descent-group ideology through the discourse on *adat* have all tended to emphasize matrilineal aspects of kin relations. The generation of the peasant political economy meant both the perpetuation of subsistence production and crisis-ridden petty commodity production, which acted in part as social bases for the perpetuation of *adat* ideology. One could argue that matrilineal kin relations have acted as the relations of production in both subsistence and petty commodity production and have been reproduced through the colonial and post-colonial jural structures governing land.

The growing ideological significance of the Malay Golden Past, at least as it is constructed in Negeri Sembilan, also harks back to the egalitarianism of the communal ideology of *adat*. This ideology is not wholly misleading; as noted above, class differences do not arise within the subsistence community as such. This egalitarian local ideology supports *adat* and its retention, and has been strengthened by women's conscious political action as women to protect *adat* when it was challenged on several occasions (De Josselin de Jong 1960).

The dissolution of adat and the rise of cognatic kinship

Much anthropology would be tempted at this point to argue that the conserved juridical structures of 'matriliny' in Rembau constitute a jural–political domain of kinship opposed to a domestic domain of close, basically cognatic kin ties and household production.[17] Nonetheless, I would be unhappy about such a division. It is not just a question of inflating a formalistic and ideological division

---

17. These issues are discussed in Yanagisako (1979), and Geertz and Geertz (1975).

of 'private' and 'public' into analytic categories. The notion of domestic kinship implies a reproductive biological core which is structurally isolated from wider social relations; such reductionism is not meaningful.

I have suggested above that a number of social forces generated by the colonial political economy acted to reconstitute aspects of Negeri Sembilan matrilineal ideology and practice. Of course other dimensions of Negeri Sembilan kin relations could always have been classified as non-unilineal, as cognatic: for example, kinship terminology does not differ from the rest of the peninsula; moreover, the father's side and a range of non-unilineal kin were always considered important in Negeri Sembilan ideology. I shall, however, concentrate my argument on the view that cognatic ties have become more important in the reproductive aspects of kin relations in the migration process.

Adat perpatih, Islam and adat temenggung

I have already noted that many villagers are very worried about the future of *adat*. It is true that few young people know who their lineage head is and many do not know what clan they belong to. This is not just a matter of expressed disinterest, but in many cases of an active hostility which allies itself to a number of counter-ideologies, Islam, 'modernization' and *adat temenggung*.

Many local commentators attribute a decline in adherence to *adat perpatih* directly to the ideological force of Islam. But one has only to point to the long history of Islam in the region to see that this in itself is an insufficient explanation. The recent rise in Islamic fundamentalism has clearly fuelled such opposition, but it seems that much of this comes from agents of 'modernization' espousing Islamic ideology as well as directly from religious authorities. The economic decline of the rural sector has clearly generated the calls for the dismantling of 'feudal' *adat* relations.

The expression of opposition to *adat* in Islamic terms has again raised the issue of structural conflict between *adat* and Islam (a topic much favoured among Malaysian dissertation writers). Although it has been argued that conflict is minimized because they occupy different spheres (Hooker 1972), there is still scope for considerable conflict, especially with land disputes.[18] Similarly, Islam and *adat* clash over marriage law and practices, yet their competing ideologies have been reconciled in the past, with varying degrees of tension.

Islamic opposition to *adat* bears directly on the issue of cognatic kinship. Much popular and scholarly discourse seems to suggest that there are two variants of *adat* in Malaysia, *adat perpatih* and *adat temenggung*. *Adat temenggung* as a term

18. I cannot agree with De Josselin de Jong that Islamic inheritance patterns are winning out, in Rembau at least. Rather land disputes reveal a confusing mix of *adat*, Islamic and bilateral principles and sometimes idiosyncratic prejudice of land officials (Hooker 1972).

is applied to the basically bilateral practices of the rest of the peninsula outside Negeri Sembilan. It is often seen as having a patrilineal bias and, importantly, as being more in accord with *syara'*, Islamic law. But as with *adat perpatih* it would be a mistake to see it as a unitary phenomenon. It seems to include elements of both bilateral and double unilineal kinship.

Opponents of *adat* in Rembau overtly contrast the perceived masculine bias of Islamic law and *adat temenggung* with the 'unfair' matrilineal principles of *adat perpatih*. Those dissatisfied with their position under *adat perpatih* often extolled the virtues of *adat temenggung* to me as a desirable alternative. They also assumed that if *adat* were dismantled, *adat temenggung* would arise in its place. The hostility to *adat perpatih* is illustrated by the following quote from a woman living on land she jointly owns with her husband's family (next door to his sister):

> My husband's family are all rich, but he doesn't get any of the property. My husband's mother had lots of land and he doesn't have any. I don't like *adat perpatih*. I think men should get a share as under *adat temenggung*. *Adat temenggung* follows Islamic law properly. God (*Tuhan*) did not want women to have property. [Significantly, her mother had had little property to leave her.]

These countering forces have found expression both at the level of individual action to avoid *adat* rules and in the form of sporadic political attacks on *adat* and matrilineal inheritance. A number of men are openly stating that they are buying land in towns because, they say, they do not want the land to become involved in *adat* rules. There is some semi-legal trading in land (mortgages and so on) which again gets around various proscriptions.

These conflicts found direct political expression in 1951: in February, the Religious Affairs Section of the Rembau Branch of UMNO issued a pamphlet suggesting that the matrilineal laws of land ownership were forbidden (*haram*) according to Islam. During a long period of tension, there were attempts to get the State Council to review the *adat* laws, shortlived support for the UMNO position by the District Officer, and various meetings of clan chiefs and Rembau Malays, in Singapore as well as Rembau. By July, women were reported to be threatening to get their husbands to repudiate them if the latter continued to support UMNO. There were several arguments in the UMNO case: that *adat* was *haram*, that it was unfair to men and that while it was needed in the old days to protect women, *adat* land tenure was hindering economic development. The proposals were finally dropped after the clan chiefs and lineage heads swore their loyalty to *adat* (De Josselin de Jong 1960).

There have been sporadic attacks since then, mainly by civil servants espousing a brand of theocratic capitalism and denouncing the 'feudal' structures of matriliny. All such attacks so far have been unsuccessful in effecting major change. But while Islamic ideology has been prominent in attacks on *adat*, and has taken hold among its opponents, I do not think we can attribute the decline in adherence among the young to Islamic forces alone. Migration in particular is progressively weakening the local substructure on which the ideology of kin relations is based. The individual wage form, bolstered by 'modernization' ideology, has led to a rising individualism that is seen as incompatible with 'feudal' *adat* relations.

Are those who see a decline in *adat* practices right? Take first the issue of corporate descent groups. In the present-day context we have to consider to what extent the matrilineal descent groups of *adat* ideology form discrete, corporate descent groups. (Of course, corporate groups as such are an elusive analytical category.) In the past, many lineages formed local kin groupings, whereas today most members of the lineages live outside the village. Moreover, not all of these *perut* are locally based: one of the villages studied consisted of a core of women from different clans whose parents had purchased *kampung* land earlier in the century. This dispersed residence inevitably means a decline in everyday co-operation among kin. The complex economic changes outlined above have been accompanied by a decline in a number of communal aspects of economic co-operation that were represented at least as being based on *adat*, although we could equally see them as based on locality. These included communal labour in the rice fields (*menyeraya*), which is sadly missed by older women who complain how lonely it is working in the *sawah* nowadays. Community exchanges of food and services within uxorilocally based kin segments could be interpreted as evidence of the continued importance of these kin ties. They clearly do reproduce kin ideology, but such exchanges can just as easily be interpreted as locality-based rather than kin-based forms.[19] Day-to-day co-operation, like help with the harvest, and calls for labour at *kenduri* (ritual meals) depend as much on proximity and locality as on genealogical ties. They certainly do not emphasize matrilineal ties to the exclusion of others nor do the participants represent them as such.

The ritual enactment of descent group ideology has also dramatically declined. Such community-wide rituals as *berpuar* centred on the pre-Islamic *padi* spirit and other traditional spirits have not been performed since the 1950s. There has also been a definite decline in *adat* elements in marriage and other ceremonies, bolstered by calls from Islamic elements to rid rituals of Hindu and other non-Muslim components. These changes have indeed progressed to the point where *adat* is often denigrated if not actively dismantled; for example, the religious authorities actively discourage ritual offerings to the *keramat* (pre-Islamic shrine)

19. Although these *kenduri* rituals act out communality and an implied egalitarianism (except for the ritual segregation of the sexes at the meal) they might equally be seen as asserting the status of the feast givers, particularly better-off villagers. Many who bring contributions and supply labour will never be able to afford to be reciprocated.

though women still secretly give offerings, especially those seeking help with fertility.

Along with the decline in importance of the descent group the traditional role of the mother's brother as guardian of his sister and her children seems to have diminished also. Fathers state very clearly that they wish to be responsible for their children and their education. Moreover, there is a growing closeness between fathers and their children which contrasts with earlier suggestions of distance in the relationship. In terms of day-to-day household organization the husband and wife are the pre-eminent unit and the mother's brother has very little say, especially among younger informants, although he is always treated with a certain ritual courtesy.

Arguments about the rise of an elementary family form raise a number of complex methodological and theoretical issues. At the beginning of this paper I suggested that such arguments are often based on faulty theoretical premises. Rather than addressing problems about structural change in kin relations, some of the debate about modern family forms in Malaysia merely focuses on the growing number of smaller, separate households.

'Traditionally', with uxorilocal residence, mothers and daughters often occupied the same compound. As noted, relationships among these co-resident women were based on co-operation in domestic and subsistence tasks. Today, although most migrants' marriages are neolocal, many women come back to the village to give birth, and some live in their home village while their husbands are away working or in the army. Therefore, while the normative pattern of most households was a homestead grouping of elementary families, migration has added extra elements to household formation. The mother's compound has become the site of reproduction in all the senses of the term. It is the place women come back to for childbirth and is the site of denuded middle-aged households and other complex patterns involving the domestic care of grandchildren and other dependents.

The elementary household is the model of the productive unit in the village economy. But it is important to note that about half of the village households in my census are headed by women, especially a large number of widows and divorcees, who are very vulnerable economically. Many households could not survive on their rural income, but are forced to depend on remittances.

All accounts of Malay kinship agree that the elementary family has been a dominant residential grouping, although many other household forms are created through developmental cycles of the household and through specific historic and economic conjunctures. There are extra pressures in modern Malay society creating this household form today. For example, many FELDA land-settlement programmes promote an elementary family household model in their selection procedures. They also treat the family household as a productive unit, with the male seen as head of the household and the wife as dependent family labour. Rising individualism, modernist ideology and the wage-labour form on which they rest are leading to increased notions of privacy, freedom and the wish to be free of the constraints of kinship on the part of some young *'moden'*. One could adduce some evidence for this from changing house form and internal organization: the traditional Malay house is being replaced by one with Western style rooms, windows and private bedrooms. Village teenagers are even demanding their own private, lockable bedrooms.

Clan exogamy was one of the mainstays of descent ideology. In the past, there were isolated transgressions of this rule, but now it is much more widely questioned by young people, although many over forty uphold it. However, few cases of lineage in-marriage occur. The pressures on traditional marriage are coming from an opposite source, with more and more Negeri Sembilan Malays choosing partners from other states. This is associated with ever-rising rates of free-choice marriage. My informants estimated that about half of all new marriages in the villages fall within this category. In the modern context, it is difficult to interpret even arranged marriages as unions between discrete kin groups as such, except in an abstract symbolic sense. Many arranged marriages seem to be taking on the character of second best, when an individual's search for a partner has been unsuccessful. The meaning of the *hantaran* ('bride-price') has been subverted by the young man himself as a wage earner often having to provide the money and I even heard of cases where the bride contributed to the sum which was formally presented to her family and back to her! Cross-cousin marriages are now very rare, again the site of ideological struggle in previous decades. ('My oldest brother and the third brother were engaged to their cousins (MBDs) when they were small but they refused. It caused an argument in the family for a while, but it's all right now.')

Several disputes about breaking clan exogamy occurred while I was there. A son of a retired soldier, for example, had met a young woman at his workplace and planned to marry her. It turned out that she was from the same clan.

'According to *adat*,' lectured one woman, to a group of young people discussing this, 'people from the same clan cannot marry.'

'What about the *Biduanda* people?' asked her teenage daughter, with a dismissive expression. [Two branches of this ruling clan may marry.]

Two days later, the young man came home and was gently reproached about his planned marriage by the same woman. He was going to stand firm even if there were opposition. After he had made a derogatory remark about *adat*, the woman retorted: 'We're strong because of *adat*.'

'I'm following Islam.'

'Yes, but you're breaking *adat* law.'

'I know, but people don't follow that these days.'

The argument continued in a spirited fashion, ending on a poignant note when the woman said, 'Maila will go back to England and say that we don't follow *adat* any more!' After all this, it turned out that the couple were members of different lineages and therefore able to marry.

It would be easy to interpret the rise in free-choice marriage as a simple product of the semi-proletarianization of young migrants. Certainly both young men and women have new economic autonomy vis-à-vis their families or new responsibilities, depending on how one interprets it, as young workers have often become the economic mainstays of their parents. I think this factor lies behind the rapidly rising age at marriage for girls. Parents concur in wishing to gain the maximum support before the child marries and children's strong sense of responsibility to parents leads them to defer marriage.[20] It is clear, however, that the move to free choice is more than a reflex of economy; notions of romantic love are very much to the fore in these unions, and most common among better-off and better-educated peasants.

The rise in romantic love ideology could be interpreted as the result of culture contact as the world mass media increasingly impinge on Malay and Malaysian culture and bring with them Western constructions of gender, sexuality and companionate marriage. (I am not sure that I strengthen my case by reporting that the favourite television viewing of my informants in the study villages in 1982 was 'Dallas' and the 'Professionals'.) This would be to oversimplify. Present-day Malay romanticism is, I think, a complex mixture of an indigenous Malay romantic tradition overlaid with modern Western and Indian romantic ideologies deriving from the media.

It is very clear that an important motive for some young people to migrate is not just their economic needs, pressing as these are, but a very real desire to escape family pressures for the relative autonomy of the urban environment. I am not, of course, proposing an ideological determination of migration, but we cannot discount the degree of potential conflict between the generations spurred on by the profound changes in the economy. There is a clear rise in individualistic concerns and a new materialism among Malays, especially among the expanding middle class, that directly conflicts with the ideology of *adat* and with other bilateral modes of kinship equally.[21] But as I shall argue below, there are other structural constraints generating kin dependence within the context of the relationship between the city and the countryside.

20. Interestingly parents preferred daughters in the past, but now want sons and daughters equally. They say explicitly that sons now bring money home.

21. This materialism is the object of a campaign mounted by Islamic fundamentalists at the present time.

Conclusions

Do all these pressures and the move to free-choice marriage mean that the elementary family is becoming the dominant kin unit? The city household of migrant Malays often consists of an elementary family, but the extended family still plays an important part. Kin often migrate to the city in chains, quite often live in the same household or in clusters of kin related more often than not through female ties and provide extensive support for each other with problems of housing, childcare and information about work. The range of persons used in this way usually extends to parents, their siblings and descendants, and Ego's siblings and descendants. City and rural households, then, are linked in a complex of relationships. I have already noted the financial contribution children make to the remittance economy and some of their ambivalence about their parents' dependence on them. The parents, however, have a considerable contribution of domestic labour to make to the extended family economy. For example, wage levels in the city and problems with housing and childcare often make it expedient for migrants to send their children to the village to the maternal grandmother. I have numerous cases of this on record. Adoption was frequent among Malays in the colonial period, but that was slightly different. These grandmothers, and sometimes other female relatives, have become responsible for a sizeable proportion of the rearing of migrants' children. Not only are the parents in the city relieved of housing problems but there are good schools nearby, piped water, electricity and by 1982, a large number of television sets bought by the migrants. The children and their grandparents are more ambivalent; the children prefer the bright lights and better schools of the urban areas, and both they and their grandparents complain about the work they are expected to do to help out.

I am arguing here then that the creation of a remittance economy and the migration process encourages a range of cognatic kin ties which maximize the welfare role of kinship. It is even possible that close kin ties are intensified by these new forms of dependence, which are often focused on women.[22] My main point is that in the modern context, this female-centredness arises or is intensified because kinship relations are domesticated, that is they become centred on the reproductive activities that are women's within the social construction of gender (Stivens 1984).

Even at the economic level, the elementary family is still embedded in kinship relations, not structurally separated. This embeddedness is secured partly through a complex moral code which enjoins the duty to help kin. This sense of

22. I do not have the space to explore the issue of the Southeast Asian 'utrolateral kindred' (Geertz and Geertz 1975). It would seem promising to explore the problem both from the perspective of cultural origins and the subsequent conditions especially favouring female-centredness, including institutionalized male absences due to trade, warfare, corvée labour and migrant labour.

moral obligation is appropriated by the state and media which both emphasize duties to kin and voice fears that people will neglect these. In neighbouring Singapore where some of my informants work, prime minister Lee Kuan Yew is talking of making it a law for children to care for their parents. Housing policy has also been revised, because it was felt that housing practices were dividing the extended family. It is clear that kin ties are important in this situation as a welfare system and that the state is only too aware of their importance as well.

An emphasis on the welfare safety net of kinship can run into the problem of painting a rosy, functionalist picture of kin ties. As I have been arguing all along, kin relations consist of a number of contradictory dimensions. There is ample scope for relations of inequality even within the loose cognatic kin grouping. Leaving aside the issue of women's subordination within the reproductive structures of kinship and the appropriation of their domestic labour, for example the childcare provided for kin, we can see other overt examples of taking advantage of kin. Middle-class Rembau Malays living in the city often drive back from a visit to their *kampung* with a car jammed full of young kinswomen (and their friends) who have been recruited as servants for the city-dweller's circle. Young women also often act as unpaid servants in their urban kin's household. Villagers were full of stories about people who had taken advantage of their kin economically, for example cheating them of their land. Moreover, while this welfare net is supported by ideology, it is no guarantee of protection against the stresses of the modern Malaysian economy. Not only may kin begrudge aid, but demographic and other factors may make kin unavailable to help.

What is at issue here is the gap between kin ideology and practice. We cannot assume that this ideology arises automatically out of family relationships as an extension of sentiment. I have tried to show for the Rembau case how competing discourses shape kin ideology. I have not had the space to explore further women's kin solidarity that finds expression at a number of levels, including both the overtly political and the domestic. It is a major force in maintaining a core of ideology which is represented as matrilineal, although I have made the point already that much that passes for 'matriliny' is not necessarily very different from other Malay patterns.

It seems likely that kinship morality will face new pressures with the continuing development of Malay and Malaysian class structure. It is probable that there will be growing class differences in kin patterns, with welfare dimensions being stressed among the poorer sections, and the new middle class emphasizing transfers of wealth and the reproduction of their class situation.

In conclusion then: I have suggested that my Rembau informants' kin practices can best be understood as an essentially cognatic core overlaid by a complex set of *adat* relations. Wider kin ties are still very significant and some of the most important reasons for this lie in the relationship between the rural economy and the wider society. The determination of the shape of kinship in Rembau can only be understood as the outcome of a complex of factors simultaneously conserving and dissolving aspects of kin relations, including the 'political economy' of land legislation, the resurgence of Islam and the intervention of the state through economic and welfare policies. There is a central contradiction between the reliance of the state on the welfare dimensions of kinship and its preservation of *adat* on the one hand, and, on the other hand, the encouragement of economic forms that put pressure on such relationships by encouraging the development of individualism and materialism.

Part II

The Territorial Domain:
Kinship and the Village Community

Processes of Kinship and Community
in North-Central Thailand

Jeremy Kemp

In 'kinship' and 'community' we have what in an older anthropology were considered to be two major if not the most important cultural and social characteristics of the primitive world. Today, many are wary of such assumptions and question the very meaning of these concepts. Nevertheless there remains a serious problem for the ethnographer as to how best to reinterpret existing village and kinship studies to create a more satisfactory framework for description and analysis. Certainly in the case of rural Thai society this older perspective has intruded into the conceptual framework of anthropologists with disappointing and sometimes disconcerting results, notably in the finally misleading assertions of 'amorphousness', 'loose structure', and relative insignificance of kinship. More recently there have been attempts to re-evaluate the community dimension (Potter 1976) and place of kinship (Kemp 1982, 1983), but on further reflection it is apparent that the analytical issues in both areas have much in common. Thus my intention in this paper is an exploration of their interrelation and the social processes involved based upon a long-term analysis of Hua Kok, a settlement in North-Central Thailand.

One aspect of the problem is the way in which the concept of community in anthropological writing on agrarian states is associated with a physical location, normally the village.[1] The peasant inhabitants of this place thus tend to be seen as representing an older, simpler social form in what has now become a far larger and more complex whole. Following Kroeber, peasant societies were 'part societies' (1948:284) and in the highly influential work of Robert Redfield the 'little community', which could be a synonym for tribe in that it encompassed the whole of a simple society, became but the village in a far more differentiated and structurally complex wider social system (Redfield 1960).

Although generally recognized as constituting neither a whole in itself nor a fully representative sample of that overall society, the peasant village community remained the focus of field-work and analysis. Apart from the practicalities of

1. A notable exception is G. W. Skinner's analysis of the existence of 'marketing communities' in China (1964).

anthropological research one reason was the supposition that the most basic and fundamental characteristics of social life were to be found there. The society had indeed become larger and far more differentiated with urban centres whence some degree of control was exercised, a surplus extracted, and so forth, yet its core was somehow manifested in the village. In this type of approach Redfield and his followers were echoing the theories of Ferdinand Tönnies' *Gemeinschaft und Gesellschaft* (1887) and Emile Durkheim's slightly later (1893) distinction between mechanical and organic solidarity. There thus emerged a kind of 'layer-cake' model of society with the primordial characteristics of social life being best retained and exemplified in the peasant village community.

These underlying, but by no means always explicit, ideas behind the study of community were of a piece with another assumed characteristic, namely its corporateness. Although Sir Henry Maine discussed both 'corporations sole' and 'corporations aggregate' (1861, 1917:110) it is the latter which have received most attention in the analysis of simpler societies. Though few anthropologists would ever have entirely endorsed the view of Evans-Pritchard that social structure is only about corporate groups (1940:262–3), the fairly general corporatist tendency is readily understandable given the search for order and stability.[2] Furthermore, such preoccupations are certainly discernible in the discussion of either the peasant village community as a whole or of its constituent parts.

The difficulty that we face today is that given certain, but by no means universal, conditions this combination of theoretical orientations and assumptions did indeed produce attractive and superficially satisfactory results. A clearly defined and socially discrete unit exhibiting patterns of interaction which emphasized local autonomy, homogeneity, interdependence and stability was duly revealed, even if at the same time these 'good' characteristics were also noted as being undermined by modern changes. One must not dismiss the significance of such characteristics, but they are obviously not the whole story and their relative absence in many rural settlements in Southeast Asia is certainly not coincident with anything approaching a state of anarchy, nor is it necessarily indicative of the consequences of rapid change.

In the assumption of an essentially corporate peasant community we have a set of misconceptions similar to those which continue to trouble the analysis of cognatic systems. For much of the past sixty years or so the importance of kinship has been sought in the occurrence and functions of descent groups. Not surprisingly, even when anthropologists at last turned to the study of cognatic systems, a disproportionate part of the discussion was involved with the classification of non-unilineal descent groups. Furthermore, it is perhaps ironic that the Iban,

---

2. This is especially so with 'structural functionalist' studies but also the case with more evolutionary frameworks charting the shift from communalism to individualism. For an attack of anthropological and sociological 'groupology' and delineation of patterns of social organization intermediate between formal corporate groups and interacting individuals see Boissevain (1968).

who through Freeman's work figure so prominently in the literature on cognatic systems, should themselves display a quite remarkable degree of corporateness at the household level in the shape of the *bilek* (see Freeman 1960). This last fact has to my mind tended to fudge or even disguise major issues which Freeman himself was confronting. Certainly in the field of Thai rural social organization one can detect a (corporate) groupist tendency in work such as that of Charles Keyes (1975) on domestic and kindred organization in Northeastern Thailand. It is also evident in the more polemical attempts of Jack Potter to re-write the Central Thai ethnography and so destroy once and for all the illusion of loose structure.

This corporatist perspective is best revealed in discussions of the kindred. Freeman was at pains to emphasize that the kindred is not a group but a category (Freeman 1961:202). It is Ego-focused in that none but full siblings share the same set of kin. Thus, although sometimes long chains of links may charter constituent relationships, its character is essentially dyadic. As Freeman points out it is 'most unlikely' that the kindred, the total set of those so linked to Ego, is ever mobilized (Freeman 1961:203), rather a particular set or selection of kin come together for a specific purpose. Even full siblings then are likely to recruit different bodies of kin for similar activities and this probability is compounded by the way in which affinally linked individuals are treated as kin. Unlike some authors I maintain the analytical distinction between kinship and affinity,[3] and those related by the latter should not be placed within the kindred. However, genealogical connection is in practice only one possible characteristic of the relationship between those who speak of and treat one another as kin. Thus affines, insofar as they become equated with genealogical kin, can and do form part of what might be called the 'effective kindred' out of which individuals are called upon in the name of kinship.

Now this is the way rituals, work parties, and so forth, are indeed arranged in the settlement of Hua Kok and its neighbourhood, but the impression of social organization given in the Thai ethnography is somewhat different. In a discussion which commences with references to unilineal and non-unilineal descent groups Keyes moves to a very different order of relationship, the dyadic ties of kinship and the way kin are recruited on various occasions. Yet he places the latter under the totally illogical and misleading heading of 'Ego-Based Descent Groups' (1975: 292 ff). To be sure, one may define groups in terms of interaction but as the starting point here is clearly permanent corporate groups of people related either by unilineal descent or kinship in conjunction with some other criterion, the whole presentation is one of confusion. This is further compounded by the perceived similarity of Thai family and domestic organization with the Japanese and Iban systems which of course do have well-defined corporate residential groups.

---

3. See the debate on the kindred in Borneo societies, notably King, this volume and 1976.

Potter falls into the same trap as Keyes in considering the kindred to be a kin group. He defines it as 'the descendants of one's uncles and aunts and their children (one's first cousins) through both one's father and mother, on both sides of the family. This group is solidary, and obligations between members of the group are considered important' (1976:158). Couched thus the definition is corporatist yet the sets so recruited are clearly ego-centred. Many of the first cousins of this 'solidary' unit are not even kin to one another! Given the apparent stability of Potter's northern research site, Chiangmai village, with its high rate of in-marriage, it is indeed possible that residential clusters of kin do develop group-like characteristics but he goes far beyond the confines of the North in claiming that the kindred (as defined by him) is 'a universal feature of Thai peasant social structure' (1976:159).[4]

In particular, focusing on the lower delta near Bangkok, he takes Kaufman's often cited but very unsatisfactory classification of family types (1960:21–5) and finds in the 'spatially extended family' that which he calls the kindred.[5] What is missing though is any reference to the fact that Kaufman fails to provide us with any descriptions of such groupings or of who actually participates in occurrences of the kind at which such closely related kin are supposed to play an important part. Nor is there any terminological evidence to show how villagers themselves conceptualized 'family' or whether they differentiated, as did Kaufman, between those brought up in the same household and others. The same kind of group fixation permeates the many publications on the village of Bang Chan situated not far from Kaufman's field-work site of Bangkhuad, and this is accordingly cited by Potter as supporting his thesis. In 1953 Sharp wrote of 'the extended family' in referring to people who could now be living in 'other parts of the realm' (1953: 80). Of course, as Sharp indicates, they might bear in mind the interests of close kin and help one another whenever possible, but this is very different from, for example, a single extended family household in traditional Chinese society (not quite a corporate group because it was not permanent)[6] or the Iban *bilek* in certain phases of the development cycle.

4. The discussion might have been better pursued by considering Freeman's discussion of 'stocks' and the effects of intermarriage which can lead to a considerable degree of consolidation so that 'while [some bilateral societies] lack the large-scale descent groups of unilineal societies, their cognatic networks are close and cohesive and so of great importance in the multiplex relations of social life' (Freeman 1961:207).

5. 'The term spatially extended family, refers to those members of a family who shared a common household during their youth and who have now moved away because of marriage or employment and are living in widely separated households, perhaps in different communities. These persons, nevertheless function as one household during the various rites of passage which take place within any one of these scattered households. The practical limits of this spatially extended family cohesion go only as far as the first cousin and involve, as mentioned before, primarily those members who were in the same household when younger.' (Kaufman 1960:23.)

6. In a comparison of the Japanese *ie* and Chinese *chia* Maurice Freedman noted '[i]n a strict Mainean sense, the *ie* is a corporate group: it never (in principle) dies. But the *chia* is in a perpetual state of dissolution, for when the partition of a family takes place, none of the resulting units retains the precise identity of the unit from which it springs.' (Freedman 1970:18.)

In creating the illusion of solidarity the group-oriented type of framework has led to much of the descriptive and analytical writing on Thai kinship resorting to such designations as 'amorphous', 'fluid', 'individualistic' and, most notoriously, 'loosely structured'. In other words, the framework adopted predicted a level of authority, permanence, genealogical ascription, and the like, which was notably lacking in Central Thailand and so generated an essentially 'negative' image. Significantly for my own analysis, it is the settlements of this area which have proved most difficult to analyse as communities and for very much the same reasons as have prejudiced the study of kinship.

My starting point then is a repudiation of the observers' externally derived, inherently group-minded formulations of kinship and community so typical of much of the literature. Groups are not the given point of departure, instead one needs to study the patterning of dyadic relations and from there move to an examination of the extent to which group formation does or does not take place. At the same time the shift of focus away from a perspective dominated by permanent groups facilitates concentration on the dynamics of social inter-action over time, and supports a diachronic (as opposed to synchronic) analysis which presents not a simple 'before and after' picture, but one of ongoing social processes within a structural framework[7] which may itself be changing. In what remains a preliminary interpretation it is evident that in response to demographic and other 'internal' changes as well as 'external' factors the communal and kin-ship organization of Hua Kok has been in constant flux over the sixteen-year period in which I conducted field-research while at the same time exhibiting many significant continuities amenable to structural analysis.[8]

Hua Kok

The ecology of the head of the central plain in Phitsanulok province is very different from that of the delta area around Bangkok. Nevertheless a pattern of social organization prevails in Hua Kok which appears to be far closer to that recorded further south in places like Bangchan and Bangkhuad, than that posited for Chiangmai village in the North. Following conventional criteria it is not immediately easy to assess the importance of the settlement of Hua Kok in sociological terms and the extent to which it constitutes a useful unit of study.

7. The concept of structure employed here consists of the various 'principles' upon which people order their behaviour. These principles are to be derived from the statements (either written or verbal) of the participants of the social system being studied. See Leach: 'I hold that social structure in practical situations (as opposed to the sociologist's abstract model) consists of a set of ideas about the distribution of power between persons and groups of persons' (1970:4).

8. Field-work in 1966–67 was sponsored by the London-Cornell Project for East and Southeast Asian Studies which was jointly financed by the Carnegie Foundation of New York and the Nuffield Foundation. Subsequent visits were supported by the Cultural Affairs Office of SEATO (1968) and the University of Kent (1975 and 1982).

96   *Jeremy Kemp*

Fig. 1. Hua Kok: Changes in housesites, 1967–1982

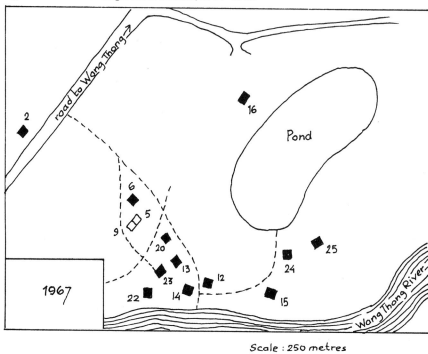

Scale : 250 metres

(Fig. 1 continued)

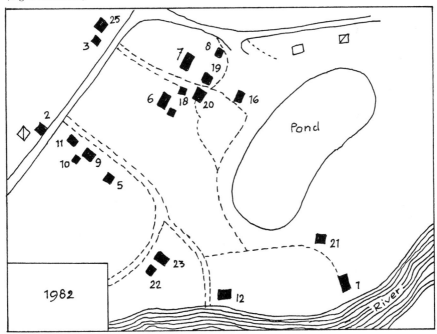

House numbers coincide with those of the households shown in Fig. 2.

The same is true of kinship, as in the published accounts of the delta region, the structure and significance of both familial and more widely defined groupings in the organization of life within and beyond Hua Kok are by no means initially clear.

In attempting to describe and capture something of the character of Hua Kok and its place in rural Thai society one possible approach is to commence by making a map of the place. This would suggest that indeed Hua Kok is a physically distinct location. The fact that further investigation would show that the land surrounding the place is frequently neither owned nor farmed by residents; that villagers are divided as far as regular temple attendance is concerned; and that the village headman in 1966 was responsible for a unit comprising two and a half named settlements, taken together question though do not necessarily undermine the choice of Hua Kok as the initial focus of study.

A second starting point would be to examine the relations of kinship and marriage which link residents one with another, and here again the time-honoured technique is the genealogical method and another map. During my first period of field-work in 1966–67 this worked very well. It was possible to eventually construct a single genealogy, admittedly with several rather than a single pair of

Fig. 2. Genealogical connections and household composition in Hua Kok: 1967, 1975
and 1982

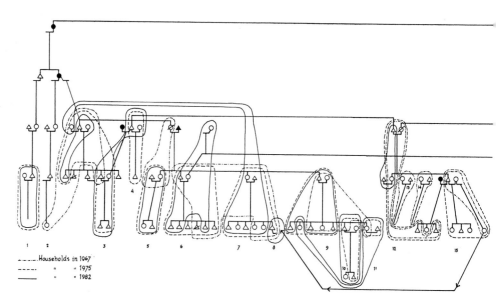

ancestors, which included every house but one, and that was headed by Wi,
a Chinese immigrant (house 16)! Illuminating though this map was (and it
certainly was of great value to a struggling anthropologist in giving him something
to hang on to) it is important to stress that this genealogy is inherently false
in the sense that it was constructed by and for the field-worker. Unlike many
other societies with corporate descent groups or even the records of certain elite
families in Bangkok, the genealogy I constructed in no way charters the organization of political resources, corporate responsibilities and the like. Furthermore,
the genealogical knowledge of individuals is limited, and in some instances the
map showed links not known to certain individuals as well as linkages different
from those which the individuals in question would claim. For example, Plang
(house 24) claimed a true kin link with Teng the village headman (house 2)
(Fig. 2) which he and his more knowledgeable elder sister denied, and my investigations finally suggested the distant affinal link indicated on the genealogy.
    Despite such reservations both maps proved useful research tools and taken
together suggest an important degree of social stability in that the extent to which
close kin resided in adjoining houses became apparent (Fig. 1), thereby suggesting a significant continuity arising from the division of parental house sites, for
example in 1966–67 households 5, 6, and 9.[9] Again, this picture though not

---

9. The members of household 7 were at that time temporarily residing in house 6 pending the
move to the site shown in 1975. Their old house which had already been dismantled and sold had
been located immediately adjacent to the other three households.

(*Fig. 2 continued*)

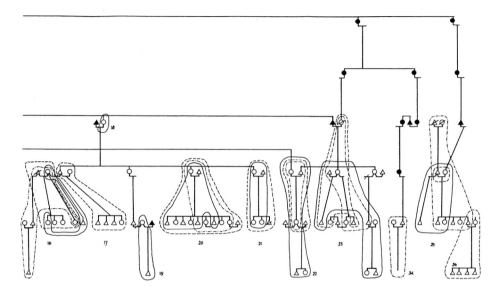

wrong is incomplete. The same image would have been conveyed by juxtaposing the settlement pattern with genealogical information collected in 1982, but when one compares the 1967 material with that of 1982 (let alone that collected on another visit in 1975) a very different impression is given, namely one of movement and change, so that by 1982 the diverging interests of household 9 and the especially close relations between houses 6 and 7 are marked in their very different use of space.

Thus the first point to be made is that although the number of households has increased only moderately over a fifteen-year period, from forty-nine to fifty-four in 1975 and finally fifty-two, the shape of the village has changed quite markedly as illustrated in the accompanying maps of one section of Hua Kok (Fig. 1). Most houses have been rebuilt, sometimes twice, and accompanying this rebuilding there have been moves from one site to another as well as more subtle movements which reflect both the general shift in orientation away from the river towards the road and the changing patterns of interaction between particular households as indicated above.[10]

10. It is necessary to note that the ease with which houses are moved is not necessarily associated with flimsiness or even poverty of the owners. Small structures of bamboo and thatch are indeed rapidly erected with minimum outlay, but more substantial and expensive houses with hardwood posts and planks, and tin roofs are also easily dismantled and re-erected. However, recent changes in style and the increasing cost of housing given the extensive use of concrete for bases and posts, and even construction of block walling seems likely to reduce the possibility of future minor moves by the more prosperous.

In an earlier paper (Kemp 1982) taking the 'ethnographic present' of 1966–67 I sought to clarify the relation between kinship and locality in order to elucidate what it is that makes the place a socially significant unit to its inhabitants and those in the adjoining neighbourhood. In terms of conventional criteria the evidence supporting some notion of community is indeed slender. In ideal 'Redfieldian' terms the village should in some way be bound together by a wide and overlapping range of common interests. As it is, the nature of the local settlement patterns determined that when the first remembered residents set up houses along the river bank in the early years of this century, any kind of neat fit between the hamlet and its farm territory was precluded. Land to the west which was fairly level and suitable for rice cultivation had already been claimed and cleared by people remaining in hamlets to the north. Hence the early settlers in Hua Kok sought land for rice fields further south, behind and beyond Wang Phom, the next hamlet.

The same kind of problem presents itself in the field of ritual. In the literature on Thailand the feature most generally signifying a community is a temple (*wat*), yet in this area the two nearest are the small, rather ramshackle structure lacking an ordination hall (*bot*) at the far end of Wang Phom and the far larger complex to the north in Bang Saphan. It is not even as if the people of Hua Kok formed part of a larger congregation; instead, those in the southern part tend to frequent *wat* Wang Phom while the rest go to *wat* Bang Saphan. Public schooling was initially closely associated with the Buddhist temple and even today primary schools are often found in or adjoining temple compounds, as is the case in both Bang Saphan and Wang Phom. There is also an association between the temple and the secular administrative structure in that the religious divisions parallel those of province, district, commune (*tambon*) and administrative village (*muu baan*). *Wat* Wang Phom is itself located in Village No. 7 (*muu thii cet*) which consists of Hua Kok, Wang Phom and part of the dispersed settlement of Wang Ja Nang, and on occasion the headman would go to that temple on major feastdays or when some announcements were to be made. However, he and his family live at the northern end of Hua Kok, and normally attend the temple in Bang Saphan.[11] Furthermore, no child from Hua Kok goes to school in Wang Phom.

The picture then is one of significantly different sets of people gathering and interacting for different purposes. Hua Kok exhibits neither the degree of local autonomy that community models suggest, nor is it integrated into some larger unit. In this somewhat fragmented set of circumstances kinship may initially seem to offer a solution as to why Hua Kok does appear to be more than just an aggregate of persons. However, it is also important to remember that while indeed all but one of the households in 1967 could be placed in the genealogy, each family had many kin beyond Hua Kok. Furthermore, in the 1960s the

---

11. By 1982 he had retired and both subsequent elections were won by Wang Phom residents.

number of marriages between Hua Kok residents was still limited by pre-existing ties of kinship and the expressed distaste for unions between kin, which was most strongly expressed in the assertion that the technically legal marriage of first cousins would result in severe misfortune to the couple and any offspring.

When looked at in more detail the significance of kinship, either in its own right or in terms of the way it makes or cements a community, remains puzzling. What are notably lacking in Hua Kok are the kinds of authority structure found in many other societies and certainly among traditional Thai elites. This situation in Hua Kok is clearly related to the lack of either fully-fledged corporate groups or units to some extent approximating to them. Unlike the Iban *bilek*, the Thai household is in no way a corporate group and it also lacks any corporate ideology. There does not appear to be any Thai equivalent for the concept of the family. *Khroobkhrua* is a primarily formal, administrative word and though usually translated as 'family' refers, in fact, to the kitchen and is rendered by Sharp and Hanks as 'cover arrangement of the hearth' (1978:52). The word normally used in Hua Kok is *baan* (house), but here again it is important to note that the same word is also used to designate a far wider social unit, the hamlet itself.

Within the household the ties that bind members other than young children tend to have a contractual nature. Given the traditional abundance of land elsewhere if not in the immediate vicinity, the young have always been able to leave should their personal relations be difficult or the rewards of staying inadequate. By the late 1970s this option had almost entirely disappeared, but it had been replaced by the lure of Bangkok. Should they remain in the parental home, however, young adults' subservience to parents remains limited. Any money that children earn is their own and does not have to be put into a household fund. Overall then, it is readily apparent that parents have very limited authority over their children and maintenance of an ongoing relationship depends to a considerable extent on mutual satisfaction.

Marriage is subject to a similar lack of constraints. With rare exceptions children choose their own partners and in the 1960s elopement had become by far the most common form of marriage irrespective of parental attitudes.[12] Although the husband is head of the household, his wife frequently looks after the money and retains the ownership of any land she has inherited. Parents often maintain a concerned interest in the unions of their children but this is limited to general support in times of difficulty and on occasion is tantamount to stirring up resentment and complaints rather than ensuring continuity. Though there is a specific term for the relation between couples whose children have married (*dong kan*) it is not useful to see marriage as uniting households or wider groupings of

---

12. Villagers draw the following distinctions: i) marriages formally negotiated through go-betweens (with or without a large ceremony); ii) elopement; iii) unions resulting from the man being caught in the girl's room; iv) capture; and v) living together without any ceremony. It continues to be the case that few unions in Hua Kok are formally registered.

kin (see Carsten, this volume). Where good relations and interaction do evolve it is on the basis of interpersonal relationships, not some wider collectivity.

Households may, and frequently do, become important social units in village life but they never achieve that permanence which marks the *bilek* or Japanese stem-family. Much stress has been placed by Keyes and others on ultimogeniture of the house and its equipment to the youngest daughter. Nevertheless there is no fixed estate or equivalent of the Iban *padi pun* and ritual whetstone. Nor is there any ideology of household/farm continuity: despite the view that they should make provision for their children, parents remain free to sell their land and draft animals as they wish. Equally, in a society where devolution of property frequently occurs before death I also came across instances where children were to be provided for, of parents consciously maintaining their control of lands as a means of guaranteeing a degree of personal security and support in old age.[13] In other cases the behaviour of the children again reveals the lack of any social value to household continuity. The headman's mother who died in early 1966 had divided her lands when living with the youngest daughter whose husband took over control of the household. Later this couple decided to move to Wang Phom and the old lady, rather than go along with them, took up residence with another daughter in Hua Kok. In 1982 an old woman dying of cancer lived alone in a small shack (house 18) provided by Hia, a man (house 7) whose wife's mother had been friends with her. (This particular link is claimed to be one of kinship though it is historically only affinal.[14]) The old woman had earlier left Hua Kok and despite the fact that some of her own children live there she has ended up living alone and primarily dependent on others than her immediate family.

The same emphasis on interpersonal relations and absence of formal associations between households (such as for irrigation as occurs in parts of the North) is found in the organization of production. Young couples residing in a parental house occasionally manage to do a little farming on their own account, and where they work the parents' land they are sometimes promised a share of the crop, or cash, as they attempt to accumulate the resources necessary to set up on their own. Even the exchange of labour for work groups transplanting or harvesting rice, which is often spoken of by reference to someone's house, is a contract between individuals. A man may send his wife, daughter or son along to fulfil an obligation, and if no one is available from within the household he may pay someone else to do the day's work, but the responsibility is his and his alone.

Despite the lack of corporate groups that give form to kinship and community organization in so many other parts of the world, kinship permeates Hua Kok

13. A careful distinction is made between the division of property (*baeng kan*) which may or may not include changes in the names entered on legal land documents, and granting usufruct (*hai chai*) which, unlike division, may be revoked.

14. In the first period of field-work statements asserting a link of true kinship with the headman (house 2) were collected from this woman's daughter (house 20) and younger sister (house 12). The headman's elder sister (house 5) denied this and cited the shown affinal link via house 23.

and plays a crucial role in what, for want of a better term, I call community life. Without becoming involved in the debate over the reality of kinship let it suffice to note that kinship is increasingly presented in the anthropological literature as an aspect of something else, production, reproduction, political life, and so forth. In many cases this approach seems to reaffirm or at least salvage the importance of kinship because it maintains an illusion of continuity with the past in that many of the activities described are managed through corporate bodies of one kind or another. That this approach and the kind of analysis it engenders of the place of kinship does not do justice to the situation found in Hua Kok is by now sufficiently obvious.

In the absence of such corporateness the issues then are: 1) How does Hua Kok 'work' as a community? and 2) What is the part played in this by kinship? The interpretation I wish to present here is essentially that taken together kinship and locality create a degree of social stability and a means of integrating and structuring the relations of individuals with the result that for them and other people from the surrounding area Hua Kok is far more than a physical locale. The basic argument has been pursued elsewhere (Kemp 1982). What I now wish to add is an appreciation of the processes involved over an extended period of time in relation to the use of space within the settlement and structuring of relations. This reinforces the anti-corporatist critique advanced above. It also confirms why the emphasis on individuals and dyadic relations does not necessarily result in a solely transactionalist analysis with its inherent repudiation of the part played by wider structural factors in the organization of daily life.

It is rapidly becoming a standard cliché to observe that kinship is polysemic, that it has multiple meanings. This is a necessary refutation of some of the simplistic, exclusively genealogical views of the past but not really satisfactory by itself. It leads far too easily to the conclusion that kinship has no analytical or even descriptive value. A very necessary distinction thus has to be made between kinship as an ideology and the institutions which often go by that name. Even at the ideational level kinship may, of course, consist of many elements expressing concepts of hierarchy, equality, proximity, authority, love, and so forth. What gives this 'package' of ideas some force though in its expression in the world of action is the fact that kinship is a moral ideology.

However, even this interpretation is insufficient by itself because such notions as deference to superiors can express other moral values, and in the Buddhist world for example the working of *karma* is seen to justify and reinforce the whole system of stratification. It therefore does seem worthwhile to go back to Fortes' formulation of the 'axiom of amity' (in spite of his own positivistic views of kinship) to specify what he also called 'the rule of prescriptive altruism' between kin (Fortes 1970). There is no need to imply that such a morality is always translated into action: in Hua Kok as anywhere else there are plenty of examples of kin cheating one another and of failing to meet their obligations — the old lady mentioned above is a poignant case. Nevertheless, through its expression of long-term moral bonds, kinship in Hua Kok and in Thailand more generally does serve, as in far simpler societies, as an important marker between insiders and outsiders (see Kemp 1984).

In Hua Kok there is no simple correlation between kinship and territory though there is a major concentration of links within the hamlet and the immediate vicinity. However, the genealogy gives a far too homogeneous and bounded image of these linkages, since some individuals have lots of close kin within the place and others only a few. It also has to be emphasized that genealogical connection itself in no way determines the existence of effectively close relations.

In this type of context it is the ideas of kinship which are significant, not the genealogical ties. But, what has to be emphasized in the Thai case, as can be done in the Malay (see Kemp 1983), is that kinship is the dominant idiom for handling close relationships. Where the Malay case differs from the Thai is in the extent to which it uses a system of markers attached to parent and sibling terms which disguises distinctions between those who are and those who are not genealogically related (Banks 1974). One must add, though, that in the Thai case, whereas no such markers are added to the 'mother' or 'father' terms, these words are not widely used other than in a very specific, though again not necessarily genealogically correct, way.

Related to this issue of genealogical veracity is the manner in which affines are handled. Analytically there is no problem as in some Borneo societies in making a distinction between kin and affines, but in practice the terms used in address and for general reference tend to be kin, not affinal. This is shown most spectacularly in the range of terms used between husband and wife (see Kemp 1976:88–90). Only one, *naang* ('Mrs'), refers to the quality of affinity, and the most polite form a wife can use to her husband is *phii*, which is normally glossed as 'elder sibling'.

Overall then we have a situation, observable elsewhere, in which kinship is not a primarily genealogical relationship and where the old assertions about kin terms ascribing social roles are especially wanting. Rather, kinship is an ideological discourse at the participants' level where it serves to create, mediate, manipulate, and express social relations. What kin terms do, among other things, is give one a social identity and mark a number of qualities quite distinct from kinship such as relative age. At the same time, however, they tap the moral content of kinship, which serves as the basis for relations of generalized reciprocity.

Within Hua Kok, kin terms and more general references to kinship reveal the web of interpersonal relations linking all residents. Unlike Riley (1972:79), who studied a Central Thai village in Chainat, I never heard people making statements to the effect that all villagers were kin by virtue of co-residence, but the actual situation is very similar. In 1982 Chan, a childless woman originally from another district, had finally left her husband (house 2) following the eruption of long-term resentments on the part of his senior wife. She then moved in with Hia and Wiang (house 7), a couple where the wife (Wiang) was a daughter of an elder sister of Chan's husband. There she remained for the time being, helping around the house and with the cooking, though there was talk of her erecting a small house of her own in the compound area.

Chan's move to Hia's house is largely explained locally in terms of kinship; the fact that there is no 'real' genealogical tie and that the link is affinal seems totally irrelevant to all involved and is not referred to. By virtue of her marriage and long residence in Hua Kok, Chan has effectively become kin (*phii noong kan*). It is also appropriate to note here that she continues to be addressed as *mae* (mother) by the adolescent son of her former co-wife. Such an extended use of this particular term is unusual, but in this case Chan had indeed helped rear him from earliest infancy and the relationship remains emotionally close.

It is Hia and Wiang who provide the shelter for the ailing old woman referred to above, plus housesites for one of her daughters and husband (house 20) who have lived there for about twelve years, and for the destitute former wife of one of her grandsons (house 19). In fact the movement of people and houses in this part of the hamlet illustrates well earlier remarks about the manner in which changing patterns of interaction are reflected in the use of geographical space. By 1982 Hia and his brother-in-law Corm were prosperous middle-aged farmers who co-operate in joint purchases of farm equipment and help (*chuai kan*) one another even in agricultural production, where either wage labour or the balanced reciprocity of labour exchange (*aw/chai raeng*) predominates. In this clustering of houses Hia and his wife in particular have built a reputation for kindness and helpfulness, and in so doing have established a following whose help can be called upon whenever required. All these relationships are handled in terms of kinship, although the links are often tenuous or even (to me) non-existent. Thus the widow (house 16) of the now dead Chinese figures in the network of those who gather under Hia's house and goes under the general title of 'Granny' (*jaai*, strictly mother's mother).

Kinship and locality thus provide a conceptual framework within which the dynamics of daily life operate. With the passage of time since the first period of field-work, it is evident that although the hamlet has changed markedly in a number of ways there remains an important thread of continuity. Alliances and friendships have changed, some people have grown old, others have left, but the basic structural patterns persist in the face of the increasing impact of economic change and improvements in communications. Indeed, an initial impression of notes taken in 1982 is that in some respects there has been a strengthening of local identity and of the bonds of kinship.

Whereas increasing diversification of crops and utilization of new if eventually distant land have been very important since the mid-1950s, resort to these opportunities is increasingly restricted. Hence the pattern of out-migration (in which sibling links are especially important) is now affecting the social organization of Hua Kok as a whole. The balance of relationships is changed in that many of the economically less-successful households tend to leave, though there are also cases of the destitute moving in, dependent on the good will of others for use of a housesite (houses 18, 19, and 21 are examples of this). Thus the pressure on productive resources, while still high, is alleviated a little, and the shortage of labour at certain times of the year exacerbated. Compared with other hamlets in the vicinity the farmers of Hua Kok have been fortunate in the extent to which they have not lost their land through undue fragmentation and indebtedness. In these changing circumstances kinship can be increasingly significant in the recruitment of help and gaining of access to scarce land resources.

This is initially surprising: what one might have expected with the kinds of changes experienced in Hua Kok and so much of Thailand is the breakdown of old networks of social interaction. In Hua Kok this was caused by a combination of factors including the progressive commercialization of the local economy via diversification rather than rice monoculture (maize and beans in the early 1960s, cassava on mountain land in the mid-1970s, with an increased emphasis on the production of tobacco and to a lesser extent vegetables in the early 1980s). Possibly because of this Hua Kok farmers have been less prone to get into the kind of debt resulting in loss of land to outside interests. Some have indeed failed to make a success of their farms, but then the resulting sales of land have tended to be within Hua Kok.

Whatever the overall pattern one can certainly see that Hia's and Corm's relative prosperity in part depends on the labour available within their own households and their following. Indeed, in Hia's case especially, his generosity to others has provided him with a useful clientele of dependents whose services he can and does call upon. In 1982 I also noted the frequency of land transactions between kin and was informed that Hua Kok people tended to sell land only to their relatives. I had never heard this kind of statement on earlier visits and it does indicate a real change. Nevertheless, this is not to reassert the primacy of genealogical connections; just who in practice are treated as kin remains influenced by locality and interaction.

Conclusion

Kinship as an ideological and moral system provides a major means of articulation and integration in Hua Kok. This is achieved not in terms of group formation but at the interpersonal level, through dyadic links between individuals. Given the passage of time and the only limited number (now apparently increasing) of marriages within the hamlet, one might have expected the role of kinship to have weakened. However, kinship must not be seen exclusively in genealogical terms but as a 'here and now' state of affairs which is constantly reinforced by interaction or alternatively weakened by its absence.

In this paper I have sought to show how chains of dyadic relations combine to create a recognizable community and how the personal ties of kinship play an important part in this continuing process. In so doing it has been my intention to redress what I see as the excessively group-minded orientation of earlier Thai village studies. In the central region, where the impact of the world economy was initially and most heavily felt, there has been such a degree of mobility and change that the illusion of group stability was destroyed. In partial contrast, Hua Kok exhibits important clusterings of relationships which could well be interpreted as signs of group formation, but it is better that we stick to an emphasis on chains of dyadic links and the extent to which they overlap and interlock with one another.

In so far as genealogies have been interpreted as a charter for the organization and interrelation of groups, one can begin to appreciate the past difficulties experienced with the Thai material. Significantly, the only sections of the Thai populace who have ever kept genealogical records and consciously seen the need to collect and formally preserve such information have been royalty and some of the leading aristocratic families like the Bunnags. In the case of the latter, the administrative system of the early and mid-nineteenth century was one with little if any upward mobility, where only members of the aristocratic families had the right to be presented to the king and so win the chance of high office. Furthermore, both groups carefully controlled the marriages of their daughters to avoid undue commitment to others and so preserve their exclusivity (see Kemp 1978). Far from Bangkok in places like Hua Kok, no such tendencies emerged and the cognatic nature of the system with its primary emphasis on dyadic relations remained unsullied by the taint of corporatism, and today provides villagers with an important tool in responding to and taking advantage of the major changes affecting the countryside.

Bisan, Equality and Community in Langkawi, Malaysia

Janet Carsten

This paper attempts to describe and account for the distinctive form which one particular kin tie takes on the island of Langkawi, Malaysia.[1] It is that between *bisan*, the two sets of parents-in-law, the husband's parents and those of his wife. While *bisan* or *besan*[2] are mentioned in many works on Malay and Indonesian kinship,[3] the relationship does not generally seem to be invested with any special significance but, rather, is often characterized by restraint and a lack of any close social interaction. In Langkawi, however, the bond is of central importance; it is continually stressed in many different social situations, with *bisan* frequently calling on each other for many kinds of mutual aid as well as socializing at every opportunity.

In order to explain why the relationship has a special prominence in Langkawi I shall first examine the way it is conceptualized and what this implies about social relations on the island. Many of the exchanges between *bisan* focus on their common grandchildren, which can be linked to the way the tie between *bisan* comes to represent relations between households. I shall argue that its significance lies in the way it is linked to a conception of the community as made up of households exchanging on an equal basis, and which have common interests in 'shared grandchildren', as well as to a wider stress on equality which is manifested in many different contexts in Langkawi.

A theme which constantly recurs in the social and cultural systems of Southeast Asia is the co-occurrence of equality and hierarchy. This is not limited to the political field but also manifests itself in the realm of kinship. It has often

1. The field-work on which this paper is based was conducted between October 1980 and April 1982. I gratefully acknowledge financial support from the Social Science Research Council (now ESRC) and the Central Research Fund of the University of London.

I wish to thank Maurice Bloch for making many valuable suggestions and comments on earlier drafts of this paper. I am also grateful to Wazir-Jahan Karim, Cornelius Simoons and members of the Thesis-Writing Seminar at the London School of Economics for their comments.
2. The form most commonly used in the literature is *besan* but both spellings are given in the *Kamus Dewan* (Iskandar 1970). I have adopted the form which most closely accords with the pronunciation of the people of Langkawi.

3. See, for example, Djamour (1959), Geertz (1961), Jay (1969) and Wilder (1982).

been pointed out that the kinship system offers models of both equality and
hierarchy each of which is stressed in appropriate social contexts. In *Political
Systems of Highland Burma* Leach describes how Kachin culture manifests both
these tendencies. While 'the *gumsa* conceive of themselves as being ruled by
chiefs who are members of an hereditary aristocracy; the *gumlao* repudiate all
notions of hereditary class difference' (1970:198). Although these two systems
are fundamentally opposed to each other they nevertheless coexist within one
cultural system:

> Of two lineages of the same clan one may be *gumsa* and the other *gumlao*; *gumsa*
> and *gumlao* speak the same languages; both in mythological and historical time *gumsa*
> communities have been converted into *gumlao* communities and *vice versa*. (Leach
> 1970:198.)

Leach describes how these two political modes crystallize in two views of the
kinship and marriage system. In one of these, aspects of kinship which are
compatible with equality come to the fore while in the other those aspects which
imply hierarchy dominate. Thus the *gumlao* system is associated with an ideology
of endogamous communities composed of three or more lineages of the same
rank and of marriage in a circle between these lineages. Marriage in *gumsa*
communities, however, takes place, ideally, between ranked lineages, with men
marrying into their own or a higher class, and there is no tendency towards
communal endogamy.

The Kachin case is one in which either hierarchical or egalitarian aspects of
kinship are emphasized, depending on context. There are other examples of
societies which use kinship to express one of these tendencies to the virtual
exclusion of the other and this too can be related to the specific sociological
context. Gibson (1986) has described how the Buid of Mindoro, who are shifting
cultivators, have been enclaved by the more powerful society of Hispanicized
peasant lowlanders. They have dealt with the threat this poses to their cultural
and social autonomy by accentuating the difference between the hierarchical
values they perceive as dominating lowland society, and the egalitarian values
which permeate their own. One aspect of Buid egalitarianism is to play down
dyadic obligations between kinsmen, whether parent and child, sibling and sibling, or husband and wife, and to emphasize the free association of individuals
in shared activity. A married Buid is expected to relinquish his or her spouse
to another person whenever the spouse wishes to terminate the marriage. Buid
marriages are highly unstable and individuals contract an average of five such
unions during their lifetime. The Buid represent an extreme example of an
inside/outside dichotomy being expressed in the form that kinship relations take.
This dichotomy also appears, albeit in a weaker form, in the perceptions of the
people of Langkawi.

The majority of villages in Pulau Langkawi are coastal communities which
derive the greater part of their income from fishing. The village in which I

conducted field-work, Kuala Teriang, has a population of about three thousand and is constituted by several smaller communities which have grown together. Almost all the cash income of the villagers is drawn from fishing but many residents have small plots of rice land which are sufficient to meet their subsistence needs. In spite of income differences between them, all fishermen and their families perceive themselves as being *orang kampong*, 'village people' or peasants, and say: 'we are all poor people' (*kami semua orang susah*). They contrast themselves with people of the town, *orang pekan*, and particularly so with those who earn regular wages or salaries, *orang makan gaji*. In comparison to this latter category they feel badly off, not only because fishermen may have a lower income but because the immense irregularity of returns from fishing gives them relatively little financial security. The elite and professional groups of Malaysia are referred to as *orang pangkat* or *pangkat tinggi*, people of rank, while villagers see themselves as *orang bawah* or *orang rendah*, people of lower stature, the *ra'ayat*, subjects. Although Langkawi forms part of the mainland state of Kedah, villagers frequently speak of 'going to Kedah' when they make trips to the mainland. In other contexts too, they refer to Kedah in a manner which indicates that they perceive Langkawi as being separate from the mainland state rather than an integral part of it. It is these contrasts which inform villagers' self-perceptions, fostering a sense of unity and equality, and which seem to them to be more significant than the minor differences of wealth and status that may exist between one villager and another.

The conceptualization of their society as distinct from the mainland and as one in which unity and equality are more important than difference and hierarchy does bear some relation to certain aspects of local social organization. The dominance of fishing in contrast to wet-rice agriculture has meant that land is of less significance as a resource than on many parts of the mainland (especially mainland Kedah which is often known as the 'rice granary of Malaysia'). Consequently, inequalities based upon the differential ownership and control of land and its inheritance have been less marked than in agricultural areas. Although ownership of boats and nets may lead to differentials of income and status, it could be argued that, on the whole, these tend to be less permanent and less significant than the kind of inequalities associated with a land-owning elite. Until recently the greater part of the fishing capital was owned by Chinese middlemen and this form of ethnic stratification may have further underlined the emphasis on equality within the Malay community.

Turning to behaviour between kin, we can see that both hierarchy and equality are expressed in the idiom of kinship. Households are female-dominated units; men are absent from the home for much of their time and often take a marginal role in the running of household affairs. Consanguineal relations within the household tend to take a hierarchical form. Children must show respect for their parents, and in particular, mothers dominate over their daughters who take on much of the household labour once they have reached adolescence. Young women carry out such work under the supervision and critical eye of their mothers and are expected to be both diligent and obedient. The sibling relationship is more ambivalent but, in general, a younger sibling owes respect to an older one and this is clearly marked when there is a large age difference, in which case the relationship takes on aspects of the parent/child bond.

Households are grouped together in compounds of up to about eight houses. The growth and expansion of compounds is a function of the developmental cycle of the domestic group, new houses usually being founded when a young couple have had one or more children. There is no marked preference for any type of post-marital residence. Thus, relationships between the different households of a compound are founded on ties of close consanguinity, with those between parents and adult children, adult married siblings, and first cousins predominating. In many respects the compound is an extension of the individual household, not just in terms of the residential cycle, but also in the interaction occurring between members of one compound.[4]

Outside the household and compound the principle of equality receives more emphasis than that of hierarchy as a model for interaction within the local community. It is notable that political and religious offices do not command markedly respectful behaviour from villagers. In their daily dealings islanders make a strong effort to treat those they come into contact with in a broadly similar manner, adopting informal codes as quickly as possible. They tend to treat non-kin as far as possible in the same way as kin, and their behaviour towards those in the former category is generally not differentiated according to any hierarchical principle. Similarly, in communal rituals such as the *kenduri*, the feast, the same spirit of egalitarianism is evident.

This 'egalitarianism' is revealed in the way kinship relations between households in the wider community are conceptualized partly in terms of affinity. The local community is often represented as a collection of households who have intermarried in the past and will continue to do so in the future. Such intermarriage operates very much in terms of a model of generalized exchange which accords well with the idiom of equality. Since *bisan* are co-parents-in-law, households which are linked through *bisan* are households linked through affinity and, since the idea of shared affinity connects with the idea of the equality of the in-marrying community, the relationship comes to represent this ideal of equality both in the realm of kinship and in terms of locality. If the community is in one sense a collection of consanguineally related households and compounds within which relationships are based on hierarchy, in another it is also a collection of affinally connected households whose relationships with each other are founded on a notion of equality.

4. Elsewhere (Carsten 1987) I have given a detailed description of interaction within the compound.

Exchanges between bisan as part of marital alliances

My attention was first drawn to the *bisan* relationship by the continual emphasis it receives in everyday situations. *Bisan* constantly visit each other's houses and are engaged in a complex web of exchange involving food, labour, services and loans. Although these exchanges may not take place between *bisan* at all, they are always described as if they did. For example, it is very common for female *bisan* to send each other dishes of cooked food, such as special curries or cakes. However, since most household labour is performed by young women rather than old, the gift might more accurately be described as passing from the daughter-in-law, who cooks the food, to her mother-in-law. Similarly, when assistance is required with agricultural labour *bisan* may be called upon, but rather than go herself a *bisan* is quite likely to send a younger member of the household. These exchanges might thus be viewed as taking place between the *households* of *bisan* rather than between *bisan* themselves. The manner in which participants single out the *bisan* as leading actors is indicative of the special significance with which this relationship is invested.

Who it is that actually participates in labour exchanges at harvesting, or house-building, in the frequent visits between households or in the sending of gifts seems to be irrelevant: what is emphasized is the exchange itself, which is then represented as taking place between *bisan*. A high value is placed upon reciprocity. Neglect of obligations to give assistance is a frequent source of bitterness and such grudges may be brought up much later in a dispute. In one way of course the mutual assistance supplied by *bisan* is of the same kind as that given to close kin or immediate neighbours, but there is a qualitative difference. Firstly, this has to do with the emphasis on reciprocity already mentioned. In the case of kin and neighbours there is greater tolerance of imbalance in the short term. Secondly, and following from this, the exchanges between *bisan* not only occur with great frequency, but they are also particularly marked. They receive constant attention in behaviour or in speech, while those between close kin and neighbours tend to be taken for granted. Nor is there any other affinal relationship that receives this kind of stress. On one level then, it is as if an attempt were being made to assimilate a bond of affinity into the realm of consanguineal kinship. On another, this attempt is belied by the very emphasis it receives, by the intensity of the exchanges and the importance of reciprocity.

If we now consider kin terms of reference and address, we may begin to understand what it is that makes the bond especially appropriate for the stress it receives in the conceptual system of the people of Langkawi. When *bisan* address each other they generally use an appropriate kin term. If, as is often the case, they knew each other or were related before the marriage of their children, they may continue to use the same term of address as before the marriage took place. Thus, there is much variation in the terms used, although sibling terms are not uncommon. The word *bisan* is principally used as a term of reference; as such, it occurs constantly in conversation and villagers rarely refer to their *bisan* in any other way.

As a term, *bisan* is almost unique in Malay kinship terminology in that it is perfectly reciprocal. It makes no distinction of age, sex, rank or generation. Terms for every consanguineal relation within the same generation differentiate according to at least one of these principles, thereby clearly implying hierarchy. The only other affinal term which is similarly symmetrical is *biras*, co-siblings-in-law, but this is not normally used in Langkawi. In addition to clearly expressing equality the *bisan* term does not distinguish between those who were related before the marriage of their children and those who were not; it is in a sense a 'purely affinal' term.

The notional equality suggested by the terminology becomes even more obvious when we examine the content of the relation between *bisan* which, as we shall see, is integral to marriage alliances from their very inception.

Traditionally, a young man's bride was chosen for him by his parents and the marital negotiations were conducted by them or their intermediaries. Increasingly, today, the young man himself initiates proceedings by informing his parents of his preferences. In the past their choice was, to a large extent, governed not by the qualities of the young woman herself but by those of her parents, their potential *bisan*. When I began asking questions about the kind of qualities that were sought for in a young bride, the answers were remarkably unrevealing. The young girl should be beautiful, I was told, and hardworking, *rajin*. At this point the conversation usually came to an inconclusive halt. However, when I asked older informants what qualities they sought in their *bisan*, their responses were altogether different in tone and correspondingly more revealing.

The most important quality in *bisan* is that they should be *orang baik*, good people. In this context *orang baik* are people who are not quarrelsome, do not gossip and are not *sombong*, proud. It is particularly important that *bisan* should be slow to take sides in a marital dispute between their children. They are expected to play a crucial role in maintaining and harmonizing the marriage. If they take sides at all, it should not be that of their own child but that of their child-in-law, whatever the rights and wrong of the particular case. If they side with their own children they put the marriage itself at risk. A young person who runs back to parents during a quarrel with his or her spouse may well be sent straight back with no more support than a moral lecture on the institution of marriage. This, of course, is ideal behaviour and, as such, examples of it were always pointed out to me when they occurred. In practice, there is an obvious conflict between the natural desire to support one's own children in a dispute and the need to promote marital stability. After marriage the close tie between parents and children is considerably loosened. This is materially expressed in the fact that unless parents cannot support themselves, they should not normally accept financial aid from non-resident married sons. To do so is seen as potentially jeopardizing the marital relationship, in that it may become a cause for dispute between the husband and wife.

Thus the pressures on *bisan* to behave in a manner that will safeguard the marital alliance are strong. They are expected to disregard their own interests in order to avoid or mitigate marital disputes. In view of the pulls that each spouse experiences to his or her natal family, it is important for *bisan* to maintain a friendly alliance with each other. Where *bisan* are not on good terms and reside close to each other, the likelihood of the marriage of their children breaking down is high and in general their behaviour is often cited as a contributory factor in cases of divorce. It seems, therefore, that one should view the responsibilities of a marital relationship as being borne as much by the *bisan* as between the spouses themselves, the stability of the latter relationship being dependent on the strength of the former.

Returning to the way in which marital partners are selected, informants emphasize the importance of the concept of *raksi* in marriage. *Raksi* means mutual compatibility;[5] it is ascertained through divination before the marriage takes place by a *bomoh* (traditional curer). The concept of compatibility in this context has to do with resemblance, sameness and equality between the people concerned. It is not a matter of blending complementary characteristics in order to create a well-balanced whole but, rather, of matching people who are already similar to each other. Ideally, the young couple should be physically of the same mould, of similar height and skin colour; they should be of roughly the same age and come from similar kinds of backgrounds; there should be no great disparity of wealth between the two sets of parents. When a village boy goes through tertiary education and becomes an urban salary-earner it is considered suitable and fitting that he should seek a wife who also has higher education and holds a professional job, rather than take a wife from his natal village. The quest for resemblance extends to the matching of the names of the young couple; to be *raksi* these should be homophonous and of the same length. At weddings the bride and groom should be dressed in exactly matching outfits. The ideal of a young couple's compatibility being achieved through their resemblance is well-expressed by the Malay proverb which describes the perfect match as being *seperti buah pinang dibelah dua*, like an areca nut that is split in two.

The concept of *raksi* is significant not only because it stresses resemblance and equality as ideals in marriage, but also because what is emphasized, as much, or

5. Wilkinson (1932 vol. 2:304) gives the following definition of *saraksi*: 'born under similar stars and like therefore to live together in perfect harmonies'. Fraser (1960:180–1) discusses how *raksi* is used in divination to determine choice of marriage partners in Rusembilan. Here the term refers to cabalistic compatibility (also mentioned by Wilkinson) which was not specifically stressed by my informants. However, it is interesting to note that in the above definitions the same emphasis on the similarity of the partners is present.

more than the young couple being *raksi*, is that their parents the *bisan* should be so. And this is also ascertained through divination. If there is a marital dispute it will not be serious, I was often told, as long as the *bisan* are *raksi*, even if the young couple are not. Villagers always say, therefore, that it is more important for the *bisan* to be *raksi* than for the husband and wife.

In spite of the close relationship that should exist between *bisan* it is notable how little contact there is between the parents of a betrothed couple prior to the marriage. All the marital negotiations are normally conducted through intermediaries. For example, at the *tetap belanja*, the settling of the marriage payment, the parents are specifically excluded from participation and the bargaining is conducted by their kin. Neither the bride's parents nor the groom's attend the *kenduri kahwin*, marriage feast, that is held in the home of their *bisan*. Informants generally say that they would be *malu*, embarrassed, to visit the home of their potential *bisan* before the marriage has been solemnized and I was occasionally told that it would be *pantang*, taboo, to do so.

During the period of betrothal of their children, the parents of the young couple should avoid one another. After the marriage, especially after the couple have children and are permanently settled, this is gradually transformed into a close relationship characterized by intense interaction. This shift on the part of *bisan* from avoidance to close interaction parallels the relationship of the couple. Appropriate behaviour for the betrothed and newly-wed is also marked by a high degree of embarrassment (*malu*). For example, it would be considered highly improper for a young girl to visit the house of her fiancé, in the same way as there is a strong taboo against her parents visiting his parents. As the years go by, married couples often become more relaxed and friendly, although they may still avoid each other in public. In view of the stress placed on the relationship between *bisan* and on the importance of their compatibility, marriage might be considered as an alliance that takes place, primarily, in the generation of the young couple's parents, as though the marital union itself were a means of uniting the *bisan*. Thus, it is not surprising to find that the two affinal relationships – that of *bisan* and that of the married couple – mirror each other in the form they take, both moving, ideally, from avoidance to friendliness.

Avoidance behaviour can be linked up to the ideal of equality, which is so central to the marital alliance. The situations in which potential *bisan* avoid contact with each other before the marriage are precisely those where either the husband's side or the wife's would risk putting themselves in an inferior position towards their future affines. It is particularly significant that the parents of the young couple do not negotiate the marriage payment directly with each other and that they do not attend the *kenduri kahwin* in each other's house. Keeping a distance during the delicate period of negotiation is a way of avoiding any imputations of hierarchy that might pervade direct interaction between the husband's parents and the wife's.

If marriage is, ideally, an egalitarian alliance, then we would expect to find an attempt to balance exchanges between the husband's kin and the wife's at the time of the marriage ceremony. The parents of both bride and groom hold a large feast for the marriage and, although one of these may happen to be bigger than the other, in general, balance is maintained. Although the marriage payments, the *belanja kahwin* and the *mas kahwin*, are paid by the groom's side to the bride's, other exchanges such as clothing, cakes and sweetmeats, and payment to the *imam* for his services are all scrupulously balanced.

The central problem, however, is the affiliation of the young couple: which set of parents will gain from the income of the husband and the labour of the wife. Here again, immediately after the marriage takes place, a careful balance is maintained. The young couple move back and forth between the groom's house and the bride's. This to-ing and fro-ing between houses is known as *sambut-menyambut* (*sambut*, to greet; *sambut-menyambut*, exchange visits). The manner in which this is done — the number of nights spent in each house, and the order of the visits — is fixed by custom and is precisely balanced; it is not a spontaneous movement subject to alteration. There are a total of six visits, three in each house. Each time the couple move they are fetched by relatives from the house to be visited. After the *sambut-menyambut* the young couple spend some time visiting and staying in the homes of kin on both sides before finally settling down in either the bride's or the groom's parental home. Even then, the couple are expected to pay extended visits to the house of whichever set of parents they are not resident with, at least until after the birth of their first child. This process of shifting to and fro between the parental homes of the groom and that of the wife is known as *berulang*, to return again. These visits are generally protracted and their order and length are not fixed but subject to the wishes of all the people concerned as well as availability of space, etc.

The residential arrangements of a couple immediately after their marriage show a very careful attempt to achieve a balance between the kin of the bride and that of the groom. However, in practice, residence up to the birth of the first child is generally mainly uxorilocal and thereafter, if possible, it is neolocal. But when asked, informants always maintain that post-marital residence is uncertain and unpredictable, being dependent on a large number of circumstantial factors such as the availability of space and the number of children already resident with each set of parents. The emphasis on the uncertainty of residence reflects the equal relationship between *bisan*. Since each set of parents has much to gain from the income and labour of the young couple, and neither side is superior to the other, it follows that neither side can be admitted to have a prior claim on the young couple's residence. This is especially so where there is a preference for uxorilocality on the part of women at the same time as a recognition that, according to Islam, it is the husband's parents that have prior rights to the income and services of the young couple and that strict adherence to Islam accords better with virilocality.

If neither the wife's kin nor the husband's have a superior claim to the residence of the young couple there will be some attempt to redress the inequalities introduced by their affiliation. The exchanges of food, labour and visits that are such an important part of the relationship between *bisan* can be seen in this light. The constant to-ing and fro-ing between the bride's parental home and that of the groom is an attempt to maintain a balance in a situation where inequalities inevitably occur, since the young couple must eventually settle down in one house or the other.

It is not surprising that gross inequalities between *bisan*, particularly in wealth, are problematic. In disputes it is not uncommon for the higher income of one set of *bisan* to be commented upon by the other. If there is a large difference in wealth, it is likely that there will be greater pressure on the richer pair to fulfil their obligations towards the poorer in order to avoid being accused of being proud, *sombong*, that is, of not acknowledging obligations towards their kin. In Langkawi, it is, in fact, rare to find great differences of wealth between *bisan*. Most marriages occur within a small locality between people of similar wealth and status. However, differentials do sometimes arise, for example, when a young man from the village who has gone through higher education and is working in the city marries into a wealthy urban family. In such cases the *bisan* will be widely separated geographically and will not interact as closely as is normal in Langkawi. One marked case of differentiation of income arose when a young unmarried brother of one married man began to make a large contribution to his parents' income. In this way inequalities may occur between *bisan* who had approximately equal incomes at the time that their children married. The ideal of equality of wealth is emphasized by informants who comment on the criteria for the choice of marital partners. Although marrying into a wealthy family may have its advantages, these have to be weighed against the possible loss of one's own child and spouse to the household of the wealthier *bisan*, where there is likely to be more space for them.

Clearly, balance and reciprocity will not be enhanced by large differences of income. When these occur one would expect to find *bisan* maintaining distance (in other words, continuing the avoidance relationship discussed above) or counteracting them with a kind of 'frenzied reciprocity', a high frequency of exchanges, periodically disrupted by disputes. This is exactly the situation which occurs in Langkawi in the infrequent instances of a marked difference of wealth between *bisan* who, at the same time, cannot avoid each other because they live rather close together.

The grandchildren of bisan

We have seen that the locality of residence of a married couple constitutes a potential source of conflict between their parents. One eventual solution to this problem is neolocality. In general, couples try to establish independent households as soon as they can afford to. However, this is never done until they have at least one child. The preference for neolocality may be viewed as an attempt to achieve a balance between rights and obligations due to the wife's kin and those due to the husband's. However, this resolution is in most cases at best only a partial one, because new households are usually founded in the same compound as either the wife's or the husband's parental home. The close daily interaction which occurs between households of one compound means that affiliation to one set of parents will still tend to be stronger than to the other.

I referred above to the central importance of grandchildren to the relation between *bisan*. This can partly be viewed as an expression of, as well as an attempt to counteract, the inevitable imbalance caused by post-marital residence. Responsibilities towards grandchildren are an important aspect of grandparents' lives and it is once again significant that many of these are conceived in terms of the link between the *bisan* themselves. These responsibilities begin with a first pregnancy, which almost always occurs in the house of a young woman's mother. In the seventh month of pregnancy the services of the village midwife, *bidan*, are secured by the husband's mother, who is responsible for her payment. It is at the seventh month when it is believed that the foetus can sustain life that the midwife performs a ritual bathing (*mandi perut*: literally, bathing of the stomach) on the pregnant mother and a small *kenduri* is held. This is only done for a woman's first pregnancy.

Without going into detail about the rituals of childbirth, it is evident that the affiliation of the couple and unborn child to the home of the wife's mother is balanced by the responsibilities undertaken by the husband's mother from the seventh month of pregnancy onwards. As the pregnancy advances she begins to buy articles of clothing and other necessities for her grandchild. At the birth itself not only does she pay for the services of the *bidan* but is herself expected to attend and in practice often stays for some days in the house of her *bisan*.

These obligations, which continue after the birth, are perceived expressly in terms of the relation between the grandparents; indeed, women say that they are a responsibility between *bisan* (*tanggungan antara bisan*). Again, the husband's mother pays for the *kenduri* and services of the *bidan* at the first shaving of the child, *cukor anak*, seven days after the birth. At these times women speak of going to see their *bisan* or of sending gifts to their *bisan*. They worry about causing offence to them should they not fulfil their duties. The relationship continues to focus on the welfare of their common grandchildren throughout the latter's childhood. Especially during the earlier years, it is important for the female *bisan* to make protracted visits to the home of her counterpart in which the young couple reside whenever a grandchild is sick or for any social occasion concerning them.

These obligations do not constitute a balanced set in themselves but are a means of counteracting the asymmetry caused by residence. If, as is normally the case, the couple reside uxorilocally at this stage the main burden of visiting falls to the husband's mother. She is expected to actively participate in looking after her grandchildren and to contribute her labour during any crisis. (Similarly, when the couple live virilocally, the wife's mother takes on this role.) Failure to fulfil these obligations quickly leads to bitterness and disputes between *bisan*. Once old enough, grandchildren are also expected to visit their grandparents frequently, and will often stay the night. Given that they and their parents normally reside with one set of grandparents, it is particularly important that they make visits to the other set, and failure to do so is likely to lead to grudges between *bisan*.

Grandparents frequently also bring up one or more of their grandchildren and are more likely to do so than any other category of kin. Hence they can avoid having to live alone in old age — something the elderly generally dislike doing. However, it is significant that grandparents often do this when their *bisan* reside with or in the same compound as the young couple and the rest of their children. In other words the arrangement is another way of balancing the affiliation of the couple and their children to one set of grandparents.[6]

This became particularly clear to me in the following dispute. The parents of a young man who resided with his wife's family were quarreling with another family over a marriage which had ended in divorce. This latter family lived next door to the son's family of marriage and these two households contained siblings in the senior generation. The family of the son's wife were thus faced with a conflict between allegiance to their *bisan* and that owed to the household of a sibling and next-door neighbour. If they continued to maintain close relations with their neighbours they risked offending their affines. If they offended their *bisan* they put at risk the continued residence of their daughter and husband. Furthermore they might well jeopardize their daughter's marriage. It was highly significant that the daughter's husband was the sole income earner of the family. They finally broke with their neighbours; the daughter's father and his brother ceased to interact in any way, as did members of their respective households. As if to reinforce this statement of allegiance between *bisan*, a child of the young couple was transferred to the husband's parents. At the time members of both households told me that this was because the child herself wanted to go. In general when children are fostered in this way adults emphasize the decisive role of the child's own wishes. However, in this case the child's actual behaviour belied their assertion.

6. Massard (1983:111–13) has also made a connection between the circulation of children in adoption and the exchange which occurs at marriage.

Forced to ally themselves with either close neighbours and kin, or the parents of their son-in-law, the senior couple had no choice but to break with the former in order to secure both the livelihood of the whole family and their daughter's marriage. The transfer of a child at a time when all relations had reached a crisis point was an extreme expression of this allegiance. I would suggest that the 'gift of a child' can in this society be seen as the 'supreme gift' in Lévi-Strauss' terms (1969:65). It is this gift which in the final analysis can correct the imbalance created by affiliation to the household of one set of parents when neolocality is not practised. It is in this sense that we can perhaps understand why grandparents so frequently bring up their grandchildren.

Similarly, it is possible to understand why villagers' vigorous denial of the a priori rights of either set of grandparents to a grandchild echoes their denial of the existence of rules of post-marital residence. I was frequently told that there was no obligation to give a child to any category of kin living without children. Neither grandparents nor any other kin can demand a child. After a divorce children should ideally be shared, boys going to their father and girls to their mother. This rule clearly expresses the ideal of symmetrical rights to the children of a marriage. The manner in which the importance of a child's own wishes in deciding his or her residence is always emphasized is another way of stating that no one has prior claims. When asked why a child lived with her grandparents, the invariable answer was because she wanted to, *ikut suka dia*, follows her own likes. The fact that in several cases known to me the child's own wishes had rather clearly been disregarded somewhat contradicts this denial of claims.

The sharing of common grandchildren is thus a crucial element in the relation between *bisan*. People often stress the particular closeness of *bisan* and that it is having grandchildren in common which makes them so. Hence it is not surprising that, although in general affines use consanguineal terms of address, *bisan* sometimes call each other *tok bisan*, grandparent *bisan*, thereby calling attention to their role as co-grandparents. It is through common grandchildren that the relation between *bisan* — one of affinity — is actually transformed into one of consanguinity. We can also understand why the birth of a first child receives such ritual stress. For not only does the first child establish the consanguineal principle in a new nuclear family, but he or she in a sense creates the kinship link between co-grandparents.

However, the stress on 'bisanship' must also be seen as an emphasis on affinity. It is an expression of the kind of relations that should ideally exist between affines where what is particularly emphasized is balance and symmetry. 'Bisanship' embodies these qualities in a way not achieved in any other relation of affinity, and its constantly reasserted equality contrasts even more strongly with close consanguineal relations.

Further, the relation between *bisan* is one between the two senior couples in their respective households. They are the joint heads of households, and the many different kinds of exchanges which take place between *bisan* are, as we have seen, in essence exchanges between households. To put it another way, exchanges between households are conceived as exchanges between *bisan*, and this is clear from the way these exchanges are conducted and described by the participants. In other words, relations between households are based on an idea of symmetrical exchanges occurring between equals.

If indeed relations between households are essentially conceived of as being between *bisan*, then grandchildren are often the means by which these links are activated as well as being their focus. Children are often used as messengers between houses. They carry words, food, gifts, loans and money. When relations are slightly tense this mediatory role becomes crucial: they interact when adults have difficulty in doing so. However, when relations break down completely, even very young children are prevented by adults from paying visits.

Hildred and Clifford Geertz (1975) have argued that in Bali teknonymy can be seen as part of a 'downward-looking' kinship system in which the stress is on future generations which seem to spread out fan-like below. In this respect they may be contrasted with African systems which can be said to 'look-upwards' towards past generations and an apical point. In a similar way I would argue that in Langkawi the stress on the production of children in marriage can equally be seen as a stress on the production of common grandchildren of *bisan* to which the latter have symmetrical rights, and this is itself intimately bound up with ideas about the reproduction of the community at large. For it is these grandchildren that in many ways constitute the practical reality of links between houses.

Conclusion

I have argued that the relationship between *bisan* in Langkawi represents an ideal of equality within the domain of kinship, and that this ideal is important not only within the marital alliance but, on a higher level, it becomes a symbol of community. Just as between *bisan* differentiation and hierarchy are ignored, so within the village, the symbolic statement 'we are all the same; we are all kin; we all owe each other aid' is being made. The relationship between *bisan* is not only a primary relationship of affinity, it is also at the very centre of the ideal notion of community. It is in this way that kinship morality becomes significant at the level of the wider community.

I do not mean to suggest that all social relationships in Langkawi conform to the ideal of equality. Of course, differences of wealth, status and class occur. And, as urban values increasingly penetrate the rural sector such differentials are likely to increase. I have discussed why the relationship between *bisan* is an appropriate symbol for equality within the kin group and the wider community. Just as in the wider community differences of wealth, status and class occur, so too do they between *bisan*. *Bisan* do get involved in disputes with each other; marriages do break down; reciprocity is not always perfectly balanced. It is because 'bisanship' is symbolically important at the level of communal solidarity that such breakdowns are particularly disruptive when they do occur.

An emphasis on the egalitarian modes of behaviour and aspects of kinship which are strongly expressed in Langkawi can be linked to the island's specific social context. An egalitarian ideology is a concomitant of the villagers' own position in the social and class structure of Malaysia as they themselves perceive it. In common with some social analysts they see the difference between the position of these classes as being, finally, of more significance than minor social differences which may distinguish members of one class from each other. It is this perception of their world which leads them to emphasize equality and unity whenever possible and to avoid making minor distinctions of rank. These tendencies may have been fostered by Langkawi's relative isolation from the centres of power on the mainland both in the past and, to some extent, still today. The absence of a land-owning aristocracy, the remoteness of the royal courts on the mainland with their elaborate ritual, and the lack of valuable natural resources to attract outside speculators, may all have contributed in allowing Langkawi to develop to a certain extent along its own lines, with kinship structures and behaviour showing tendencies which are less marked elsewhere.

Although egalitarianism can be expressed in the idiom of kinship, it may take other forms, for example, fostering specific modes of economic co-operation or appearing in political rhetoric. The particular form that it takes in Langkawi has to do with a parallel emphasis on the notion of the community as an in-marrying unit in which households are linked together through shared affinity.

Finally, it should be emphasized that a stress on egalitarianism does not imply actual equality in the social system. We know from our own experience of political rhetoric that speakers who express a concern for this theme may in reality be more concerned to maintain existing social differences than to abolish them. Values may be disconnected from the social situation, they may mask it or they may themselves be inconsistent. In Langkawi it is possible to build up a totally different model of kinship from the one I have described here: one based on hierarchy and drawn from consanguineal relations within the household. Such a model could, no doubt, be linked to real differences of income and wealth that exist between fishermen; however, it is not this model which is stressed in Langkawi. Bloch (1981) has shown that similarly conflicting models can be constructed from the Merina kinship system. The way in which one particular set of values is emphasized in a society relates to social and historical circumstances, but such values cannot give an accurate account of the social reality of which they are themselves a part.

Kinship, Community, and the Structure of Pahang Malay Kindreds

Bill Wilder

But my uncle-father and aunt-mother are deceived.
(*Hamlet* II,ii.)

Kinship is, thus, far more ambiguous in practice than some kinship studies seem to indicate; it has, moreover, a great many unconscious roots.
(George Devereux)

The argument

My paper is about the concepts of descent known to Pahang Malays who live at Kampung Kuala Bera, Temerloh District. It is an attempt to outline the working structure of Pahang Malay kindreds, in contradistinction to their ideal and typological structures. The quotations I have used as epigrams give a hint of the nature of the problem: like every people known to ethnographers, the Malays of Kampung Kuala Bera possess concepts about their 'kin universe'. One such concept is that every person (or sibling group) is surrounded if not totally then at least by a great many kinsmen plus a few 'outsiders'. In this respect Kampung Kuala Bera is like perhaps a hundred thousand other traditional settlements around the world. But kinship in this particular village is, as I shall show, fluid and highly malleable. It is not a question of 'kin' and 'non-kin', or that kinship (or much of it) consists of many elements intertwined with other parts of the social organization such that it has no separate existence: it is a question of numerous ambiguities within the kin universe itself.

The descent collectivities with which this paper — and the people of Kampung Kuala Bera — is concerned are briefly as follows:

1. The unrestricted agnatic stock, *bangsa Syed* (also *Sayyid* or *Said*)
2. The restricted agnatic descent line of the Pahang royalty
3. The ego-centred kindred, *saudara*
4. The bilateral, ancestor-centred 'kindreds' (stocks).

These are, in a sense, 'types' of kinship organization, but it would be misleading to try to compartmentalize them and thereby give the impression that the social structure of even one village, let alone many, belongs to one type or the other.

How do we avoid the abstractions of a typology like 'Hawaiian terms' or 'cognatic descent', which may turn out to be, at the very least, unnecessary to the analysis? One way to do so is by focusing upon the major dimensions of a kinship system. The first and most salient characteristic is its range (Radcliffe-Brown 1950:6); what concepts of 'distance' are used to define and qualify descent ties or other relationship ties within and between kindreds? Let us look at the Malay kindred concept referred to by the word *saudara*. Initially, the notion of *saudara* appears very vague and semantically pliable. I heard it used quite frequently and very freely in Kampung Kuala Bera in the 1960s and 1970s when I was there. It had the extremely general senses of 'relative', 'kinperson', and 'co-descendant'. Its application was highly flexible and varied according to a wide range of circumstances. Cognation, or notions of kindred, is a property of all kinship systems, and *saudara* seems to have this level of generality. (Thus, instead of 'kindreds' in the title of this paper, I could just as easily have written 'kin terms' or 'genealogies' or possibly even 'local groupings'.)

And yet, as is true of most common words, *saudara* has a narrower and specific meaning; used in this way, it generally signifies 'fourth-cousin circle of relatives'. This meaning apparently gets us on to more secure ground. I take it to correspond to the sense of the term kindred as many anthropologists use it, in other words, to mean 'field of recognized kinship' (Appell 1976, Freeman 1961).

Another aspect of this problem of range in kinship is the distinction, frequently met with both in anthropological accounts and in native categorizations, between 'kin', 'affines', and 'non-kin'; even finer and more extensive categorizations may be encountered. It is easy to transpose these notions into literal and exact 'kinship', whereas I suggest that, in most cases, they may be simply — in native eyes anyway — 'classificatory' approximations serving as concepts of social distance (see Leach 1958). Perhaps the exact categorizations are more specifically characteristic of narrow-range kinship systems. In such cases, the temptation, with ethnographers and natives alike, to present them as literal computations of ancestral relatedness becomes much greater. I suspect that the wider the range of the system the more absorptive and flexible its categorization is, the more metaphorical the ideas of 'kin' and 'non-kin' are. For this reason, I suspect that my argument differs from — and may actually be opposed to — those of students of Malay or similar kinship systems who seem to think that 'real' kinsmen are unambiguous and stand in complete contrast to the ambiguity of 'artificial' kinsmen (see Bloch 1973, Nagata 1976, Banks 1972). This type of distinction seems to me unnecessary.

The reader of this paper who, at this stage, expects an unorthodox approach will I hope not be disappointed. I shall argue that the village in question is affected by some four recognized and ostensibly 'alternative' or semi-autonomous (Hammel 1968) kinship concepts, as listed above. They are, for purposes of this paper, only four in number; though there are in fact several others (Wilder 1982) either mentioned in passing or omitted in the interests of clarity. It makes sense to spell these out rather than to try to subsume them within the Procrustean ideal of the 'kindred'. My concern is to present an overview of the operations of Pahang village kinship rather than a complete inventory; thus, the argument is limited to an attempt to show the ways kindreds or part-kindreds of various kinds are mobilized — by residential propinquity and by a degree of endogamy — rather than to see them as simple descent idioms. In partial agreement with some other students of the kindred I argue that the social situation in Kampung Kuala Bera produces kinship-defined local groups, not localized kin-groups (Sather 1976) and that affines, neighbours, and friends are largely interchangeable with kin under local conditions of recruitment and participation (King 1976).

Agnation

It will be convenient to first dispose of the concepts of agnatic descent: *bangsa Syed* and the Pahang royalty. Neither unit is confined to the village, but both affect the village in significant ways.

A *Syed* is a male descendant of the Prophet Muhammad in the male line. Female descendants, the daughters of *syeds*, take the title *Syarifah*. Such persons theoretically command respect — though in a typical village this may be hardly noticeable — and the kinship example they present lends prestige to the notion of agnation. In Kampung Kuala Bera, there are two *syed*-families (adjacent houses linked mother-to-daughter); these are in turn linked, through exchange of spouses, to a village in north-central Pahang consisting, it is said, almost entirely of *syeds*. There is, then, a preference for endogamy within this class which, through a tendency to exclusiveness, helps to reinforce its prestige. On the other hand, this is a title-group or class in which membership is in principle very large; it is an unlimited descent category, not an organized group.

Far more influential is the traditional Pahang Sultanate. Here the group is explicitly organized for the consolidation of political power. This power resides in the throne, the office of ruler. Figure 1 reproduces an official record of agnatic descent including all Pahang rulers since the late nineteenth century (Pertabalan 1975). The existence of such a record shows the importance of pedigrees as a way to prove or assert the legitimacy of the power holders.

The Pahang royal 'house' affects Pahang Malay villages in at least two ways. First, it is a design for the consolidation of power, through presumed agnation in the determination of succession. In the villages, the corresponding office of government headman *penghulu* is strongly patrilineal; the office in itself does not have a specific tradition of patrilineality, but these local headmen or minor chiefs seem to emulate the agnatic ideals as practised by the aristocratic and royal classes. How far is an agnatic effect achieved? An indication is given in Figure 2,

Fig. 1. Descent pedigree of the rulers of Pahang, 1863–present

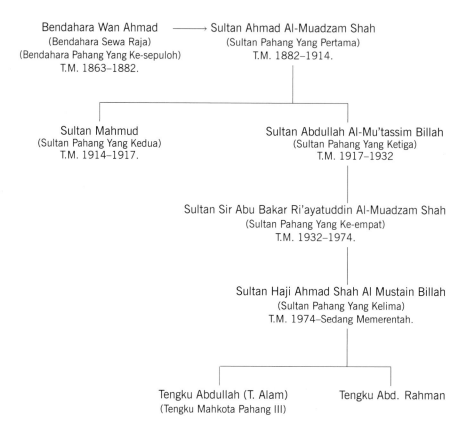

where both fraternal and father-to-son forms of agnatic succession occur. Notice that both of these were present in the Pahang royal succession (Figure 1). However, it is also the case that the ties found in the headmen's genealogies, while forming a close-knit circle, do not amount to an organized group of the same order as the Pahang Sultanate. The ties among the headmen rest much more on marriage and affinity (the second point to be discussed) than on strict agnation as an organizing principle. But before discussing the second point, let us consider further the question of how far agnation gives rise to organized corporate groups in the village. In some parts of the Malay peninsula, immigrant Malay (e.g. Bugis) communities recognize unilineal descent in a major way, but in Kampung Kuala Bera the descent concepts *salasilah, keturunan,* and *kerabat-kerabat* refer to genealogical categories, or descent lines, and not to organized groups. This suggests that while the Sultanate provides a model of power, embodied in office, it is not that of a *system* of groups using the descent principle (see Gullick 1958; Kahar 1970). The same is true of most Malay villages in Temerloh District, if not in most of Pahang. (The partial exception of a *syed*-village has been noted. It is also to be noted that in Kampung Kuala Bera, and perhaps elsewhere, the religious office of Imam has, at times, followed patrilineal succession.)

There is no strong idiom in Pahang villages for conceptualizing solidary kin groupings, that is, the vocabulary of groupings (as opposed to categories) is not elaborate. Neither group name nor genealogical tracing predominates in defining descent units. *Bangsa* (race, kind), *puak* (family, party), and *saudara* refer to some kinds of groupings; much less often villagers use the words *kaum* (faction, section), *waris* (heirs), or *adik-beradik* (relative of mine, siblings). Expressions for 'house', 'household', 'family', even 'village' and 'community' are not popular, and are usually encountered as ecological rather than socio-political notions. Kin are reckoned, as a rule, between individuals and between sibling groups. Some villagers keep rough sketch-genealogies, apparently for their own use, but many do not even see kinship in genealogical terms and, as stated, the circles or sets of kin they do recognize are not named nor are they ever validated by reference to a common ancestor. There is no strict ideology of descent which involves the average villager. The only word for 'descent' (*turun-temurun*) covers genealogical reckoning and this tends to be patrilateral beyond the second ascending generation.

Descent ties in Kampung Kuala Bera really amount to selective cousinship. Genealogical knowledge is, in general, of little concern. Where it is necessary, or desirable, to compute precise relationships, this is done by sorting out, first, generation-level, and then degree of collaterality. The latter is the major criterion of relationship, a form of distance (described below in connection with Table 1). I found this method of kinship computation remarkably accurate, particularly to third or fourth cousin (*tiga-pupu, empat-pupu*). The villagers are at pains to distinguish *their* 'descent' records as separate from, and lesser than, those of royalty. When I began taking genealogies in Kampung Kuala Bera, I used the word *salasilah* in asking for villagers' trees. They laughed at this and insisted that they don't have such things.

The Sultanate influences the villages in a second way, through marriages, and this may be the more significant influence. As might be expected, the descendants of the Pahang Sultans and their brothers are very numerous; this situation makes it possible for commoner women (often *penghulus'* daughters) to become attached through marriage to the agnatic relatives of the ruler or to the Four Major Chiefs (*Orang Kaya Indera Besar Berempat*, or *Orang Besar Berempat*), the latter being offices next below the Sultan's circle in the hierarchy of traditional political ranks. In such a way, connections of prestige are established but, because they need not be maintained, the separateness and the superiority of the royal and aristocratic sides are not compromised. Two *penghulus* of Mukim Bera (both alive in 1976) had married off a daughter and a sister, respectively, in this way and thus set up close affinal ties with the traditional Pahang elite.

Fig. 2. Genealogical ties of 'headmen' in Kuala Bera region, 1965 (Wilder 1982:66)

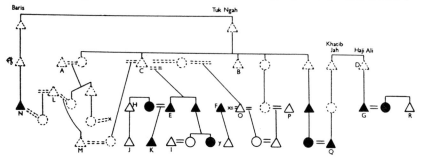

Penghulus (government of subdistrict headmen)

Dead
A. Penghulu, Mukim Bera
B. Penghulu, Mukim Bera
C. Penghulu, Mukim Bera
D. Penghulu, Mukim Bohor

Living 1965
E. Formerly Penghulu, Mukim Bera
F. Formerly Temporary Penghulu, Mukim Bera
G. Penghulu, Mukim Bera
H. Penghulu, Mukim Kertau
I. Penghulu, Mukim Cenor (formerly Penghulu Mukim Bera)
J. Penghulu, Mukim Kertau (1976)
K. Penghulu, Mukim Bera (1976)

Tuk Empats (village headmen = *ketua kampung*)

Dead
L. Tuk Empat, Kg. Batu Papan
M. Tuk Empat, Kg. Kuala Bera

Living 1965
N. Tuk Empat, Kg. Batu Papan
O. Tuk Empat, Kg. Paya Hitam
P. Tuk Empat, Sembrang Pahang (Kg. Serendang)
Q. Tuk Empat, Kg. Kuala Bera
R. Tuk Empat, Kg. Sebrang Gui

xx   previous marriage
y   impending engagement (*tunang senyap*) 1965

That this pattern of prestige marriages rather than the sustained alliance of
groups is of primary significance in the Pahang political arena is suggested in
Figure 2. This diagram shows all the *penghulus*, or government headmen, in
the Kuala Bera region during a period of one hundred years or more. The next
political rank below *penghulu*, the village headman or *tuk empat*, is also well

represented. Neither of the two kinds of office shown is strictly hereditary, so it is striking to see that the *penghulus'* sons often do succeed and that office holders in the Bera region are concentrated within a small circle of common descent and intermarriage. All the Bera *penghulus* since at least 1889 (when British colonial administration takes account of them), as well as *penghulus* of two neighbouring *mukims* and many of the village headmen of the region, are included. Figure 2 shows this relationship. In short, we find that the local political elites are drawn together through a mixture of preferential agnation and preferential endogamy.

Kindreds and the village

We have seen that agnation in Pahang Malay kinship depends, in varying degrees, upon the existence of traditional offices or titles: *syed, imam,* Sultan, *orang besar, penghulu, tuk empat.* The average villager, in contrast, is involved in circles of kin reckoned, on the whole, bilaterally, and mobilized, or recognized, by diffuse means. Formally, the *saudara* or kindred presents a picture of an ordered kinship domain, structured by concepts of distance (Table 1). But, having said this, I must add that a category of 'non-kin' (*bukan saudara, orang lain, orang*) is also recognized, so we are not dealing here with a simple 'kin-based' community. And yet, as stated earlier, such social categorizations are not necessarily mutually exclusive. How might this point be demonstrated?

One possible definition of the kindred is by a strict marriage rule, with spouses determined according to cognatic distance, in other words, a form of exogamy. Such a rule is not recognized in Pahang, but an analogous operation does emerge, in that first and second cousins are frequently chosen in marriage, with second cousins more frequently so than first (Wilder 1982:62). Thus the Pahang Malay kindred is, if anything, highly endogamous. To some extent, marriage of 'kin' is actually formulated in kinship categories (Wilder 1982:51–65). Conscious preferences are expressed in Kampung Kuala Bera for marriage of both kin *and* affines. Some half-dozen types of affinal marriages are recognized in addition to various types of kin marriages; for example, one possibility is with a 'step-grandmother' (*wan saudara tiri*) widowed as a young woman (*bini muda*).

In a similar vein, 'kin-marriages' may evolve from the genealogical metamorphosis of an affinal relative into a consanguineal relative, as shown in the example (Figure 3). In the diagram, Ishak and Mat Aris stand, genealogically, in an affinal relationship, or, to be accurate, in two affinal relationships. Yet in my village census, I was told that they were 'not kin, not related'. On another occasion, however, Ishak told me that he addressed Mat Aris as *abang* 'because he is *dua-pupu* (second cousin)'. What is the 'true' picture here? Ishak was at the time twenty-eight years old, Mat Aris between forty and forty-five. Ishak, as the husband of Mat Aris's daughter, would not use the term *abang* (older sibling,

Table 1. Consanguineal distance, Kampung Kuala Bera, 1965

Distance	Approximate category	Category range
saudara dekat 'near kinsman'	± sa-pupu 'first-cousin'	bapak saudara anak saudara sa-pupu bapak saudara sa-pupu anak saudara sa-pupu
saudara jauh sikit 'kinsman a little distant'	± dua-pupu 'second-cousin'	bapak saudara-pupu anak saudara sa-pupu dua-pupu bapak saudara dua-pupu anak saudara dua-pupu
saudara jauh 'distant kinsman'	± tiga-pupu 'third-cousin'	bapak saudara dua-pupu anak saudara dua-pupu tiga-pupu bapak saudara tiga-pupu anak saudara tiga-pupu
	= empat-pupu 'fourth-cousin'	empat-pupu

male) to Mat Aris if that affinal link were being observed; but *abang* is the correct term for second cousin, and is the one preferred by Ishak. As far as I could determine on quite sound genealogical evidence, the relevant parts of which are shown in the diagram, the two men are not descended from a common ancestor; they are not cousins (consanguineal relatives), but are, rather, involved in a *kin-like* connection, that is, a relationship of approximately third cousin distance, as the diagram suggests.

I interpret this example as showing that a marriage tie can have the same kinship value as a descent tie. Genealogical substitutions like this occur widely in Kampung Kuala Bera and, I am sure, in many Pahang Malay villages. Thus, while kin-marriage, or the marriage of *consanguineal* relatives, plays an important part in local solidarity, so too does the marriage of *affines*, and the links in individual cases may be multiple.

At least two general features of the kindred in Kampung Kuala Bera may be inferred from the foregoing: kinship ties are dense and they are malleable. The latter feature has just been illustrated. The former could also be shown (see Wilder 1982:95–100 on personal kindreds). These data, showing range of kin reckoning (Table 1), marriages of kin, and marriages of affines, suggest, furthermore, that in practice the two features are interdependent and they are so to a greater degree than the conventional formal and typological perspectives on kindreds would indicate.

The evidence presented so far seems to recommend caution in any attempt at 'true' or strict genealogical representation of the cognatic kindred; at the same

Fig. 3. Marriage and kinship: Ishak and Mat Aris, 1965

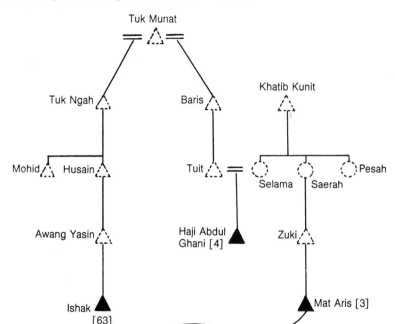

time, it shows the importance of the concept of 'distance' (*jauh/jauh sikit/dekat*) in Pahang Malay kinship. I have not so far mentioned one highly significant factor in the collocation of social groupings in Kampung Kuala Bera, that of residence. Here the notions of spatial and social distance seem to converge. The kindred, or *saudara*, category referred to in Table 1 is the theoretically unlimited circle of kin to which any, and therefore all, ancestral ties are relevant. However, another form of cognatic kinship operates in the village; it seems to be divided, if only in a latent fashion, into a half a dozen cognatic 'stocks' (to use Freeman's terminology). These are, by definition, ancestor-focused. They are also, to a measurable degree, localized collections of households, and together they make up the great majority of the population (81 out of 127 houses), and almost all of the houses of native-born villagers. The ancestral origins of the groupings are sketched in Figure 4.

The ancestral figures shown above the broken line in the diagram have living descendants in Kampung Kuala Bera today who are, despite considerable disruption and internal shifts of population (especially from Dalam Bera and Kuala Bera to Lubuk Lian), arranged into groupings territorially distinguished from each other. In short, these territorial groupings can in each case be referred back to a single common ancestor, as I shall explain.

Bill Wilder

Fig. 4. Ancestors: Kampung Kuala Bera. (Letters below broken line refer to Table 2)

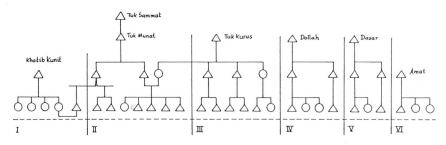

Most villagers know the names of these ancestors, since they are descended from one or more of them, but in no case was I given to believe that the ancestors embodied common group interests which carry down to the present time; rather, the ancestors are recalled selectively (as the genealogical sketch is intended to imply), and with some pride (on grounds of former eminence), no more than that. These proposed descent collectivities are admittedly statistical constructs but they tend to coincide with the four sub-territories into which Kampung Kuala Bera is divided, each with a different topography and settlement history. Table 2 shows the existence of such a pattern: to the extent that one or more members of the eighty-one households have a certain ancestor in common, their houses tend to cluster together. The table gives the actual count by household units. (The remaining forty-six houses in the village are not classified or belong to outsiders.)

Table 2. Settlement pattern and common descent, Kampung Kuala Bera, 1965

	Locality				
Descendants of	Tanjung Bera	Dalam Bera	Kuala Bera	Lubuk Lian	Total houses all localities
I Khatib Kunit	**15**	–	–	–	15
VI Ahmat	–	**12**	–	–	12
V Dasar	–	8	–	7	15
II Tuk Munat	–	1	8	**13**	22
IV Dollah	–	1	3	6	10
III Tuk Kurus	–	2	2	3	7
Totals, each locality	15	24	13	29	81

The eighty-one household groupings shown in the table belong to an ancestral 'community' of no more than six individuals, all traceable at a level (in 1965) two to four generations above living persons. The largest concentrations of co-descendants are shown in the table in bold print. Khatib Kunit's and Ahmat's descendants represent the most localized contemporary groupings; Dasar and

Tuk Munat are also strongly localized when it is recalled that Lubuk Lian is a new settlement and the people there used to live at Dalam Bera and Kuala Bera respectively. These four are also the largest groupings.

We are now, inevitably, faced with the question of why these restricted kindreds should exist. They are descent units corresponding to what are technically known as stocks in that they are limited by an ancestor focus. They are strongly bilateral. They are also maintained as restricted groups by a degree of endogamy and by residence preferences. The restriction, however, is not overtly formalized, a negative feature which makes them problematical. The argument of this paper leads me to the suggestion that these latent groupings may be — or may be seen as — bilateral, clan-like images of the agnatic stocks of the *syeds* and Sultans of Pahang. That these localized descent groupings are latent and require a statistical or organizational (Firth 1964) model to elucidate does not make them too unimportant to enter into the analysis of the structure of kindreds; on the contrary, if they are truly resonant of the agnatic descent forms, then we achieve a better grasp of kinship in Pahang Malay villages than if we exclude agnation, on the one hand, and latent descent groupings on the other.

The question is intriguing, but without more sophisticated treatment of the data than I have yet been able to carry out, and despite the valiant efforts of comparativists on the structure of cognation (e.g. Appell 1976; Needham 1975), I cannot offer a more decisive analysis at this stage.

Conclusion

The study of kinship groups and categories, including the kindred, is in some anthropological writing overconcerned, it seems to me, to convey a sense of the unambiguous. Thus in some of this work the distinction is made between 'real kinsmen' and others. I note in Freeman's own article on the kindred an uncertainty as to how kinsmen are to be identified, when he shifts between the nondistinct qualifications of known relatives to include variously 'all', 'some', 'certain', 'many', and 'any who happen to be known'. Freeman himself acknowledges (in his Note 29) that genealogical relatedness may mean not just descent but also adoption, affinity, friendship, and co-residence; as he says, any person who has 'assumed the status of cognate' (1960:216). These apparent certainties turn out to be deceptive, as well they might. All kinship is 'cognatic'; it would then follow from this that all kinship is highly ambiguous, and that anthropologists do not spend enough of their time asking just what counts as 'kinship' for the people they study.

In the Pahang Malay context, as I have tried to show, kinship relations are both abundant and mutable. And yet there are discernible units, corresponding to several notions of descent, or relatedness. At a general level, there is probably a concept in Pahang villages of a 'complete' genealogy. Such is one of the overtones of the descent of *syeds* (or *sayyids*), the descendants of the Prophet Muhammad. A more limited and localized form of unilineal descent is presupposed by the Pahang Sultanate; rather than involving all agnates, the Sultanate concentrates on the direct agnatic line. Such concepts of more or less restricted cognation are known and reflected in village life in Pahang. In Kampung Kuala Bera there are diffuse networks of kin (*saudara*) selectively but comprehensively recognized on what one might call pan-genealogical or unrestricted grounds, that is, when an adoptive or affinal or some other tie is swapped into a straight tie of common descent. Restriction is exercised in a kinship idiom of consanguineal 'distance' but, like descent, this too is mutable, in terms of residence space. Thus, finally, cognation may manifest itself in stocks with some degree of territorial cohesion. These groupings are ancestor-focused; they consist of the locally residing descendants of six prominent ancestral figures, reinforced by other factors such as preferential endogamy. Descent in these units, as in the kindred itself, is strongly bilateral, both normatively and statistically.

In this brief essay I have attempted to specify some of the materials which, it seems to me, are essential for any study of Malay kindreds. If it has a specific, immediate purpose, it is an appeal to field-workers, not to theorists. I see no strong case for arguing that Malays use one form of descent or kindred or cognation over any other. It seems to be the case, rather, that Malay kinship is many things at once: language, genealogy, locality, matrimony, sentiment, symbolism, and more besides. Kinship is acted out in all these spheres, and each should be treated in its own right.

Kinship and Exchange Practices
in a Malay Village

Josiane Massard

Kampong Kiambang is the long-established village, situated along the banks of the Pahang river, in which I did field-work between 1978 and 1980.[1] As defined by administrative maps it consists of sixty-four households with a total population of just over three hundred. Yet, though initially selected as a unit of study, I soon discovered that in many respects it does not function as a discrete social entity but that its social universe merges with two neighbouring officially designated villages. This is especially apparent in the case of exchange practices where the networks of participants are not restricted to administrative boundaries but extend beyond the limits of Kampong Kiambang. Furthermore, the people of these three villages consider themselves part of the same social entity, Ganchong, which constitutes a subdistrict (*mukim*) according to the usual Malaysian administrative pattern. This discrepancy between the bureaucratic and social realities of the community is made all the stronger by the local distribution of power, in which the very competent and influential *ketua kampong* of Kiambang enjoys almost as much prestige as the *penghulu* of Ganchong, even though the latter has a far higher formal status. In other words, personal characteristics compete with the formal attributes of status in a social context in which the significance of relative rank is of considerable importance in interpersonal relations.

If we turn to the economic sphere it is apparent that the rather homogeneous picture often given of rural Malay society conceals a far more diversified reality. It is true that most people in Kampong Kiambang derive a meagre income from mixed farming, a combination of rice and vegetable growing with cattle-raising, fishing and rubber tapping. Yet a few households do exhibit signs of material wealth, whether in the traditional forms of land, jewelry and cattle, or the more modern possession of cars and electrical appliances, which stand in sharp contrast to the poverty of others. One might argue that this economic

1. The funding for the first phase of field-work (March 1978 to March 1979) was provided by the Délégation Générale de la Recherche Scientifique et Technique (Bureau du Premier Ministre); the second phase (May to August 1980) was financed by the Centre National de la Recherche Scientifique (Paris).

stratification is due to the presence of villagers who as active or retired government employees — teachers, nurses, military men — are or have been able to both
save and simultaneously live in comfort. Yet even if government employment is
the main source of financial advantage it is not the only one, and wealth can be
acquired within the social and economic boundaries of the village through inheritance and access to the control of state resources. Such fortunate individuals not
only have financial security but, partly because of it, also enjoy prestige within
the village community. The latter is thus, as a whole, internally differentiated by
variations in prestige and control of economic resources, which often partly coincide. However, economic success and/or being well-born are not in themselves
sufficient to gain respect, for which a third factor, that of religiosity, comes into
play. The importance attached by people to the observance of Islamic codes of
conduct is such that wealth has to be matched by religious devotion. Well-born
or wealthy villagers are honoured and admired as long as they are pious Muslims.

Most forms of social intercourse in a Malay rural community are explicitly justified by villagers in terms of either kinship or religion. I have shown elsewhere
(Massard 1983a) how exchange practices, which constitute an important aspect
of such intercourse, in fact follow two distinct and mutually exclusive patterns,
egalitarian and hierarchical. Insofar as informants often claim that relations between kin are marked by generosity and sometimes by equality, it seems necessary
to consider further the implications of exchange for kinship and the part the
latter plays in village life with particular reference to social differentiation.

In this paper I maintain that the only sense in which the central Malay concept
of kin — *saudara* — can be understood is from the perspective of the individual.
Only *adik-beradik benar* (real brothers and sisters) born of the same mother and
father share the same set of consanguineal kin. *Saudara* relationships, whether
they be matrilateral or patrilateral, are established on a dyadic basis, the category
of *saudara* thus constituting the kindred as defined by Freeman (1961). Whereas
the genealogical boundaries of a kindred can be defined, its social limits are
hardly predictable and forever fluctuating because of the element of choice. Thus
even in the smallest social unit, the household, which functions as an economic,
residential and emotionally close-knit group in most circumstances, minor differences may and do occur between members which reflect variation in wealth
and actual social relations as well as the heavy emphasis on differences between
generations, and to a lesser degree between elder and younger siblings. Contrary
to any impression of equality, relationships between close kin are thus almost
always coloured by status evaluations.

Villagers express a preference for marriage with kin, more precisely with
first-degree cousins (*sa-pupu*), though this seldom materializes.[2] Similarly, people

2. Out of the 174 marriages referred to in one genealogical chart, only 26 or less than 15%
concerned people who had a *sa-pupu*, *dua-pupu* or *tiga-pupu* relationship.

assert that if marriage with kin is not possible then it is arranged with co-villagers, yet this also occurs only in a minority of cases.[3] Here is not the place to investigate such discrepancies between cultural ideals and practices, but simply note the still not insignificant rate of village in-marriage and its slight matrifocal trend. Of the sixty-four households, eleven were matrilocal, eight virilocal and four ambilocal in that both sets of parents resided in the village.

As for 'exchange', which of course is a Western-made concept, here I use the term very broadly to encompass a whole series of practices which include *sedekah* (almsgiving), *tolong-menolong* (mutual help), *berderau* (rotating team work), *bagi dua* (sharecropping), and *upah* (paid labour) among many others. It thus refers to any circulation of wealth either on a temporary or permanent basis from an individual villager (or grouping of people) to another individual or grouping. Wealth in this sense includes locally valued resources such as land, food or money, services within the agricultural, technical or even ritual contexts, less tangible items such as political power or religious or social status, as well as people circulating in marriage or in various forms of adoption.[4] Despite the problems of evaluation for equivalence, exchanges cannot be treated as one-way because the return is relatively intangible. I have thus chosen cases where, however crudely, a relative symmetry or imbalance can be determined. In order to give as broad a picture as possible, I have selected examples from different aspects of village life; the first two relate to the circulation of cooked food, the third and fourth deal with agricultural activities, and the last example pertains to the ritual cycle.

Cooked food made public

Following the routes taken by cooked food during the Muslim fasting month of Ramadan can be very rewarding[5] because of the way activities become far more focused on the household, given the restrictions on normal daytime sociability. At sunset members of the household gather to break the fast with home-made delicacies (*kueh-kueh*). Earlier in the afternoon the cook often prepares more than is required by her own household to send *hantar*, 'extra shares', to other houses just before sunset. It appears that the recipients, who can number up to six households, remain the same throughout the period even if food is not exchanged every day. The first criterion in their selection appears to be physical proximity, they will be at the most a few minutes walk away. Given the residence

3. Out of the above total, only 33 other marriages had linked village people (*orang sini*).

4. Except for the transfer of individuals, our use of the term 'exchange' coincides more or less with what Banks has called 'gift' (Banks 1976:576–7). I differ from Sahlins (1974) in not isolating material goods from other valued resources involved in general circulation.

5. Among the Minangkabau of West Sumatra, cooked food circulates before the beginning of the fasting month, see Prindiville (n. d.).

pattern mentioned above, this physical proximity can coincide with genealogical ties and when it does the latter are emphasized. In most cases these gifts are reciprocated (*balas*) in kind the same evening or at the latest within one or two days. One would be ashamed (*malu*) of returning an empty container via the child go-between more than once. Such symmetrical or balanced exchanges are said to operate between both relatives and those who are just neighbours (*jiran sahaja*).

However, sometimes there is no return, as when the beneficiary is too old or poor to be able to cook anything besides rice and fish. This may be referred to as a 'free gift' (*bagi sahaja*) from a younger to an older relative. Alternatively the explanation can be economic, as when the offering is explicitly spoken of as 'alms' (*sedekah*) and, as observed by Nagata (1976), this can occur even when there is a genealogical tie. The converse of these gifts occurs where the recipient's household enjoys a far higher achieved or ascribed status than that of the donor. In such circumstances the gift is a sign of respect and in Kampong Kiambang the government midwife is often presented with gifts of *kueh* as is the house of the *penghulu*.

Finally, one must note that although some women never send cooked food to others during this period, they do regularly prepare *kueh-kueh* to be sent or personally taken to the neighbouring prayer-house (*surau*), where the dishes are served in between prayer-sessions. If there are any left-overs these are distributed and taken home afterwards. These gifts are also referred to as alms.

From the preceding it appears that the preparation of delicacies beyond the household's own requirements during Ramadan can be motivated by a variety of factors among which the desire to honour kinship ties is not paramount. The egalitarian or asymmetrical forms taken by such gifts is not predetermined by the existence of blood ties. According to Bloch (1973) the cases in which fairly immediate and balanced reciprocity is stressed should coincide with those loose/versatile social ties that need to be frequently re-activated, yet in fact these exchanges include consanguineal kin. This not only contradicts Bloch's model, it is also in discordance with the villagers' statements that real brothers and sisters 'do not keep accounts' (*tidak kira*) of what is given or received and consequently should feel no obligation to reciprocate so quickly. Applying equally to kin and non-kin, the need to reciprocate is meant to express an egalitarian relationship between those involved and has nothing to do with a lack of trust or weakness of ties. Furthermore, partners who exchange *kueh* on an equal footing in the fasting month during the rest of the year visit one another's homes informally and regularly, when frequently though not necessarily food is served. Can one thus say that the sending back and forth of Ramadan dishes is a substitute for temporarily interrupted visits? This would appear to be so, as the routes followed are those otherwise taken throughout the year.

The fact that kin and non-kin partners are treated identically does not mean that they are considered as identical in other respects. That neighbours are perceived as irrevocably different from blood kin is perhaps the very reason they must be treated 'like brothers and sisters' (*macam adik-beradik*), because they are encountered and needed in everyday interaction. Kinship here is important in that, broadly speaking, local standards of etiquette offer two different social codes, one for strangers, 'unrelated people' (*orang lain*), and one that applies to kin (*saudara*). Obviously, next-door neighbours cannot be treated as strangers and, on a wider though looser basis, it makes social life smoother and more reassuring if one can talk of the village community as one large family, *orang sini, semua saudara* (the people here are all relatives). As distinct from the Kedah people studied by Banks (1972) my Kiambang informants are dealing with nothing new or disturbing when they socialize with non-kin neighbours. The use of kin terms towards non-kin thus does not generate any confusion for those concerned, while it does enable actors to conduct apparently harmonious relationships. Such practices become even more important where unrelated people have to live together in close proximity, as happens with people who have moved to the new settlements in the land schemes of the Federal Land Development Agency (FELDA). There the dishes tend to be sent to two or three neighbouring households, usually following the practice of balanced reciprocity outlined above, and female informants insist that they treat one another like sisters (*macam adik-beradik*). Again, one can see how kinship provides a code of interpersonal behaviour which is all the more important in a recently created community without a common past in which new exchange networks have to be developed.

Now what about the various gifts of delicacies which are not returned in kind and the structural principles underlying them? In dealing with an intergenerational link presented, for example, as mother/daughter or grandmother/granddaughter irrespective of whether a blood tie actually exists, we certainly have an illustration of an important item in kinship ideology: children should help their parents when they reach socially defined old age and provide for them if necessary. They do not expect anything in return, at least not from the parent who is being helped; rather they hope their own children will show the same generosity or consideration when they too grow old. The gift has a rebounding effect: compensation does not come from the recipient, it is stretched along the generational chain.

In contrast, where a one-way gift from a younger/better-off villager to an older/poorer one is accounted for as 'alms', kinship ideology gives way to the realm of religion. Muslims are enjoined to practise charity and the very notion of charity presupposes the existence of economic disparities[6] in the same way that

6. Of course, this is not to say that the advent of Islam resulted in socio-economic differentiation within Malay society. If anything, Islam further validated the existing order which was already stratified.

generosity implies an at least temporary imbalance. In neither case is any tangible return expected, but the Islamic gift *sedekah* is such that villagers explicitly hope for rewards in the afterlife (*pahala*) as they do for other good deeds such as providing free religious tuition to children or giving used clothing to poorer villagers. Again, when these delicacies instead of going down the social scale go from ordinary villagers to holders of a valued function or high status, we have another expression of asymmetrical exchange. Historically, the sending of gifts by peasants has been but one way of paying tribute to overlords (Gullick 1958). While in the old days such forms of tribute were a means of securing protection, in modern times they can be construed as honouring the established order. Here again no tangible return is expected, yet the sender may hope for easier access to help or advice from the beneficiary which will in no way cancel the imbalance.

If by way of provisional conclusion one had to qualify Ramadan dishes, one could say that they are polysemic. Whatever diversity they have as far as social and symbolic meaning is concerned, they express a limited geographical mobility in that they always circulate within the village.[7] This is not true of another type of cooked food which is associated not with the Muslim calendar but with the agricultural cycle.

At the beginning of the rice harvest when the crop has barely ripened, groups of two or three female villagers get together in the evening to prepare *emping* or 'new rice'.[8] In the days that follow, this 'new rice' which will keep for days or even months does 'travel' almost exclusively beyond the village limits. Again, depending on destination the gift carries different social messages. It is most often sent to close relatives such as daughters or granddaughters, in which case it might be taken by a member of the harvesting household to that of, for example, a married daughter living seventy kilometres away. Very different are villagers' recollections of how in the 1960s they still sent 'new rice' to the Sultan's palace some twenty kilometres away. Thus, as opposed to Ramadan dishes which circulate along numerous routes and can be reciprocated with similar counter gifts, the 'new rice' is a one-way transaction and the recipients few in number. The care shown in their selection can, in a very general way, be linked with the symbolic value of rice: *emping* is the 'first fruit' from the rice field and is produced on land which will one day be inherited and shared by lineal kin, the very people who are given *emping*. The fact that the other partner used to be the ruler is a reminder that traditionally the Raja enjoyed some higher control over his subjects' land and was thus entitled to its first fruits. With the former pattern the movement of *emping* illustrates the association between long-term and enduring links said to

7. Because of climatic conditions, they must be consumed the day they are cooked so they could not in any case go very far outside the village limits.
8. In fact it is freshly harvested new rice that is first soaked for a few hours then grilled dry and finally pounded in the wooden mortar or *lesong*.

be typical of kinship ties. In the latter, travelling up the social scale it plays the role of a tribute in showing the acceptance of a certain power relationship. In both cases the distribution expresses the asymmetrical quality of relationships.

Who works for whom? Labour and kinship

In the preceding section I showed first how non-relatives can be treated 'like' kin, then how real relatives can be distinguished from others. I now turn to the organization of work on rubber holdings and rice fields to consider on what basis labour is asked and granted. At the time of observation twenty-five village households depended for a living on rubber tapping; fourteen tapped their own trees while the rest were related to the owners of the rubber smallholdings. In nine cases the link was close, such as between siblings or a mother and daughter; in the remaining two it was more distant. The latter had been recruited on a *bagi dua* basis[9] which is a common form of labour contract between non-kin: what about the others?

One man worked his brother's plantation on a *bagi dua* arrangement, though with five school-going children and no land or property of his own he seemed all the more deserving of his brother's generosity, especially given that the latter was a school teacher. The other tappers who were working their relatives' trees retained all the profits from the sale of the rubber sheets. For example, a divorced lady with two children attending secondary school depended on her father's trees and commented that she was 'her father's real child' (*anak benar*). It appears that close blood ties are respected, as generosity normally prevails among such kin; the man referred to above was the only exception of someone being treated as a distant relative by a sibling. Nevertheless, it seems unlikely that owners willingly accept an apparently disadvantageous deal; further observation reveals that they were not left with much of a choice, as few villagers were willing to tap others' trees and recruitment of outsiders proved unfeasible. At least they knew that by entrusting their trees to close relatives the latter would not damage them[10] and would carry out essential maintenance work. Kinship ideology proved effective in that other than for the brothers mentioned earlier the *bagi dua* arrangement seemed unthinkable between close kin and, since owners could not find others to accept this contract, they saw no alternative but to allow their close relations to work the plantations for free.

In comparison to tapping, the types of work distribution in rice growing seem almost infinite. Several of these can occur in a single plot during a given season

---

9. This means that half the profits derived from the sale of dried rubber sheets go to the plantation owner, the tapper retaining the other half.

10. As opposed to outside labourers — mainly Indian coolies — who are often accused of damaging the trees by cutting too deeply into the bark in order to get more latex.

and can be combined quite differently the following year. Not only may the extra
help utilized be provided by different people, but even when the same individuals
help for two consecutive years on the same plot the terms of the contract may differ. This instability of work teams among Malay rice growers has been especially
striking to observers from another rice-growing culture, the Japanese, where a
unilineal descent system results in rigidly organized work groups (Kuchiba and
Tsubouchi 1968). In Kampong Kiambang kinship does not act as a strict determinant; kin are not necessarily asked to participate, and even household
members — especially unemployed teenagers — can escape the obligation to help.
In fact the percentage of kin in work teams is so low that one can hardly speak of
'kindred based action groups' (Freeman 1961). Furthermore, other than household members some of the kin participants work on no better terms than non-
kin.

When Aminah asked 'Teh, a widowed half-sister with four young children,
to help with the harvesting, she let her retain only half of what she had cut. Yet
when an 'aunt' (father's first cousin) helped, she was allowed to keep all the paddy
she had harvested. There was, in addition, an old lady described as *orang dagang*
as she was without any relatives and she too kept everything she cut. Finally,
two other non-relatives worked according to the same *bagi dua* arrangement as
did 'Teh. In every instance a different explanation was advanced: 'Teh worked
on a *bagi dua* basis because 'she harvested a lot', Aminah's aunt kept everything
because they 'consider one another as mother and daughter' (*kira 'mak sama
anak*), the *orang dagang* lady kept everything because 'she is old and poor', and
the other two people worked on a *bagi dua* basis because they are not related
(*orang lain*) to Aminah.

It appears that kinship and economic referents are very skilfully manipulated
and can sometimes be used interchangeably as in 'Teh's case. According to
Aminah's strategy, some blood relatives were indeed treated as kinship ideology
demands and in accordance with Sahlins' category of 'generalized reciprocity'
(1976:193–4), while other kin were treated as outsiders. However, while all
helpers were poor enough to deserve Aminah's generosity in retaining all the rice
they harvested, she herself could not afford to part with so much of her crop.
At the same time she alone could not accomplish the work of harvesting fast
enough on her own, and required at least part of the help recruited and so had to
impose harsher terms on some of them. The little choice she had was in deciding
how much each might keep and even though I have argued elsewhere that *bagi
dua* contracts are in the owner's favour (Massard 1983a),[11] this advantage is
limited. That same harvesting season some villagers were recruited on a *bagi tiga*
or even *bagi empat* basis keeping only one third or even one fourth of what they

---

11. Perhaps because of the way the practice is worded or because the profit is shared into two
equal parts, some authors have seen in *bagi dua* a form of egalitarian exchange (Wilson 1967) or an
act of generosity (Nagata 1976).

cut.[12] Kinship did play its part in Aminah's choice in that she felt she had to ask her half-sister and so in a sense pay homage to kin ties. Moreover kinship played a major ideological role in providing a plausible justification to the way Aminah's aunt and the two strangers were rewarded. Reference was also made to the religious duty of charity in the case of the *orang dagang* lady. Economic interests were only explicitly referred to in 'Teh's case although they played a part in all other instances. This is not to say that the economic interests are pre-eminent. The one who 'controls the means of production' is impeded in dictating his or her terms by two series of factors. In the first place there are ethical reasons — whether they be phrased in kinship or religious terms — which make it difficult to push exploitation beyond a socially acceptable point. Secondly there are demographic and economic factors: just as with rubber tapping, though to a lesser degree, the pool of willing and/or able helpers is limited[13] and the latter therefore enjoy some choice as to for whom they work. They sometimes turn down offers which appear unprofitable to them even when they have been put forward by a close relative. This is true of people who only wish to harvest a little paddy in order to meet part of their consumption needs. Villagers who need to stock enough to live on most of the year cannot afford to be so choosy and have no alternative but to accept *bagi dua* (or *tiga* or *empat*) contracts. 'Teh belonged to the latter category and was given the opportunity to harvest a reasonable amount of paddy at a relatively moderate labour cost.[14] In contrast Aminah's aunt and the *orang dagang* lady deprived Aminah of little (their output being low because of their age) and were offered a much better deal. Only in their case — despite the fact that they harvested little — could one say that their employment was an act of generosity (Kuchiba and Tsubouchi 1968). In fact no one is expected to display such generosity; what matters is a willingness to share the work of harvesting, and those who try to escape this obligation by harvesting with no outside help are regarded as mean by fellow villagers. They are condemned not so much because they exclude their relatives but because they do not share their resources with anybody outside the household. Such an inward-looking production — and con-sumption — process goes further than seeking mere autonomy (to which villagers have no objection), it is tantamount to a form of 'social incest' and is in private considered as deviant. It is nevertheless condoned publicly and the members of such a household can still be part of other exchange networks which involve social and ceremonial production rather than so-called economic production.

12. Even in such cases, the arrangement was referred to as *bagi dua* and the precise percentage was only revealed after further investigation.

13. In this sense Pahang would contrast with other states of the Malay peninsula such as Kedah which suffers from a shortage of rice land. The shortage of labour in the community studied can be partly accounted for by massive out-migration towards FELDA land schemes.

14. Again, as compared with less favourable work terms that non-relatives might have offered her; yet the arrangement which tied her to her sister must have involved some emotional cost which one cannot evaluate but which must be borne in mind.

Relatives and ceremonial production

On ceremonial occasions such as weddings or circumcisions which on account of the large number of guests, sometimes up to five hundred, require the organization of a large labour force in their preparation, the composition of the work teams is subject to totally different criteria.

When Meriam and Jalil were making preparations for their daughter's wedding they asked Meriam's mother's brother, Jafar, to be the chief cook. They also recruited twenty-nine other people, nineteen of whom were kin and the rest affines. All of them were busy preparing the meal from Saturday afternoon until late into the night. They all received snacks and meals at Jalil's house, and then took home raw meat on the Saturday and cooked food (*lauk*-accompanying dishes) the next day. The shares were identical, apart from that of Jafar who received choice pieces because of his more honorific role. All of the participants were of Meriam's or her mother's generation and were recruited on the maternal side, as Jalil was an *orang dagang* without local relatives. The ties extended to her mother's third cousin. These contributions of labour are explicitly regarded as work that can only be compensated by a similar contribution in identical circumstances. The gifts of food constitute an immediate payment but the organizers of the celebration are also either receiving retribution for help given earlier or incurring a long-term debt. We are here dealing with a kindred-based action group as kin are in the majority, and all participants are treated the same. People do exchange as 'brothers and sisters' on an equal footing, yet the sharing of such ritual services brings together people who might in other circumstances be exchanging on asymmetrical terms: one might be working in another's rubber plantation on a *bagi dua* basis, or the household or one of the helpers could be the beneficiary (because of his/her high status) of one-way food gifts. This shows that existing economic gaps can be blurred temporarily, that certain circumstances in fact require the basis to be egalitarian; there is no alternative but to ask people to help *tolong menolong*, which is why the service can only be repaid by a similar service. Thus one female informant explained that she had stopped participating in large ritual celebrations once all of her three daughters were married because her work contribution could not be repaid. This is also why a childless couple remains socially isolated: how could they give their share of social production as fully-fledged members of the community if they have no son to circumcise or daughter to marry? This is where the need appears to create kinship ties where there are none. One possible answer is the practice of adoption by which the adopting couple is enabled to take part in the more valuable moments of the exchange game (Massard 1983b). Whereas children are not expressly needed in the other forms of wealth circulation previously referred to, they are indispensable to ritual participation and this is even truer of marriage practices themselves, from which childless people are excluded as acting partners.

Conclusion

Out of the different cases of Malay exchange practices presented in the preceding pages, there does not seem to emerge any single coherent rationale which motivates people's choices and in which the status of kinship would be determined once and for all. Yet, the lack of prescription — specific to cognatic kinship — should not be equated with a state of confusion or even with a possible unlimited individualism. Without pretending to offer a typology of Malay exchange practices, I think that by centering on resources in circulation and within the limits of one particular context, it is possible to indulge in predictions as to the various strategies available to villagers and to the part played by kinship in each of them. While exchange practices between kin as well as non-kin can be put into two broad categories — those that circulate on a strictly reciprocal basis (e.g. ritual production, Ramadan *kueh-kueh*), and those that are not met with an equivalent counter-gift (agricultural work, land) — there seems to emerge another distinction which might be more relevant to our study. In cases which have long-term implications, wealth ('new rice', land, ritual production) circulates strictly along kinship lines, either on an egalitarian or in an asymmetrical way. Such resources convey a precisely defined social message.

Kinship ties can be subordinated to other factors; when physical proximity prevails, relatives are generally treated the same way as ordinary neighbours; in these cases strict and immediate reciprocity is expected, which is another way of saying that people are considered equal as they can reciprocate. When economic motives become pre-eminent, relatives are again treated as strangers, and not as equals, as they are dependent upon work offers from the better-off partner. This second type of local resources lends itself to manipulation by villagers and hence can imply a variety of social messages. Depending on the relative status of the partner and on the possible absence of any equivalent counter-gift, the items in circulation will have a different social meaning.

In no way are exchange practices expected to blur out economic disparities between kin. Hierarchy and stratification are part and parcel of Malay village life and I have tried to show that wealth circulation is meant to illustrate them rather than cancel them out. We now need to collect more information concerning such symbolic forms of communication so that we can elaborate not only a typology of locally valued resources in circulation but determine a possible hierarchy among them, as to which act as more highly valued media of social communication, or have more 'meaning'. The study of the relationship between the village socio-economic stratification and the way resources are valued would help in our understanding of Malay exchange practices and of the role of kinship.

Part III

Access to Resources:
Kinship and Social Differentiation

Power, Property and Parentage in a Central Javanese Village

Frans Hüsken

'What the social anthropologist calls kinship structure
is just a way of talking about property relations.'
(Leach 1961:305)

Koentjaraningrat commences his contribution to *Social Structure in Southeast Asia* (1960) with a complaint about the paucity of information on Javanese kinship. It is indeed remarkable that both colonial and early post-colonial anthropology produced only a limited number of studies devoted to the subject. In an extensive bibliography of anthropological research in Indonesia which Koentjaraningrat published in 1975 approximately 800 titles were listed but among them publications on kinship refer overwhelmingly to the 'Outer Islands' and less than a dozen pre-war titles discuss kinship in Java. The situation did not change much after the Second World War. During the years immediately following Independence the little anthropological field-work there was in Java was mainly carried out through the so-called Modjokuto-project whose members — with one noted exception — mention kinship matters only in passing.

More than a quarter of a century after Koentjaraningrat's complaint about the state of Javanese kinship research many more anthropological analyses of Javanese culture and society have been published, but on the whole his comments remain valid; there are still remarkably few studies of Javanese cognatic organization.[1]

The impression of anthropological neglect is compounded by the fact that the few accounts that are available present cognation as a relatively irrelevant dimension of Javanese social organization. Most authors confine themselves to a description of terminology and to a few general statements about the limited

1. Post-war studies include Berthe (1965), Dhofier (1980), J. Fox (1986), Franke (1971), H. Geertz (1961), Hiroko (1976), Jay (1969), Koentjaraningrat (1961; 1968), Palmier (1960), Pandam Guritno (1958), Sjafri Sairin (1982), Ukun Suryaman (n.d.).

importance of kin ties in Java. Kinship tends to be discussed as if it had few or no linkages to social domains other than the moral and ceremonial.[2]

Another striking feature of this limited number of kinship studies is the unanimity about the central position of the nuclear family and the minor role played by larger and more encompassing kinship units, a view which is most explicit in the work of members of the 'Modjokuto'-team. Hildred Geertz, who wrote the main report on Javanese family life, designates 'the nuclear family [as] the only important kinship unit' (1961:3). Similarly, Alice Dewey in her ethnography of peasant marketing states that, because of the very diffuse character of kin ties, 'the nuclear family is the almost universal economic unit' (1962:28). These authors relate the dominance of the nuclear family and the practical absence of important supra-nuclear kin ties to the cognatic character of the Javanese kinship system. The idea is that given the Javanese lack of strict rules for assigning individuals to 'lineages', the ties of cognatic kinship do not permit the formation of corporate descent groups with their more or less clearly defined collective rights and duties and, most important, common property.

By stressing the role of the nuclear family post-war anthropologists follow in the footsteps of the colonial scholars, who were even more adamant in their assertion that Java knew no larger kin groups. In their search for the dominant structural principles of the Indonesian village communities, the so-called *adat* (customary) law scholars were particularly convinced that Java was an example of an exclusively territorially-based society: the Javanese *desa* belonged to those types of 'communities in which the kinship factor had no significance' (Ter Haar 1962:55). In addition, anthropological discourse in the Netherlands Indies was still very much engaged in the search for unilineal descent. This may have been one of the reasons why, in colonial times, when anthropology put such strong emphasis on kinship studies, far less research was devoted to Java than to the eastern and western parts of Indonesia where unilineal descent prevailed.

In this respect, colonial Dutch ethnologists were not that different from British social anthropologists who at the time were concentrating mainly on the study of African societies with their unilineal systems (cf. R. Fox 1967:163; Kuper 1982:91–3; Van Baal 1977:291). From that perspective, it is not surprising that even in the few colonial accounts that did discuss Javanese kinship a (sometimes evolutionistically-inclined) unilineal bias is apparent. Being confronted with a bilateral social organization the authors, generally of the Dutch structuralist school, were concerned not so much with analysing the existing system as a form

---

2. It is remarkable that while the colonial literature emphasized the dimension of customary law (*adat*) in its analysis of kinship, this focus nearly completely disappeared from sight in more recent research. What is available discusses 'Javanese kinship' with hardly any attention to regional variation or urban–rural differences. So the first full-fledged modern study of the Javanese family (Geertz 1961) generalizes for the whole of the island on the basis of research in a small East Javanese town. Only a few recent studies differentiate between specific socio-cultural strata like the Javanese nobility (*priyayi*), the orthodox Muslim clergy (*kyai*), and the peasantry (Dhofier 1980; Hiroko 1976; Sairin 1982).

of social organization in itself, but with explaining it in terms of its origins. With eastern and western Indonesian cultures (the heartlands of Dutch structuralist theories) in mind they saw Javanese kinship preferably as the outcome of adaptational changes from unilineal (or, more specifically, patrilineal) systems whose corporate character had been lost in the course of history.[3]

While most post-war studies also emphasize the nuclear family as the pivot of contemporary Javanese society and consequently pay little attention to units including more remote relatives, there are occasional deviations from this general trend of playing down the significance of extra-nuclear relations. Some authors (notably Jay and Koentjaraningrat) mention links beyond the nuclear family, although they consider them to be of a rather minor local significance. These links come to the fore in discussing the role of the kindred: the category of close kinsmen which in Java usually extends to the second collateral degree. Koentjaraningrat (1968:53–4) uses the term *golongan* to designate a unit which functions as an occasional bilateral kin group whose members 'contribute to or participate in life-cycle ceremonies [...] and at other ceremonies and occasions'. Even so it has only a limited importance outside the ceremonial sphere, as it 'does not co-operate or act as a unit in economic activities or enterprises'.

Even what Koentjaraningrat referred to as an 'ambilineal descent group' which he came across in South Central Java, the *alur waris*, was considered of limited significance. 'An ancestor-oriented group which shares the obligation for its ancestors' graves and of meeting the expenses of the ceremonies and the *slametan* which this care involves' (Koentjaraningrat 1968:54), it did reveal some conception of 'corporateness' among kinsmen, but these common responsibilities were only occasionally exercised and were of little consequence for its members.

---

3. I here refer inter alia to the studies of Van Ossenbruggen (1917), Rassers (1959) and Bertling (1936) who tried to prove that present-day Javanese kinship is an atrophied form of an originally patrilineal society. This line of reasoning was continued by Louis Berthe (1970) who on the basis of an analysis of kinship terminologies came to the conclusion that: 'Les nomenclatures centrales, ou distributives, sont donc le résultat d'une série de transformations opérées d'une autre type. On est par ailleurs assuré que les nomenclatures antérieures étaient assignatives. Or, on l'a montré, les premières sont constamment associées aux sociétés à groups, et les secondes aux sociétés à réseaux. Il est donc possible d'engendrer celles-ci à partir de celles-là.'
This transformation of the Javanese kinship system, according to Berthe, dates back from the fifth century when during the reign of king Purnavarman the first large irrigation canal was built: 'Ainsi, non seulement il n'y a pas d'impossibilité logique qu'une société à groupes se transforme en une société à réseaux, mais le phénomène s'est certainement produit à une moment donné de l'histoire de Java. Le moment où il s'est produit n'a pu que coïncider avec l'introduction du riz et des techniques d'irrigation.' (Berthe 1970:727.)
The 'Asiatic State' which was the outcome of this technological development considered the existence of permanent groups, interrelated by marriage bonds and disposing of their own power and autonomy, as a threat to its central authority.
Berthe's theory is an interesting but still hypothetical explanation. Possibly, the present-day marriage rules are survivals from this original form of kinship organization. Lacking sufficient information on local social structures antedating the foundation of 'Asiatic empires' little can be said on the validity of the hypothesis.
Recently, however, James Fox (1986) on the basis of a linguistic analysis concluded that the 'original' Javanese kinship system was cognatic.

In the light of the above it comes as no real surprise to find the Javanese village as far as kinship is concerned being described as 'loosely structured' (Koentjara-ningrat 1960:114)[4] or as striking for the 'general formlessness of life there, the essential vagueness of social structure, [and] the looseness of ties between indi-viduals' (Geertz 1959:34). Geertz implies that in such a situation kinship is not a viable means of either exerting economic control or pursuing political conflicts.[5] Given this line of interpretation and reasoning it is also quite understandable why the villagers described by another member of the Modjokuto-team 'were little interested in the details of any kinsman's connecting links' and why their knowledge of kin had little genealogical depth (Jay 1969:170–1).

The resurrection of kinship

On the basis of this accepted anthropological wisdom I did not anticipate vil-lagers' reactions to questions on the topic when I commenced field-work in Gondosari, a relatively large village of 3100 inhabitants in Pati regency, North Central Java. I began by making a census while at the same time collecting genealogical information from all households, mainly for very practical purposes like bringing order to the immense number of names but also to create an op-portunity to talk freely about other people in the village. Quite unexpectedly the questions on genealogy in many cases aroused enthusiastic responses, which were rather different to those on the admittedly not very exciting questionnaire on household composition and land tenure. Most household members were very keen to give as many names of ancestors and relatives as they could think of and they liked the classical anthropological way of making diagrams so much that I was frequently asked for a copy to be kept with the family papers and land titles.

The latter was only true for those villagers who did own a piece of land, and in Gondosari, they were only a minority. More than three-quarters of the village households owned no land at all or just a tiny plot, while among the remaining quarter of land owners a few dozen households owned more than half the village land.[6] It was this small group that dominated village life not only economic-ally but also politically as they were quite well represented in local positions of

4. The use of the term 'loose structure' in describing Thai villages is interesting as it reflects some of the views of its originator (Embree 1950) and some of the preoccupations of the Bang Chan research team which used the term as a major frame of reference (cf. Evers 1980). Usually Javanese villages are presented as a marked contrast because of their supposedly high level of inte-gration and corporateness (Geertz 1963). Obviously what Koentjaraningrat wanted to emphasize in applying the 'loose-structure' concept, is the organization of interpersonal relations: relations between individuals as such — i.e. non-(corporate) groups.

5. Elsewhere, Geertz (1965:144) seems to have abandoned this view, however, as he there de-scribes the village ethos as 'a peculiar combination of what has been called familistic individualism and a strong sense of the common fate of all village members'.

6. For a general overview of land tenure and social organization in Gondosari (a pseudonym), see Hüsken (1988; 1989).

power: the *desa* administration is nearly completely in the hands of this local elite and the leadership of the local chapters of the two main political parties — the government-backed Golkar and the Muslim PPP — rests also with them.

While interest in genealogy was rather general, there proved to be a remarkable variation in the extent of knowledge about genealogical depth and breadth which was closely correlated with differences in social class. Landless and small peasants often lacked any memory of deceased relatives outside their own nuclear families. When I tried to obtain information on their kin, these people had great difficulty in telling me the names of grandparents, uncles, aunts or cousins who had lived in the same village. In some exceptional cases, old people did not even remember those of their fathers and/or mothers as they had left their families at a very young age to go and work as domestic servants in other people's places.

In marked contrast, members of well-to-do households in the village were very proud to belong to long-established 'families' (*pamili*) which could trace their origins back to an illustrious ancestor. In fact the terminology used even had the connotation of a descent group. People referred to their 'recognized relatives' as linked through a common great-grandfather (*satunggal buyut*) or as offspring, descendants (*turunane* or *turune*). In one case, a family possessed an elaborate pedigree or 'book of inheritance' (*buku waris*) in which six generations of descendants of a certain Sutosaridin — an early-19th-century immigrant to the region — were registered. The book was kept and regularly updated by the village secretary. It was of more than just private genealogical interest to him as it was frequently consulted for different purposes by people who were linked into the 'family'.

Pedigrees are a rare phenomenon among Javanese peasants, although among the aristocracy (*priyayi*) they are the major justification of rights to ranks, titles and position, as well as important symbolic expressions with which to close their ranks as against the 'common people' (*wong cilik*). The presence of a 'book of inheritance' among the Gondosari elite indicated that this *priyayi* practice was disseminating among villagers. Although not of noble descent, demonstrating that they were descendants or relatives of former village headmen and the old landowning elite was a useful means of strengthening their contemporary social and political status. At the same time, it enabled them, if need be, to call on the help or support of even remote relatives (*prenah*).[7]

> This was well illustrated during the first month of my stay in the village. One afternoon a minibus crowded with some twenty people from two villages in the neighbouring regency of Jepara drove into Gondosari. They introduced themselves as descendants (*turunane*) of Sutosaridin and therefore 'somehow' related to the Gondosari village elite. They had made big efforts to trace their remote relatives and said they had come to talk about a family matter, the reconstruction of Sutosaridin's grave. They proposed erecting a luxurious tomb in the prestigious classical *pendopo*-style with a tin

7. *Prenah* means 'somehow related'. It literally refers to a 'relative position in a structure', hence to 'family tie'.

roof, and sought financial support for the undertaking. After the initial surprise they were received with clear pride by their Gondosari kin.

Some months later the project was indeed implemented with the greater part of the expenses coming from the Gondosari branch of the *turunane*. This proved, however, not to be the only effect of the renewal of kin ties. In the course of the frequent contacts and discussions about the construction of the tomb, other 'business deals' were concluded. For the previous couple of years the people from Jepara had been in great financial difficulties which could only be resolved by sale of their family land (in this case rather unusually designated as *tanah pusaka*: heirloom land[8]). If the Gondosari relatives were to buy the 2.5 hectares at a reasonable price, this land would still remain 'within the family'. Its present owners would not face too great a degradation in social status: they could still behave as 'managers' or 'caretakers' while in fact they would work the land as a kind of sharecropper.

This transaction was duly completed and at the same time the youngest son from Jepara was sent to Gondosari to become the 'foster child' or domestic quasi-servant of one of the members of the village administration.

Such a well-prepared relief operation was not a rare phenomenon although, in the above case, geographically as well as relationally the distance was rather great. Between relatives within the village references to the moral imperative for co-operation and reciprocity are more common. Kinship ideology stresses the fundamental egalitarianism of members of the same 'family'. This is, however, only one side of the coin because 'kinship' also in Gondosari is polyvalent. When social statuses of relatives differ considerably, it is not the ethos of equality which is stressed but the hierarchical dimension between seniors and juniors which permeates Javanese kinship terminology. Then it is not so much co-operation between equals and mutual help which are stressed, but rather the generosity of the seniors and reciprocal loyalty of the juniors. People refer to this dimension when better-off farmers support poor relatives by allowing them to become sharecroppers on their land. When I asked landowners why they did so, the general reply was that it was 'out of sympathy' (*welas, kasihan*) with their landless relatives. For less well-to-do villagers, therefore, ties with remote richer kin are a crucial resource which they can use to apply for a relatively advantageous status as sharecroppers.

Before 1965, Kusno, then a man in his early forties, was the secretary of the Gondosari branch of the Communist Party. As a descendant of a rather well-to-do family closely related to the mighty Sutosaridin 'offspring' he had inherited some land in the village. He also inherited the leftist political orientation which had been strong within his family. He followed in the footsteps of two of his older cousins who had been exiled by the Dutch to New Guinea because of their alleged involvement in the communist uprising of 1926. Besides working part of his own *sawah* Kusno was also a leading member of the Sugar Workers Union at the nearby sugar factory. Like many other left-wing activists he was arrested in the week following the coup d'état of October

8. The term is generally used in Indonesian lineal societies, denoting some kind of 'corporate' property of the family.

1965. Without trial he was kept prisoner in the regency's capital until 1972 when he was released on parole.

Returning to the village he found himself without any land as his wife — herself a descendant of a line of Gondosari village headmen — had had to sell the *sawah* as well as their house in the course of his imprisonment. As work in the sugar factory was out of the question because of his political background he was forced to live off charity. Thereupon he approached two of his 'uncles' (his mother's brother as well as his mother's brother's wife's brother — whom he addressed with the same term *pak dhe*) to ask for support. While others would have offered him a job as a farm-hand, 'this is not done among *prenah*'. Instead, he was — be it condescendingly — appointed sharecropper of half a hectare of dry land to grow citrus and clove trees and was given a garden plot to build a modest house.

Others, less dramatically downward mobile, were given land by their well-to-do relatives as well. In fact, a major reason to appoint a sharecropper was that he was considered to be *isih pamili*, still related.

On other occasions, the richer Gondosari branch of the Sutosaridin offspring acted as intermediary when relatives of theirs were involved in legal problems. People who lost money in land speculations or by misappropriating tax funds, would look for shelter and protection from the police as well as financial support.

One day when I left the village very early on my way to the market I met a rather wild-looking man walking from the main road through the lane leading to Gondosari. He looked rather shabby and extremely tired and I was surprised when he introduced himself as Suhar, the village secretary (*carik*) of a village in the southern part of the district. It turned out that I had met him several months before at a wedding where I had gone with my landlord.

Suhar was on his way to his Gondosari relatives and told me in an unexpectedly open-hearted way that he was fleeing from a creditor who had lent him Rp. 300,000 (more than twice the annual salary of a schoolteacher). As Suhar was not able to repay his debt, the creditor had sent the police after him and threatened to confiscate his house which was the collateral for the loan. The house, a beautiful teakwood structure, was worth at least double the amount of his debt. To prevent the confiscation of the house 'which had been built by his great-grandfather' he was looking for his relatives' support. Together we went to his mother's mother's brother, a powerful member of the village administration in Gondosari, who was in charge inter alia of police affairs. There a temporary solution was reached: Suhar was to go into hiding with another relative in Gondosari. As long as he could not be found by his creditor, his house could not be sold as such a transaction needed the owner's signature. In the meantime, Suhar could try to raise enough money to redeem his loan.

For some days this strategy seemed to work well, but then the fund-raising campaign ran into problems. People learned that Suhar was a compulsive gambler who had still more debts to repay as well as to face charges for embezzling money from the village purse. With this information only a small number of relatives was prepared to spend their money in such a dubious case.

When I visited Suhar a few weeks later his house — in Java a movable good — was gone and Suhar was living in a makeshift bamboo dwelling all alone as his wife and children had left him. His fortune had gone but things could have been even worse, he said: through an all-out effort several relatives who wanted to prevent a further humiliation were able to get him off the legal charges for embezzling village money.

Of course, it was mainly among the well-to-do that these examples of 'class-linked' behaviour occurred. Those without resources would rarely ever appeal to relatives who themselves tended to be in the same economically and politically weak position.

The examples cited above showed me that there was ostensibly more to Javanese kinship than accepted anthropological wisdom would have. It was also clear that kinship carried differential weight among the social classes in Gondosari, as there seemed to be a direct association between the importance of kin ties and economic and political power. As noted it was particularly the elite households who stressed their kin ties. Before answering the question of why and how kinship and descent were important parameters for the village elite, I will briefly describe the local setting.

The village of Gondosari

The village (*desa*) of Gondosari is located in the northern part of Pati regency, some 100 kilometres by road northeast of Semarang, the provincial capital of Central Java. It lies close to the sea on the gently sloping foothills of the Muria and Clering mountains.

Gondosari is mainly a rice-growing village. More than half of its 328 hectares of land consists of *sawah* fields yielding two and sometimes three rice harvests a year. Next in importance to rice cultivation is the production of cash crops which are grown on the dry fields (*tegalan*), consisting mainly of peanuts, cassava, kapok, cloves and citrus fruits. In the past decade part of the villagers' *sawah* has also been planted with sugar-cane which is processed at a nearby sugar factory.

As said before, the distribution of land is highly skewed. Only about a quarter of the village households own a piece of land which is sufficiently large to subsist off (more than 0.25 hectare). The remaining three quarters more or less depend for their livelihood on working the land of others (either as sharecroppers or as wage-labourers). There is a small but strong group of major landowners consisting of a mere 31 households (5 per cent of the total population) who together own and control 56 per cent of the fields.

It is this group of wealthy landowners, being in control of most village resources, which has taken advantage of the commercialization of agricultural production that started in the late 1960s. They are gradually becoming rural entrepreneurs by investing heavily in agriculture and by extending their activities to other sectors such as the local rice-milling industry and the trade in rice and peanuts. They have, moreover, adopted a more business-like attitude to farm management in reducing the number of agricultural labourers employed on their *sawah* and *tegalan* and by cutting real wages.

The political economy of kinship

Nearly all the elite households are located close to the centre of the village. Their large and spacious houses along the main roads make it easy to tell who are the *wong koyo* (rich people) in Gondosari.

> At the beginning of my stay, Tolib, who is a Quran teacher and sharecropper of the local *haji*, tried to explain to me who it was that had a say in village affairs. For him this was neither a difficult nor a complicated task: 'Oh, of course, there are only a few people here who own a lot of land here, and in one way or another they are all *prenah* [relatives] of each other. The rich all live closely together in several blocks [residential clusters]: *Blok Dongkol*, where the former village head lives and the *haji* with their children and clients; *Blok Carik* which is the centre of the former nationalist party [PNI] leaders, *Blok Kasdan*, the rich misers [...] Since the new village headman was elected in 1975, he has become the centre of a cluster which has become powerful again, *Blok Petinggi*. Some of these clusters consist of *wong agama* [religious people], others have less strict beliefs [*abangan*]. This difference never used to be a problem for them as they are all relatives. However, over the past couple of years since the last election of the village headman they haven't got along well with one another.'

Diagram 1 shows how nearly all these 'blocs' of elite households are closely related and the extent to which there is an overall division into two major sections which are linked to one another through marriage. The smaller, which includes the present village headman (Basuki), consists of a rather homogeneous group of *santri* or *wong agama*. These are the descendants of the nineteenth-century Gondosari elite who had ruled the village until the 1880s and whose control of land dates back to that period.[9]

The other section traces its descent and wealth back to another nineteenth-century figure, Martruna. His father (Sutosaridin) was one of a number of immigrants who settled in the area somewhere between 1820 and 1840. He cleared large tracts of the dense forest which at the time still covered most of the northern part of the regency. Later Martruna became head (*petinggi*) of the village of Gesengan, a few kilometres to the west of Gondosari. He too succeeded in opening up new land and in his later years (1905) is mentioned in a government report as the largest landowner in the whole of Pati regency, with more than 100 *bahu* (appr. 70 hectares) of *sawah*-land (cf. Hüsken 1988:196–8). In addition to their inheritance Martruna's children followed in their father's footsteps by acquiring yet more land in Gondosari and neighbouring villages.

9. For the sake of convenience the diagram is given here only in an abridged form. It neither includes all descendants (mainly those born in or moved to other villages have been left out) nor indicates genealogical order.

Diagram 1. Kin ties between Gondosari landlord families (1977)

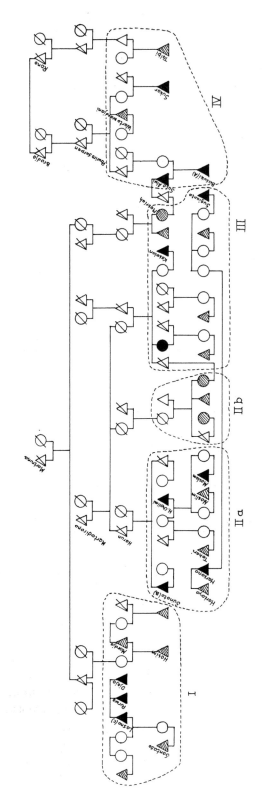

Remarks:
1. This is a simplified kinship diagram which does not take into account genealogical order;
2. Black symbols refer to households owning more than 5 hectares of *sawah* land;
   hatched symbols refer to households with more than 2.5 hectares;
3. Dotted areas refer to the clusters of landlord families: I = *Blok Carik*;
   IIa and IIb = *Blok Dongkol*; III = *Blok Kasdan*; IV = *Blok Petinggi*.

By the first decades of this century practically all the forest had been claimed and the gradual expansion of landholding by Martruna's children came to an end. Over time, the inheritance system by which all children of both sexes receive approximately equal shares (though sometimes modified by ultimogeniture with respect to the house) might thus have been expected to produce a complete fragmentation of the family's assets within one or two generations. However, Martruna's descendants have managed to maintain their position as rich landowners up to the present. The village land registration records which go back to 1928 reveal that throughout this period they have continued to own about half of Gondosari's *sawah* and approximately one-sixth of the less valuable *tegalan* fields (Hüsken 1989:309–10).

The longstanding character of this elite's economic power is even more pronounced in the political domain. Positions in village government (*sarekat desa*) have been attractive since the nineteenth century, both because of the important salary lands (*bengkok*) connected with it and because of the opportunities for controlling rural labour and money taxes. Salary lands, which in Gondosari consisted of 30 hectares of the best *sawah* and 20 hectares of *tegalan*, have been a continuous attraction. Formerly the right to manage corvée labour (*pancen*) which had to be rendered to the village head must also have been an important benefit at a time when labour was not as abundantly available as it is nowadays.[10] The access to such lucrative resources has caused village elections since the late nineteenth century to be periods of fierce political competition among several candidates. (Diagram 2 provides an overview of the main contestants during these elections and their kin relations.)

Once Martruna had become wealthy, several of his sons engaged in the competition for village headmanships in the surrounding villages. In Gondosari one of them succeeded in wringing political power from the hands of the old local elite, and for the following three-quarters of a century Martruna's descendants played a dominant role in the village administration. Martruna's son-in-law became *petinggi* in 1903 and ruled as an autocrat for thirty years. In the elections held in 1933 following his retirement due to ill health, and 1945 in the aftermath of the revolution, it proved relatively easy for the members of Martruna's 'stock' (*turunane*) to retain political dominance. Given their land holdings, they controlled a large client-following of sharecroppers and other dependants, and were able to finance expensive campaigns. Two of Martruna's great-grandchildren (*buyut*) won the 1933 and 1945 elections and, as their predecessors had done,

---

10. The agrarian structure in Java has changed considerably since the turn of the century: during the revolution (1945–1949) salary lands were reduced in size, and in 1960 legislation on land reform did away with the communal lands. On the other hand, average landholding has decreased dramatically, mainly because of demographic growth. As agricultural modernization in the 1970s and 1980s has led to booming rice harvests, salary lands are nowadays even more important than previously.

Diagram 2. Kin relations between major contestants during village elections in Gondosari, 1870–1980

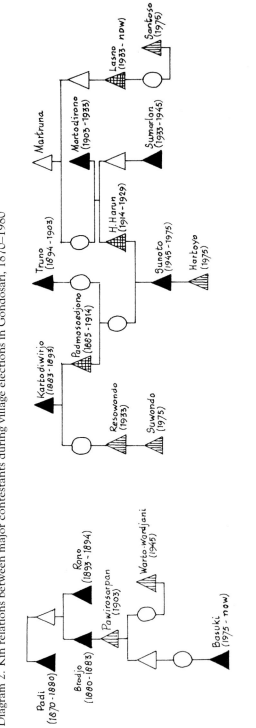

▲ = village headman   ◮ = village secretary   ◭ = candidates in village-headman elections

they appointed close relatives to the other important and lucrative positions in the village administration.

The last *petinggi* from this stock ruled from the days of the Indonesian Revolution in 1945 until 1975, when the provincial government issued a decree enforcing the retirement of village headmen over the age of sixty. During his term of office he had initially followed a nationalist and then, in the early 1960s, a rather leftist political course. Following Sukarno's fall and the destruction of the Communist Party in 1965, this led to open political frictions with his Muslim relatives which he was, nevertheless, able to survive.

The 1975 elections were one of the hardest-fought political battles of the decade. Because of the increasing influence of Islam in Indonesian politics after 1965 the *santri* group, which since the end of the nineteenth century had had to yield political primacy to Martruna's descendants, regained some of its former prestige in the village. When the Muslim United Development Party (PPP) locally fell short by only a few votes of obtaining a majority in the national elections of 1972, this was a clear signal that the political balance of power in the village was changing.[11] Once several members of Martruna's *turunane* under the guidance of the local *haji* (a brother-in-law of the old *petinggi*) decided not to support a close relative during the 1975 elections but to side with their Islamic brethren, the fate of the Martruna 'stock' was decided. The young *santri* candidate, who received considerable economic and religious support from the most prominent Muslim leaders, thus became the new *petinggi*.

This *circulation des élites* aroused confusion and tension within the *desa* and within the village administration itself, which still consisted of the former *petinggi*'s relatives and clients. Usually a new village headman would change the composition of the *sarekat desa*, but the district officer, fearing too strong a Muslim influence in village affairs, prevented him from doing so. The new *petinggi* was thus unable to convert his election victory into effective political domination. The result was that he was more or less openly confronted with obstruction by the members of the village administration who stuck to their influential positions. When I revisited Gondosari in 1982 this political conflict was still continuing and had culminated in a long-lasting *cul de sac*, though with rumours that the present *petinggi* would be forced to resign in the near future.[12]

11. In the 1950s the nationalist party and the communist party dominated the local political scene (Bachtiar Rifai 1958). In subsequent years, until its downfall in 1965, the communist party probably had the largest following in Gondosari.

12. These rumours turned out not to be true. In 1989, new elections were held as part of a complete overhaul of Indonesian village administration and policy making. Loyalties had changed over the years, and Basuki was re-elected with a broader support than in 1975. Gradually he is appointing his own relatives and clients into the administration as old members of the *sarekat desa* retire.

Social closure and intermarriages

The retention of political power, property and prestige within the hands of the small Gondosari elite for such a long period required a high degree of social closure[13] and it is precisely in that respect that kin ties and kin solidarity played such an important part. However, descent from a common ancestor alone did not ensure this. As indicated earlier, in the normal course of events the prevailing high birth rates and the system of bilateral inheritance could have been expected to lead to fragmentation of land holdings and a gradual erosion of political power. Other mechanisms were also important and the co-residence of elite households in 'blocs' was one such factor. Most of these families lived very close to one another, having built their houses within a large compound owned by one of their ancestors. Although this occasionally leads to minor inter-household frictions it proved to be a useful means of forming kin clusters[14] with a relatively high degree of social cohesion in day-to-day contacts as well as in ceremonial festivities.

The most important mechanism effecting social closure was the high incidence of intermarriages within the 'stock', as already explained by Freeman in his analysis of the role of the kindred in cognatic societies:

> If the marriage of cousins is continued generation by generation, this results in a continuing consolidation of stocks and produces a closer cognatic network than in societies in which the marriage of close cognates does not occur. This, I would suggest, is a most significant feature of some bilateral societies, for while they lack the large-scale descent groups of unilineal societies, their cognatic networks are close and cohesive and so of great importance in the multiplex relations of social life. (Freeman 1961:207.)

In an article on cognatic descent and social stratification Kemp has elaborated this idea of Freeman's by examining the ways in which the aristocracies of Siam and Malaya managed to obtain and consolidate their power, influence and wealth by a combination of female hypergamy and marriage with kin (Kemp 1978:63–84).

Similar marriage strategies are also familiar among the traditional Javanese *priyayi* as Palmier pointed out in his study of marriage patterns in a Javanese regent's family: there was a high incidence of marriage with kin (half of all marriages are between first and second cousins). According to Palmier,

---

13. In recent years the concept of *social closure*, coined by Max Weber, has been revived by Parkin (1979). I use it here in the Weberian sense as 'the monopolization by members of an interest group of social and economic opportunities by closing off those opportunities to outsiders' (Murphy 1983: 632; cf. Weber 1922:631–41).

14. I prefer to use the term 'clusters' instead of 'networks' as social interaction among these households is more intense. On the other hand, terms like 'quasi-groups', or 'semi-corporate groups' stress far too much a kind of corporate identity (cf. Boissevain 1968).

[This] marriage pattern [...] was part and parcel of the system of social status of the nobility in general and the Regents in particular. Position and marriage were related to one another. The highest positions were reserved, ideally at least, for those who were connected by both descent lines with those already in the highest positions; and they were supposed to take as official consorts women similarly connected, thus ensuring that their children would have the same advantages. (Palmier 1960:55.)

What has not been recognized is that such strategies are not confined to the Javanese *priyayi* circles: if we map out the descendants of Martruna we discover among this peasant elite a relatively high number of inter-marriages. It is not feasible to reproduce all these alliances in a single chart, but Diagram 3 serves to illustrate the types of intra-stock marriages that I was able to trace in Gondosari.[15]

As was the case in the regent's family studied by Palmier, the majority of marriages among Martruna's descendants are between first or second cousins (respectively *misanan* [PBCh; PZCh] and *mindoan* [PPPBChCh; PPZChCh]). The incidence of *mindoan* marriages is especially striking, as throughout Java marriages between second cousins are strongly disapproved of or even prohibited. Similar objections are raised against marriages between patrilateral parallel cousins (the so-called *pancer wali*), against marrying genealogically senior kinswomen (*sepuh estri*) and against marriages which imply an exchange of women between two families (*mlumah murep*).[16]

Nevertheless, within the Gondosari elite examples of unions violating these rules and prohibitions do exist, as illustrated in the diagram. Marriages nos. 4, 6, 7, 8 and 9 belong to the *mindoan* type; nos. 2, 3, 9 and 10 involve *pancer wali*; nos. 2, 8 and 9 imply *sepuh estri* and marriages nos. 2 and 3 include *mlumah murep*.

There exist special ceremonies through which the dangers of such alliances can be avoided, but most villagers do not dare to defy these prohibitions. These rules, however, do not apply to the *priyayi*: among them *misanan* and *mindoan* marriages are considered to be preferential and the other impediments like *pancer wali* and *sepuh estri* can be ritually overcome by the nobility (Koentjaraningrat 1957:55; Ter Haar 1923:221; Jay 1969:127).

Although the village elite in Gondosari cannot claim even remote *priyayi* status, they have adopted the nobility's marriage practices, and for apparently the same reasons, namely the consolidation of power and wealth by creating a high degree of social closure.

---

15. The diagram is incomplete as it was well nigh impossible to trace kin ties between spouses of the older generations or between younger members who had moved out of Gondosari.

16. For a discussion of these marriage prohibitions see: Berthe (1970:725); Bertling (1936:122–5); Holleman (1919:139; 1921:208); Jay (1969:127–30) and Koentjaraningrat (1967:256).

Diagram 3. Intermarriages within the Martruna family

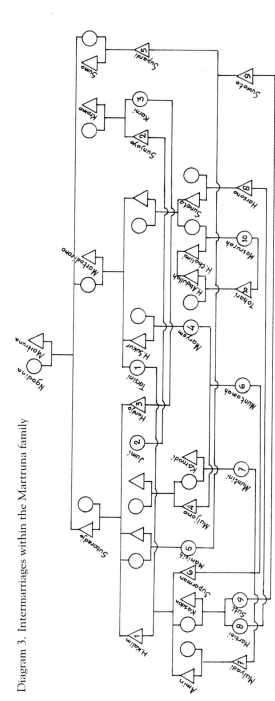

This diagram is a simplified and incomplete representation of Martruna's descendants and can therefore only be used to illustrate intermarriages (insofar as I was able to trace them during field-work).

These marriages, numbered 1 through 10, are classified in the table on the right.

Marriage of man with:	Cross cousin/ parallel cousin	Local term of reference for spouse
1. FZD	cross cousin	adik misanan
2. FBD	parallel cousin	mbakyu misanan
3. FBD	parallel cousin	adik misanan
4. MFZSD	cross cousin	adik mindoan
5. MBSD	cross cousin	keponakan misanan
6. FFZSDD	cross cousin	keponakan mindoan
7. FFZDD	cross cousin	adik mindoan
8. FFZDD (also: FFMBSDD)	cross cousin	mbakyu mindoan
9. MFBDD	parallel cousin	mbakyu mindoan
10. FBD	parallel cousin	adik misanan

F=father, M=mother, B=brother, Z=sister, S=son, D=daughter

Conclusion

In this paper I have tried to show that there is far more to Javanese cognatic kinship than nuclear families and personal kindreds. What turns out to be of particular interest is the great variation in the range as well as the importance of kin ties between the different classes of village society. While these links may carry little weight or none at all for the rural poor who lack all kinds of resources, such ties are of considerably more significance to the wealthier strata of the village. Here I have confined myself to an analysis of the ways in which the elite of a North Javanese village managed to attain a high degree of social closure by developing a conception of semi-corporateness among kinsmen and kinswomen. For more than a century this proved to be a very effective strategy in controlling both local political power and economic resources. Only recently have some rifts appeared within the tightly-knit network of elite kin ties causing a considerable loss of influence in village affairs for Martruna's descendants. National political and religious developments and the rapid transformation of the rural economy might be held responsible for this crumbling of kin solidarity as these processes tend to create new orientations towards bases of power and wealth on the supra-village level. In the 1970s and 1980s lucrative economic opportunities outside agriculture came within the reach of rich villagers, and they could afford to partly turn away from local resources. Moreover, many of their children have moved off the local scene, initially to go to high school, college or university, and later to find employment in the state bureaucracy or in the commercial sector. Their outlook and lifestyle are much more urban but they have not severed their links with the village economy; access to its major resources, land in particular, is still important. If among the younger generation these urban tendencies get stronger elite households will no longer primarily concentrate upon village resources; in principle, they do not need to rely upon their nearby relatives alone. But since kin ties still appear to be such convenient and reliable assets it seems highly improbable that their importance in local politics and economics will drastically diminish in the near future.

The Political Economy of Kinship and Marriage Strategies in Java and Central Luzon

Willem Wolters

Research on cognatic kinship in peasant societies has suffered from a double theoretical handicap. In the first place, anthropologists concerned with kinship focused their attention on unilineal systems. Conceptualization and theory thus developed around the existence of corporate groups, and where these were absent the role and importance of kinship tended to be played down with the observed network of kinship relations being seen as loose, shapeless and unstructured. At the same time, the significance of kinship in peasant societies was considered to be very different from and certainly less important than the place it occupied in the 'classical' field of anthropological study, tribal society. Domination by the ideology of kinship was replaced by a concern with class and territory (Fried 1967:121) and many students of peasant society have indeed given only limited attention to kin-based social organization.

The analysis of cognatic organization in the peasant societies of Southeast Asia cannot therefore readily rely on established theoretical frameworks. What one might call 'kinship centred theory' explaining 'one aspect of kinship in terms of another' (Gibbs 1965:161) must be replaced by an emphasis on the interplay between the varied dimensions of social life. Kinship is not an autonomous system and its importance is to be found in its interconnection with such areas as economic activity, political conflict, alliance and coalition formation, and in its strategic and tactical use in power struggles and exercise of political control.

The networks of relations of kinship and affinity can perform various functions for those so linked, and subsequent marriages can be contracted with a view to furthering specific interests. One can distinguish two types of marriage strategy. The first is marrying into a local group, which often entails unions with close relatives (cousin marriages), thereby creating dense kinship networks which exhibit some measure of group cohesion and facilitate social closure. This social closure ensures the retention of property and power within the group, either in terms of individual rights or in some corporate form. The second is marrying out, that is, marrying into a territorially wider group but still within one's own or a higher social stratum. If the ensuing ties are widespread, forming supra-local networks, they do not acquire the same measure of density as in relatively closed local groups. Marrying out reflects interests other than the retention of property, namely interaction with regional higher-status groups and access to the national elite; in other words, the politics of the right connections.

It is with elucidating the relationship between such strategies and the political economy of rural life in Southeast Asia that I am concerned here, albeit in a necessarily very limited and restricted way. In particular, it is with class-specific patterns of kinship and marriage organization in a Central Javanese village and the way in which comparison with the different political and economic context of a village in Central Luzon can clarify the character of the relationship.

Watulawang

The village (*desa*) of Watulawang in which I did research in 1978–79, is located in the northern uplands of Banjarnegara regency (Central Java) at about eleven hundred metres above sea level. The area is extremely hilly with steep inclines and rivers which in some places have carved deep gorges into the landscape. In general, the land around the village is not very fertile, most of it (213 hectares) consisting of dry fields (*tegalan*) on which corn is planted, with only an additional twenty-nine hectares of land which is irrigated during the rainy season for rice cultivation (*sawah*).

On the *tegalan* land a pattern of mixed farming is practised, the corn stalks being interplanted with other crops, most commonly roots and tubers such as cassava, taro and ganyong (*canna edulis*), though various vegetables are also grown. On the *sawah* a single crop of rice is possible which is then followed by one of corn. The various agricultural tasks require a great deal of labour as animal traction and use of the plough is not practicable on *tegalan* fields where the different crops are planted too close together and so are worked with hoes (*cangkul*) and pickaxes (*pacol*). Nevertheless, agriculture is closely linked with animal husbandry, particularly with the raising of goats which are kept in pens and whose dung is used for manure. Some also raise cattle for working the *sawah* and for their meat.

At the end of 1978 Watulawang had a total population of 1,373 inhabitants living in 283 households. The village is sub-divided into five distinct settlements, which are formally recognized as hamlets (*dukuh*). The pattern of land tenure in this upland village as shown in Table 1 manifests a degree of inequality though one which is apparently less skewed than on the plains of the North coast (see Schulte Nordholt 1981). By far the largest land holder is the village headman (*lurah*) who owns 13.5 hectares and controls more.

Farming is the primary means of subsistence in the village: work opportunities outside agriculture or animal husbandry are limited. However, there are a few

Table 1. Distribution of landownership in Desa Watulawang, 1978
            (in *sawah*-equivalents)*

Size of holding	Number of households	Area owned (in ha.)
1. Large landowners (more than 2.5 ha.)	6 (2%)	27 (19%)
2. Better-off peasants (1–2.5 ha.)	26 (10%)	35 (25%)
3. Middle peasants (0.5–1 ha.)	60 (21%)	41 (30%)
4. Small and poor peasants (0.25–0.5 ha.)	66 (23%)	25 (18%)
5. Marginal peasants (less than 0.25 ha.)	81 (29%)	11 (8%)
6. Landless peasants	43 (15%)	– –
Total	282 (100%)	139 (100%)

* A common denominator of *sawah*-equivalents is used in these calculations by halving the area of *tegalan* land which is less productive than the *sawah*.

artisans working as stone-cutters, carpenters, and basket weavers. Those living in the hamlets close to the large market in the sub-district town can also find jobs there as bearers on the weekly market days. Finally, one must note a small number of elementary-school teachers, religious teachers, and civil servants who reside in the village.

The rather fragmented and closed character of the local labour market is a striking feature of the area. Indeed, Watukumpul, which is the largest hamlet in the village with 109 households, constitutes a small labour market in itself. Virtually no people from outside the *dukuh* are employed in agriculture there and the residents themselves rarely work outside the confines of the hamlet. In contrast, for those from the hamlets closer to town there are greater opportunities for both menial work and agricultural labour. Most peasant households sell any surplus to other villagers, townspeople, or to merchant-truckers who act as middlemen. Agriculture, however, is not strongly commercialized and to a large extent retains its subsistence character.

Kinship and social stratification

In the absence of clearly-defined corporate social groups the strategic development and manipulation of relations of kinship and marriage can do much towards the creation of a mutual moral solidarity, a common identity, the establishment of contacts, mutual help and various forms of co-operation. Just what pattern emerges, however, clearly depends on the economic and political resources commanded, and so within the socially complex and stratified world of the village there is considerable variation in both the structuring of ties and the ways they are employed.

Diagram 1. Genealogy of Sumarmo's family

Generation

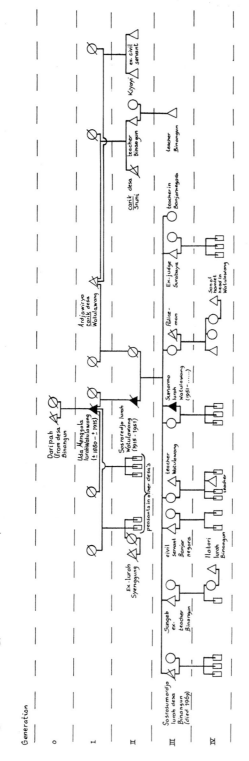

Sumarmo, the present village head, is a descendant of an old *lurah* family which has monopolized the office for three generations, ever since the 1880s. Perusal of the genealogy of this family (Diagram 1) reveals a number of significant features. The first is that neither Sumarmo nor his father married within the village, but sought their wives outside the *desa* from the somewhat elevated stratum of teachers, civil servants and other *lurah* families. Presumably this was also the case with the grandfather, though no precise information is available. The same pattern is observable with respect to the *lurah*'s siblings and in-laws who have achieved the positions of teacher, civil servant, *lurah* of a neighbouring *desa*, trader, and big-city judge. All married outside the village, though one sister who married a teacher from the town did eventually settle in Watulawang. This pattern of out-marriage thus clearly sets off the *lurah*'s network from that of the other established families in the *desa*.[1]

Furthermore, when one examines the geographical spread of marriages over time, a widening range is noticeable. The network of the second generation was supra-local in focusing on ties with other important non-peasant families in the area. This developed further with the *lurah*'s own generation, which benefitted from the increased educational opportunities of the last decades of colonial rule. Some members of the third generation were able to obtain jobs in the district town, the regency capital, or even a big city like Surabaya, and there intermarry with civil-servant families. The process has now gone even further in the fourth generation with some entering jobs in other parts of Indonesia, though in recent years one must also note a degree of joblessness. Overall, one can readily see how the geographical and social dispersal of the family reflects wider changes in mobility within Indonesia, the increased opportunities of the post-Independence period and then, more recently, the increasingly difficult employment situation.

The *lurah* family apparently kept its distance from other established families in the *desa* at least partly for status reasons, viewing educated townspeople as of equal rank to themselves whereas the village peasant elite was of lower status. Political considerations also probably played their part in that channels to the higher echelons of administration were important to the *lurah* as a semi-government official, and these were protected by keeping distant from the established peasant families in the village and avoiding any of the claims generated by intermarriage. Land ownership remained important to the *lurah*, but again his interests were pursued not through marrying the daughter of a wealthy farmer but by using his advantageous position in other ways, such as purchasing fields from those unable to pay the land tax.

Sumarmo and his father both actively accumulated land. According to the village land-register, in 1938 the latter owned nearly ten hectares of private

---

1. The stratum of larger and middle peasants shows a marriage pattern which is mainly restricted to the village and even to the hamlet. The poor peasants and landless households had their marriage ties outside the village.

land in addition to having the use of some eight hectares of *bengkok*, salary land. Upon his death in 1951 the private land was divided among his eight sons and daughters. Sumarmo, who by then had already been elected *lurah*, did not immediately hand over all the various portions to the legitimate heirs, but kept control of several hectares until the mid-1970s. By paying the land tax on this land he retained usufructuary rights until he eventually transferred it. The reasons for this delay may well have been primarily political. Sumarmo and his father had allowed villagers without a housesite to squat on some of the land, this being partly the benevolence of a landowner towards his servants and partly out of a sense of responsibility as a village head towards his people. Sumarmo was well aware that once the land was transferred to the legitimate heirs the squatters would either have to pay rent or vacate their sites, something which could easily cause considerable social tension and possibly unrest.

In addition to his inheritance, Sumarmo acquired property rights in other fields in the village, bringing his total property to thirteen and a half hectares. He also controlled two hectares of *bengkok* land (which had become reduced in the course of time). With a total of fifteen and a half hectares the *lurah's* household was the richest in the village.

The benefits derived from pursuing a strategy of marriage with the regional stratum of civil servants and educated people were apparently status and prestige, which in turn were valuable assets in manoeuvres to gain access to higher-level resources. In the colonial period paternalistic ties between higher-level officials, particularly those between the regent, *wedana* (district head) and *lurah*, made possible the selection of the *lurah's* children for higher education. Furthermore, after about 1920 the colonial government had also followed a policy of inviting the children of the village elite to follow a secondary education, though the Japanese occupation had prevented Sumarmo himself from receiving more than five grades of elementary schooling. Since Independence these traditional, long-established particularistic ties between *bupati* elite families and *lurah* families in the village have tended to break down as offices became positions of appointment rather than succession.

Without control of any common property the *lurah's* kin network does not constitute a corporate group though it does have a clear identity which bears some resemblance to the ancestor-oriented kin groups, *golongan* and *alur waris*, described by Koentjaraningrat in South-Central Java (1968:53–4). Despite this common identity it is important to note that the interests of the *lurah* do not always coincide with those of his relatives. His close kin express a degree of resentment in envious remarks about his landholdings, one of the main grievances being the retention for many years of control of between two and three hectares of his siblings' inheritance.

Most of the other farming households in the five hamlets of Watulawang are interrelated by kinship or marriage, though individual networks are for the greater part confined to the home hamlet. Only a relatively small number of households have relatives or affines in other hamlets, and it is mainly teachers, government officials or religious teachers who have married outside the confines of their natal place. The data on hamlet in-marriage by the better-off peasants is too complicated to be presented here in full, but is well illustrated by the example of the descendants of a couple from one of the hamlets, Watukumpul.

Table 2. Intermarriage of the descendants of Kakek and Nenek Bai

Generation	No. of descendants marrying	No. of marrying co-descendants	No. of persons in misanan unions
2 – Children	6	0	0
3 – Grandchildren	20	2	0
4 – Great-grandchildren	60	20	14

Kakek and Nenek Bai, who lived in the late nineteenth century, had six children. Table 2 shows the number of their third and fourth generation descendants who married, treating each person individually so that in the fourth generation twenty descendants intermarried, thus constituting ten couples, which puts the total number of descendant households in that generation at fifty. Of these twenty persons who intermarried, fourteen did so with second cousins (*misanan*), a category of union forbidden by Javanese *adat* (Bertling 1936; Palmier 1960). In fact, had descent been traced from all of a couple's four sets of grandparents the number of *misanan* unions would have shown up as even higher. However, what requires emphasis here is that five out of the six village landowners with more than two and a half hectares of land live in Watukumpul, where all are the descendants of Kakek and Nenek Bai. Moreover, two of them are among those who married co-descendants. The other intermarrying descendants fall within the categories of better-off and middle peasants. It is clear that this strategy of marrying kin-related persons successfully keeps landed property within a relatively small circle of households, and can be termed a strategy of social closure.

Forty-three households in the village neither own land nor can expect to inherit any from either parents or other relatives. In one of the smaller hamlets a number of these households share a common background as newcomers, recruited from other poorer *desas* in the region by the *lurah* family which employed them as household servants and labourers. Some are still dependents of the household of the present village head. Only rarely do these landless households have kin or affinal ties in Watulawang, and most look to their home areas for marriage partners. For them the wider network of kin and marriage ties does not play any major part in everyday life. With the one exception of a household containing a descendant of Kakek and Nenek Bai and consequent ties with some of the better-off peasants, a similar situation prevails in Watukumpul itself where there are eight landless households whose members work as dependent labourers (*janggol*) for the large landowners.

The organization of labour relations

Kin and economic relationships emphasize different principles of association. Kinship entails a notion of equity with close relatives showing, to some extent, a feeling of in-group solidarity, adherence to the norms of generosity and mutual help. In contrast, economic relationships belong to the domain of production and distribution, and are characterized by a calculating attitude and principle of maximization. The issue, then, is the extent to which kin ties overlap with, or exclude, various types of labour relations. It is important, not only for the light it throws on the functions of kinship in the village, but also for the way it clarifies the pattern of labour relations and the extent to which capitalist orientations have penetrated the local peasant society.

In Watukumpul it is possible to distinguish six types of dyadic relationship which are typically fairly long-lasting. Two exist with regard to land and concern sharecropping (*maro*) and leasing (*sewa*). The rest concern work itself, namely labour exchange (*sambatan*), contractual wage labour for agricultural purposes (*buruh harian* — day labourer), the employment of a stockman (*gamel*), and finally the employment of a contract-labourer in return for advance payment (*janggol*).

Maro is a sharecropping relationship between landowner and peasant farmer where the latter cultivates the land and divides the harvest on a fifty-fifty basis. In Watulawang, teachers, government officials and wealthy peasants have their land cultivated in this way, as they do not have the time to work it themselves. The sharecropping contract is generally considered to be rather favourable to the actual cultivator, and this advantage is even more marked in the *sewa* relationship, where a landowner cedes all rights to his land for a specific period for a cash rent paid in advance. In return for a fairly small sum the contract can be for up to ten or fifteen years, so this type of arrangement is only resorted to when the landlord is in urgent need of cash.

In the *sambatan* reciprocal exchange of labour there exists an established relationship between households which call upon one another for labour in the fields. The arrangement is concerned with the timing of inputs and contrasts markedly with the practice of some farmers who regularly employ labourers paid by the day at rates according to the season (Rp. 100 to 130 in 1979) for such tasks as hoeing, ploughing, weeding, and so forth.

The literal meaning of *janggol* is 'a person liable for corvée labour', but today it refers to a cash contract between a landowner and labourer. In return for an advance the *janggol* is contracted to work one day a week throughout the year, and he also receives three meals, a drink and some tobacco on the days worked.

In 1979 the sum paid was 1,500 rupiah for one year which, at an average of about 39 rupiah per day, is less than one third of the usual day wage of a casual labourer. *Janggol* contracts are clearly in the category of debt labour. The work is also heavy, as a *janggol* can be charged with carrying out all kinds of odd tasks in both the fields and the house of the employer. The burden of work is also very heavy for the *gamel* or *buruh merumput*, who is employed to go out every morning to gather fodder for domestic animals. For 6,000 rupiah per year and a daily meal on his return, the employee often has to walk long distances to find sufficient grass on the hillsides to cut and gather.

A number of conclusions about the importance of kinship can be drawn from plotting these contractual arrangements against the presence or absence of kin ties between the parties involved (Table 3). Although kinship links and these long-term economic relationships neither fully coincide nor exclude one another, there are significant and varied degrees of association. *Maro* relationships are to a large extent (70%) between relatives, thereby supporting the idea that this arrangement is mutually advantageous to both parties and therefore compatible with the norm of equality. On the other hand, the *sewa* contract is mainly between non-kin, and this reflects the predominantly economic and calculative character of the relationship. Where labour is concerned, a clear contrast emerges between the horizontal relations of equals and the vertical ones existing between superior and inferior. Thus the *sambatan* relationship is mainly (83%) between relatives, whereas those between landowner and, respectively, *gamel*, labourer, and *janggol* all reveal a low incidence of kin ties (25, 20 and 7 per cent).

Table 3. Long-term economic relationships and kin ties in hamlet Watukumpul (*desa* Watulawang) in 1978/79

Type of relationship	Total No.	With kin ties No.	%
1. Labour exchange (*sambatan*)	376	312	83
2. Landowner–sharecropper (*maro*)	21	14	70
3. Landowner–stockman (*gamel*)	24	6	25
4. Landowner–labourer (*buruh harian*)	61	12	20
5. Landowner–leaseholder (*sewa*)	21	3	14
6. Landowner–bonded labourer (*janggol*)	45	3	7

Notwithstanding conclusions to the contrary drawn by Hildred Geertz (1961:77) and Koentjaraningrat (1967:262), extended kin networks do play an important part in the social organization of village life in Watulawang and, I would suggest, more generally in Java. Inheritance is still the primary way of acquiring the most valued asset in an agricultural economy, and descent still determines one's chances of achieving the influential and powerful position of village head even though the occupant is now elected. Together, kinship and marriage are important determinants of social status and a significant means of maintaining and expanding control over crucial resources.

In Watulawang it is clear that different social strata pursue varying marriage strategies. 'Reaching out' was resorted to by the *lurah* family in particular in order to strengthen its political base by marrying out of the village and up the social scale. In marked contrast was the reaction of the middle echelon of peasants who used marriage as a means of social closure to safeguard their landed property. It was only for the landless that kinship was relatively unimportant since by virtue of their lack of resources they were unable, in general, to participate in or mobilize any significant social networks.

Java and the Philippines compared

The intricate relationship between the domains of kinship, politics and economics as evinced in Watulawang may be further elucidated by comparing Java with another Southeast Asian peasant society in which a cognatic system prevails. In Central Luzon in the Philippines, where I did field-work in the early 1970s, local and regional political competition is firmly embedded in kin-based social networks to the extent that political factions are generally labelled by the surnames of their main leaders and protagonists. In Java we do not encounter such a close relationship between kinship and political factionalism above the local village level. In order to interpret these differences one must know something of the social and political history of the respective areas.

The landlord class, which dominated Central Luzon from the early nineteenth century until very recently, was able to consolidate its position by controlling the means of production—capital and land—in the local setting. It also used its political power and influence at the local, provincial, and national levels to protect these economic interests. Most parts of Central Luzon were frontier areas from the first half of the nineteenth century till well into the twentieth century. The land was opened up by Tagalog migrants coming from the South and Ilocanos from the North, most of whom aspired to become homesteaders. Landlords owning rice-growing estates (*haciendas*) tried in various ways to increase their holdings: they claimed wasteland and took their tenants from other estates to open up new areas. They also resorted to landgrabbing, contesting the rights of illiterate smallholders and making use of political connections to settle disputes in their favour.

The histories of these landlord families, or *principalia* as they were termed, reveal that they acquired their properties over a long period involving several generations. Most of these families are themselves descendants of Tagalog migrants from the South. Their command of local government positions provided them with the political leverage to legalize the expropriation of land. This process of expansion was necessary for the protection of their interests because landholdings were subject to fragmentation following their division upon the death of the family head.

The marriage patterns of the landed gentry in Luzon indicate a strategy of out-marriage. Initially unions were restricted to the local municipality, but when during the American occupation they were allowed access to higher-level political positions the limits were extended to incorporate the whole province. There was no necessity for in-marriage and the creation of social closure even in the first decades of the twentieth century, as there was still plenty of land to be acquired. Furthermore, marrying out into other towns provided even better opportunities for the acquisition of wealth. At the same time kinship played an important part in the local and provincial politics of the period in that family networks proved useful in winning elections and influence-peddling with the state bureaucracy.

Even after Luzon had lost its frontier character in the 1930s and land had become scarce, the provincial elite did not aspire to social closure. This was because their interests were no longer exclusively limited to land, but extended to include professional careers, urban real estate, government positions and business. The leading families also tended to leave the province for the capital, Manila, whereas the smaller landholding families usually stayed in the province but sold part of their landholdings. Investing in education for their children who then developed careers as professionals, teachers, and employees, they gradually changed into an increasingly urban-oriented provincial middle class.

Among the peasant population a somewhat different kinship and marriage pattern emerged. Field-work in the village of Tabon in Nueva Ecija province (see Wolters 1983) revealed that while the household is the principal economic unit, some economic and political co-operation can and does occur between neighbouring and related households. Nevertheless, the functions of networks established by kinship and marriage are less easy to establish. One can discern a pattern of intermarriage among the better-off peasants in the village and within the municipality. However, this network is less dense than that observed in the Javanese village of Watulawang. In Tabon there is a much higher percentage of marriages with non-villagers and unions with first or second cousins are virtually absent. The reason for this development can be found in the history of the region.

The area surrounding Tabon had first been settled and opened up around the turn of the century. On the one hand, landlords of Tagalog origin took possession of large tracts of land which they registered in their names. On the other, large numbers of migrants from Ilocos moved in, opening up land for rice cultivation and trying to officially claim the land they had cleared. Some succeeded in getting their property rights recognized, but most became sharecroppers (*kasamá*) on the lands of the landlords. Some intermarriage occurred between these settlers who themselves had often come in small kin groups. In the 1970s people could still trace their connections to one another through the intermarriage of parents and grandparents. Most of the established families still active in village politics are descended from these early immigrants.

However, in-marriage did not become a preferred strategy in the second and third generations because sharecroppers do not have any landed property to be conserved through marriage. Although there are individual cases of smallholders benefitting from such a strategy, they were too few for any consistent pattern of intermarriage to emerge. Access to sharecropping contracts remains limited mainly to the older established peasant families because landlords have tended to view dividing the land on the death of a sharecropper as uneconomic. Furthermore, even a son was only able to take over the farm if known to be an industrious worker.

Kinship plays an important role in the formation of political alliances. The set of households with the same surname traced back to a common ancestor is considered to be a unit (*angkan*),[2] whether or not they actually form a coalition. There is also a prohibition, not always observed, on marriage between people with the same surname. In Tabon a surname referring to the *angkan* 'founder' who had migrated to the area around 1900 was thus closely linked with status and prestige in the village, given the higher esteem of the old established families. Even so, the *angkan* does not function politically as a closed group because member households often have diverging interests, ties with different landlords, jobs in the businesses of rival politicians and so forth. A clash of interests might occur at any time which could split the *angkan* into conflicting groups. This and the relative economic autonomy of constituent households, their involvement in vertical ties and their varying political affiliations, all combined to make the *angkan* a rather weak entity. Essentially it is a set of kin which can be mobilized as an interest group but which can also lie dormant for long periods.

Finally, *compadrazgo* relationships, ritual bonds of kinship established between families by godparenthood may also exercise a political importance. In utilizing many of the values of kinship the institution plays an important role in consolidating and moulding social relations between parents and godparents. In the Philippines the *compadre* system has been, and still is, used 'horizontally' to further relations within the middle-class and landlord strata and thus serves as an important linkage in the everlasting game of influence-peddling. It is also used, though on a much smaller scale, to cement 'vertical' ties between the better-off peasants or lower middle-class people on the one hand and wealthy landlords, businesspeople or popular politicians on the other.

---

2. The term refers to both patrilateral and matrilateral kin as well as affines. Women are supposed to identify with the *angkan* of their husbands, though a son-in-law from an insignificant family will usually identify with that of this father-in-law.

Conclusions

Any conclusions based on these two community studies must be tentative given the variations in milieux and circumstances within both societies. However, the material suggests that cognatic systems are rather flexible and that kin relations and marriage strategies are readily adjusted to changing conditions. With respect to the field of political economy, the contrasting cases of Java and the Philippines suggest that kin relations have more political functions in the Luzon village than in the Javanese. In the latter, political rivalry has not been allowed except for a brief period in the 1950s and early 1960s so that the use of kinship-based political coalitions could not become institutionalized. However, the occurrence of other factors pertaining to the wider social context have resulted in particular patterns of kin relations and the emergence of clear-cut marriage strategies.

Java is characterized historically by its heavy state bureaucracy, a strong control from the top, the long-term dominance of a Dutch colonial administration which was impenetrable to the native elite, the absence of an independent land-lord class, the *priyayi* elite with its exclusively bureaucratic orientation, a stratum of village officials forming a supra-local network but without the power and independence of a landlord class, and a relatively strong bureaucratic emphasis on public affairs. Overall there emerged a system of closed social strata with relatively little social mobility and limited possibilities for the establishment of vertical patron–client ties. Within this context extended kin networks were confined to the social strata in which they emerged, and could only acquire limited functions for those involved.

Among the nineteenth-century Javanese *priyayi* a high degree of in-marriage took place, that is, unions between people who were related and of high social status (Palmier 1960:58–80). Given a colonial state bureaucracy with the limited number of positions reserved for native officials, the *priyayi* families apparently tried to enhance their claims by keeping their high social status undiluted. Given their lack of an independent power base and the colonial government's prohibition on economic activities by native officials, the only means of upward mobility was by achieving a position in the indigenous administrative bureaucracy.

In contrast, the family of the village head of Watulawang followed a strategy of out-marrying, at least since the late nineteenth century. For members of this stratum new chances for upward mobility emerged as the colonial government increasingly required lower-level civil servants, clerks, judges and teachers, and consequently expanded the educational system to prepare people for these positions. After Independence the rapidly expanding state bureaucracy offered even better opportunities for these upwardly mobile educated families. It is possible that kinship networks between village officials and the lower echelons of the state bureaucracy became politically significant, particularly in the 1950s when elections were held and political parties organized. More obvious though is the fact that the marriage strategies followed by this *desa* elite reveal its inclination to assimilate with the urban middle class.

Yet another pattern is revealed by the better-off peasants in Watulawang who have followed a strategy of in-marriage within the community. These families did not have access to education during the late-colonial period, and only achieved this in the 1950s and 1960s. For them, holding on to land was of primary import-ance in a situation of extreme land scarcity and an ever-expanding population. In-marriage served the purpose of keeping land within the family, and prevented it from becoming widely distributed.

Since the colonial period the Philippines have been characterized by a weak state apparatus, limited control from the centre, a strong and independent land-lord class, a pervasive value orientation fostering private interests over public duties, a relatively high degree of social mobility and the use of personalistic ties for the promotion of one's interests. The American colonial government started to turn the administration over to Filipinos in the 1920s and consequently introduced a system of elections in which political parties vied for power at the various administrative levels. In this framework kinship ties became important, acquiring functions for the individuals and households involved.

In this frontier society where economic assets were 'up for grabs' for those with positions of power, the landlord class by and large followed a strategy of marrying out, thereby creating a wide network of kinship relationships which reached into the administrative apparatus and the judiciary. This network was not focused on the retention of rural property, but rather on the politics of influence and the acquisition of new forms of wealth. A possible contributory factor was the overall decline in the importance of landed wealth by the 1930s and 1940s in a heavily commercialized society in which business provided far better chances for self-enrichment. Since political influence often facilitated access to this commercial wealth, political careers were highly sought after.

Among better-off peasants the *angkan*, coalitions of kin-related households, played an important role in political rivalry at the village level. Power and con-trol within the village enabled these peasants to appropriate pork-barrel funds coming from higher-level politicians, and to win control of the best plots of land. Until very recently an important element was the fact that within this landlord–tenant system the peasants owned hardly any of the land themselves, so that they had to play the game of the 'politics of the right connections' in a situation where an ability to deliver the vote was their chief resource. Under these conditions it was not marriage strategies but kin relations which were major ingredients in the formation of political coalitions.

Class and Kin: Conflicting Loyalties on a Philippine Hacienda

Rosanne Rutten

Rural communities in Philippine lowland society resemble what Wolf (1966) terms 'open' communities, where in the absence of corporate groups dyadic ties of kinship, friendship, and patron-clientage are of strategic importance in gaining access to resources. Conditions appear somewhat different in the sugar-cane producing areas of Negros Occidental, where many local communities are part of hacienda enterprises and consist of worker families employed by the hacienda and residing on its premises. Hacienda employment in itself entitles workers to credit and housing, and the status of wage-labourer officially provides access to such state-controlled 'resources' as protective labour laws and medical insurance. Nevertheless, although the hacienda enterprise and state regulations guarantee, at least in theory, the subsistence security of worker families, personal relations remain crucial for workers in claiming their collective rights and furthering their subsistence interests.

Hacienda Milagros

The province of Negros Occidental, with its several thousand sugar-cane haciendas and fifteen sugar mills, is one of the main sugar-producing regions of Southeast Asia. Commercial cultivation was initiated in the 1850s by numerous entrepreneurs, many from the neighbouring island of Panay, who established haciendas in the then sparsely populated province (McCoy 1982). Labour was mainly provided by landless families who migrated from Panay and other nearby islands to settle permanently on the haciendas, and by migrant seasonal workers. Today, most haciendas broadly fall within the category of what Mintz (1966) calls 'family-type haciendas' in being relatively small and unmechanized, owned by individuals or families, and with personalized paternalistic relationships between planters and workers. Most planters employ resident wage labour (men, women, and children) to cultivate the cane and migrant labourers to help with the harvest during the annual 'milling season'. The production of sugar, partly for the world market, has made possible a considerable accumulation of wealth, which remains largely in the hands of mill owners and planters; relatively little has trickled down to the workers themselves. The legal minimum wage for labourers is low and spells poverty to the estimated 150,000 hacienda workers in the province.[1] Even so, many planters pay wages below the legal minimum and some resort to blacklisting those who demand their legal due. The state does not strictly enforce labour laws and cases filed by workers often turn out in favour of the planter (AMRSP 1975; Wiersma 1982).

The personal dependency of workers on their planter has gradually decreased since the haciendas' establishment. Planters initially dictated wage rates and hours of work, and any help in cases of illness depended on their 'generosity'. Owners of large haciendas lived on their properties and exerted a daily personal control over the workers. On account of labour shortages they tried to bind workers to the hacienda by extending credit and allowing them to cultivate small plots for subsistence crops. With the development of province-wide labour unions at the beginning of this century, and the introduction of protective labour legislation and a social security system in the 1950s, the state took some control over the labour and living conditions of hacienda workers, while unions began to organize them along class lines. At the same time personal relations between workers and planters weakened as planter families moved out to settle in nearby towns or the provincial capital, and as the need to tie workers to the hacienda diminished with supply of workers eventually exceeding demand. Still, workers today remain to some degree dependent on planter paternalism and a willingness to give them what is their due by law, given the poor enforcement of labour laws despite union pressures. Furthermore, workers continue to need credit from their planters to tide them over the lean season and meet financial emergencies.

Hacienda Milagros is located in the municipality of Murcia, some twenty kilometres from Bacolod City, the provincial capital. The owner resides in Bacolod City but visits the hacienda once or twice a week. The hacienda covers 134 hectares and has forty-six families living on it. Of these, ten are those of salaried employees (an overseer, two foremen, a timekeeper, a watchman, three truck drivers, a tractor driver, and a security guard), while the rest are families of workers. Each of the latter includes one or more members with the status of permanent labourer (*duma-an*), which implies a right to available work, credit, and free housing on the hacienda. In return they are obliged to work whenever their labour is required. Altogether there are about eighty permanent workers (forty-nine men and thirty-one women) plus fifteen casual workers, some of whom

1. In 1977–78, the period of my main research, the legal minimum wage for sugar-cane hacienda workers was 8.00 pesos a day, including a daily cost of living allowance; second-class rice cost 2.10 pesos a kilo. Since then, the minimum wage has been raised in stages to 18.33 pesos a day in 1981; in the same period the price of rice almost doubled and general consumer prices trebled. (See also Rutten 1982.)

live outside the hacienda. Each milling season some twenty migrant workers supplement this local labour force.

The overseer and other salaried employees (*empleados*) do not form a clearly separate socio-economic group, although the overseer and to a lesser extent the foremen have positions of power. They are almost as poor as the workers, to whom they are socially close. Except for the overseer and a foreman, all are of hacienda-worker background. Many have relatives and friends among the workers, and the wives and elder children of most *empleados* are also employed as labourers.

The main problem for the resident workers is the low and irregular income derived from hacienda work. In many families two or more people earn a wage, but their combined income still barely covers basic household expenses. The situation is exacerbated by the fact that most of the work, which is paid by the day or by task performed, is concentrated in the six-month milling season when the cane is cut and the fields replanted. At other times the available work is limited to some weeding and maintenance tasks, with employment being offered for only part of the week. During much of this 'lean' season, labourers depend on the planter for cash advances and rice on credit. It is this insecurity of income which distinguishes them from the salaried employees, who are paid all the year round.

Worker families supplement their incomes with vegetables and fruit grown in their yards for home consumption, and by rearing chickens and a pig or two to sell. The latter part of the lean season in the sugar-cane cycle coincides with the rice harvest, when there is work on the three hectares of hacienda rice fields and on neighbouring haciendas and small rice farms for payment in kind. Some women keep a small store at their house, others retail fish and rice, prepare rice cakes for sale, or earn money as dressmakers or traditional midwives. A number of families receive small remittances from children living elsewhere, mostly daughters working as domestic servants in town.

It is against this general background that one must set the two contrasting types of relationship which are crucial to the families of Hacienda Milagros in the endeavour to further their subsistence interests. These are the relations of dependency with the planter and overseer on the one hand and those of mutual aid amongst themselves as expressed along lines of kinship, friendship, and neighbourhood on the other. To gain access to employment and credit, workers depend to some extent on their personal good standing with the planter. Those who show him loyalty may be rewarded with favours such as promotion to the position of salaried employee, whereas those who are 'disloyal' can be punished by being denied help or even work. As the planter's representative on the hacienda, the overseer is also in a position to grant or withhold assistance. His is an important office since it is he who allocates the daily work among the labourers and regulates the repair of their houses.

Forming a social community the workers of Hacienda Milagros feel a certain obligation to assist one another in times of need, and mutual aid does indeed alleviate short-term difficulties. Small quantities of the less valuable food items are shared with others who are less fortunate, and households with large vegetable plots feel obliged to give produce to anyone from the hacienda who requests it. Such patterns of minor help are quite intensive between neighbours and friends, while help with respect to more valuable items like rice and cash is provided by kin.

Instrumental and moral aspects of kin relations

Though the cognatic Philippine kinship system lacks a basis for corporate group membership, it does provide people with an effective model for maintaining and strengthening special ties with others. Individuals have a wide range of bilateral kin, and affines are also included to form a significant part of one's circle of relatives. Within this set of relations one is quite free to choose with whom to maintain close contact and with whom not. Indeed, the rights and obligations inherent in kin relations which specify support and assistance are 'selectively implemented' (Eggan 1967:199). The choice of effective kin is often guided by practical considerations. As one observer noted, 'some people narrow the range of their recognition of kin to one side or the other in this bilateral complex, depending upon which group is useful in achieving certain goals (mostly economic) in life' (Jocano 1983:125). This instrumental element is also clear in the establishment of *compadrazgo* (godparenthood) relations of ritual kinship, which may strengthen existing bonds of friendship or kinship as well as serve to create closer relations with people of wealth and influence (Hart 1977).

Such instrumental considerations are interwoven with social and moral ones. Close association with many kin is highly valued in itself, and individuals without relatives living nearby are pitied not just because they lack dependable people who can be asked for help, but also because of their initial social isolation. Moreover, the moral duties towards kin are impressed so deeply from one's childhood onwards, that should a person 'not conform to his expected role in relation to kinsmen who have been close to him, he feels guilty and suffers the social disapproval of his family' (Hollnsteiner 1963:68).

Kin are, therefore, often the first to be called upon in times of need and seldom refuse assistance. Given the relative openness and trust among kin, they are also more accessible for a request of favours and there is less risk of shame or loss of face should the response be negative. Within the total set of relatives the actual degree of closeness and co-operation of course varies; ties of consanguinity are generally more intimate than those of affinity, and relations with kin of the first degree are the closest. It is also necessary to recognize that physical proximity and personal characteristics affect kin relationships and that relatives do not always take precedence over others.

Among the Ilongo-speaking people of the Western Visayas, of which Negros Occidental forms part, the kinship system resembles that of the lowland Philippines in general. Kin are recognized up to the third or fourth degree and equal importance is attached to maternal and paternal kin, to whom the same forms of address and reference are used (Gonzales 1965; Jocano 1983). Affines are not rigidly distinguished from kin and are addressed and referred to as though the link were consanguineal. Residence is neolocal after the first year or two of marriage; a couple usually resides for some time after the wedding with the wife's parents unless it is more convenient and advantageous for them to live with those of the husband. As elsewhere in the Philippines, kinship implies for the people of the Western Visayas the ideas and values of 'reciprocity, cooperation, and favored bias' (Gonzales 1965:29).

In Hacienda Milagros, kin links are an important part of the labourers' social networks, as many people on the hacienda are interrelated. This might appear surprising, given the lack of such bonds as common property in land, and the high mobility of the worker population to the extent that most present adult residents were not born on the hacienda. The influence of kin links on migration patterns partly explains the density of kin relations. Many of those who settled in Hacienda Milagros had relatives there who informed them about the place and through whom they gained permission from the overseer to settle as resident workers.[2] As it is the overseer alone who grants such permission, it is crucial for those seeking employment on the hacienda to be either acquainted with him or to have links of kinship, friendship, or godparenthood with residents who will approach him on their behalf.

Another reason for the prevalence of kinship ties is the intermarriage of a few large families who now comprise more than half the hacienda population. Children of these couples have married others on the hacienda and remained there because they, as the offspring of permanent workers, are themselves more readily granted the same status with its attendant access to regular work, credit, and a house of their own after marriage. Because the planter prefers a stable labour supply and labourers depend in part on kin linkages to gain access to the scarce resources associated with the position of permanent worker, relatives are thus kept together far more than might otherwise be expected. The network of kin relations is further consolidated by exchanges and mutual help. Ties are certainly more dense within the confines of the hacienda, though by no means restricted to it. Contacts with relatives elsewhere may be more sporadic, but are

2. Women's kin were, in this respect, as important as men's. Of eighteen families on which I have information, ten settled on the hacienda through relatives of the wife, and eight through those of the husband.

activated on such occasions as the need to gain access to rice-harvesting work on neighbouring haciendas (see Sibley 1957).

By using kinship forms of address in their daily interaction, relatives and ritual kin reaffirm the personal bonds uniting them and the implicit claims each has on the other's help. Similarly, in using the term *toto* in addressing the planter — a term of endearment normally used for the eldest or youngest boy in the family — workers express some measure of loyalty and respect to the planter while simultaneously reminding him of his own personal obligations towards them.

Kinship versus class: conflicting loyalties in unionization

In the preceding pages I have briefly outlined the kinship system of Hacienda Milagros and the social organization of the hacienda itself. Whereas the ideals of kinship support the kind of interdependence between workers described earlier, there are circumstances in which the bonds of kinship and the advantages these convey divide families against one another. Kinship may then hamper the emergence and effectiveness of other forms of affiliation, which in the following case is one of class mobilization.

People in need expect assistance from relatives in a position to help. In Hacienda Milagros the person holding a strategic position in this respect is the overseer: although he has to implement the planter's directives and safeguard his interests, the overseer has some room for manoeuvre given his power to distribute hacienda work and house-repair materials. In a situation where some labour is lighter and pays more than others, where work is scarce during the lean season, and where house-repair materials are in short supply and repairs go slowly, it pays to be on good terms with the overseer and to be in a position to appeal effectively to him for help.

At the time of the events described below, the overseer was a young man with many relatives on the hacienda.[3] He belonged to one of the older families and had married a woman whose parents and siblings were also fellow residents. Among his close relatives were three other salaried employees: his father was a foreman, one brother-in-law was a timekeeper, and another was a truck driver. The cluster of relatives around the overseer and these three *empleados* was the largest in the hacienda; the other six salaried workers either had no relatives on the hacienda, or only a few.

The overseer felt obliged to help his kin and close affines and they, on their part, could pressure him to fulfil this obligation. A disproportionately large

3. Six households were consanguineally related to him: those of his parents, his two married siblings, and three first cousins of his father. A further six households were linked by marriage: those of his wife's parents, her three married brothers, and two married siblings of his own sister's husband.

number of his worker relatives thus had access to light work paid on a daily basis and to scarce work during the lean season, and their houses were kept in better condition. Some of his close friends who had become ritual kin also shared in these advantages. Those denied such favours were well aware of the preferential treatment given by the overseer and felt discriminated against.

The division among workers became manifest in 1975 when some labourers started to organize into a local union chapter, following a radio programme that explained the legal wages and benefits of hacienda workers and that advised them to join the National Union of Sugar Industries (NUSI) to obtain their legal due. At that time the workers of Hacienda Milagros received the legal minimum wage and were covered by social and medical insurance. Their complaints concerned the non-payment of obligatory annual bonuses, though for some the overseer's preferential treatment of relatives and friends was also a motive for joining. Two workers actively recruited a membership which soon totalled forty-nine men and women from eighteen families. With the union's help they filed a complaint at the Department of Labour against non-payment of the bonuses.

Those with special relations with the overseer or planter kept out of the union. They included the kin of the overseer and his wife, some of their ritual kin, as well as the salaried employees, who could only maintain their privileged position by remaining loyal to the planter. Fearing reprisals by the planter some newcomer and other worker families also refused to join.

The overseer felt especially loyal to the planter because of the long-standing support the planter had given his family. After his truck driver father was afflicted by rheumatism in one of his hands the planter had appointed him a foreman. The overseer himself, slightly built and unable to work hard in the fields, was first employed as a houseboy in the planter's home where he tended the garden and swept the yard. After his marriage he became a foreman and later, when the old overseer left, he took over that position. A deep debt of gratitude marked his bond with the planter.

With the overseer's position in the conflict so clear-cut, his relatives rallied behind him for both moral and instrumental motives. They viewed the unionization of workers not only as an attack on the planter but also as directed against the overseer himself. Even though many of them were labourers, as close kin and affines they felt the obligation to come to the overseer's aid and to show him support in return for the assistance he had given them. Because of the small size of the hacienda community, with all the residents well aware of each other's dealings, the social pressures to conform to the norm of reciprocity were strong. From a more strategic point of view, they may have felt it necessary to demonstrate their loyalty so as not to lose out on possible future assistance – in particular his affines, who were less close emotionally to the overseer. Thus, what formerly had been a cluster of kin and affines living in close proximity and related on an individual basis now became an effective group with common interests and objectives. That these relatives viewed the unionization as an 'external' threat, guided by 'outsiders' to their group who had a grudge against them, further encouraged this.

The workers' affiliation with NUSI lasted for about two years. The planter did all he could to suppress the organization, ordering the overseer to refuse work to the most militant members and to limit the work assigned to the others. He pitted members against non-members by inviting a company union into the hacienda to counteract the NUSI. Many who were not members of the latter joined, among them kin and affines of the overseer. For a time some NUSI members sought work elsewhere, others tried to survive on the little work they obtained on the hacienda, but in the end they felt the sacrifice was no longer worthwhile. Although their action did have some success in that after many court hearings they received their benefit payment, the union organization slowly disintegrated.

The division between workers who were relatives of the overseer and those who were not remained, however. Some time after the NUSI episode, workers began to join the National Federation of Sugar Workers (NFSW), which is linked to progressive groups within the Roman Catholic Church. They were contacted through Catholic Sisters and lay leaders active in the municipality. Those who joined or were sympathetic to it were former NUSI members plus some of the other non-relatives of the overseer who had previously kept aloof. Workers who were relatives of the overseer and his wife, as well as the salaried employees, were against the union and the Sisters and, suspicious of their activities, branded them as 'subversive' and 'against the government'. Despite their own poverty they saw these activities as an attack on the status quo on which they depended for the few meagre privileges they gained over others on the hacienda.

Things changed significantly in 1977 when the planter gradually eased the overseer out of his position and demoted him to foreman to make way for an outsider. The background to this change was the sharp drop in the planter's income as a result of a slump in the sugar price on the world market, and his consequent decision to rationalize the production process. Skilled management was required to improve production methods, reduce labour costs, and exercise greater control over the work performed. The old overseer, who had only an elementary school education, was thus replaced by one who had been to high school and by an administrator with a college degree in agriculture. Neither man had ever been in Hacienda Milagros before, nor did they have any relatives or friends there.

The ex-overseer felt repudiated by the planter and, taking his demotion as a rejection of his personal allegiance, his loyalty made way to a sense of grievance. He soon began to seek contacts with his previous adversaries, the members of the union NFSW. His parents, brothers and sisters, and the close kin of his wife, all eventually joined the NFSW, with one of his wife's sisters even becoming an 'officer' of the hacienda union chapter. There were several reasons for these moves. Showing solidarity with a relative in need was one, but the relatives also regarded the demotion as an insult to the whole group and thus found little reason to remain loyal to the planter. Furthermore, having lost their preferential access to scarce resources, their interests now coincided with those of the other workers. Fear of reprisals by the planter, which might otherwise have kept them out of the union, was now possibly countered by the feeling that the increasing power of the NFSW in the province assured them of effective support.

These developments have fostered unity among the workers of Hacienda Milagros. The new overseer, who had no relatives on the hacienda, provided less occasion for divide and rule, and the backing of a strong union offered some security against possible retaliation by the planter. Since the planter soon replaced the new overseer and likewise employed his successor for only a short time, workers had little opportunity to develop individual bonds of friendship or ritual kinship with these local men of authority. Eventually, in 1982, the workers succeeded in making a united effort to reach a collective bargaining agreement with the planter.

Conclusion

In Philippine society, where personal relations are crucial in gaining access to scarce resources, kinship can be of great instrumental importance to people living in poverty who need to safeguard their subsistence security through mutual help. The workers of Hacienda Milagros maintain relations of mutual aid with consanguines, affines, and to a lesser extent with ritual kin, with whom they exchange assistance in food, cash, and labour. Such assistance is mainly given among relatives on the hacienda itself as well as on nearby haciendas. Together with relations of friendship and neighbourhood, which also involve a moral claim on support, these reciprocal ties link the hacienda families and may contribute to the organization and co-operation of workers on a class basis.

On the other hand, for a number of years relations of kinship and affinity between workers and the overseer constituted a barrier to the unionization of all the hacienda's workers. With his influence and control of scarce resources the overseer was able to help his worker relatives in favouring them in the allocation of work and supply of materials for house repair. This preferential treatment divided the hacienda worker population in those who benefitted — the overseer's relatives and close friends — and those who did not. The rift became manifest when the latter joined a labour union and the former remained loyal to the planter. Only when the overseer was demoted to the rank of foreman and lost his influence and capacity to assist his relatives did the situation change.

The study of kin relations among working-class people may thus provide important evidence of their role in the individual survival strategies of worker families as well as enlighten certain aspects of the organization of workers as a class. But whether kin solidarity actually enhances or counteracts solidarity of a wider group of workers clearly depends on the interplay of other relations — in this case the changing interrelations of workers, overseers, planters, unions, and the state itself.

Kinship and the Domestic Development Cycle in a Kedah Village, Malaysia

Diana Wong

This paper draws upon a study of the social organization of peasant production in a Malay village located on the North Kedah Plains some seventeen miles north of Alor Star.[1] Up to the 1950s most of the area was covered by swamp forest, which has since been cleared. However, Kampong Gelung Rambai is a long-established village which in 1979–80 consisted of 133 households clustered together. It is situated along the Jalan Perlis river which used to be the main transport artery between the states of Kedah and Perlis. Thus in the past the village was by no means economically isolated and its economy has become even more commercialized since the area became part of the huge Muda irrigation scheme in 1970. The village is primarily agricultural (its major crops include wet rice and rubber), though non-farm employment (construction and other kinds of wage labour in the nearby towns) is also quite an important source of income for most villagers. Because of this multiplicity of income sources landownership as such is not a sufficiently useful indicator of social differentiation. If we apply a more general measure, using village standards, we could say that sixteen households belong to the 'well-to-do' category and seventy to the 'middle' band, while forty-seven are considered 'poor'.

Despite the clear differentiation and despite the process of agrarian commercialization in the area, it appeared that access to land and labour resources within the village rice economy was only partly mediated by market forces. It is here that kinship comes into play. This is most noticeable with respect to inheritance and usufruct patterns as well as in the control of household labour, which are all associated with significant differences in household composition between the social classes in the village. Although the nuclear family is the norm it is most frequent among the middle category of households, while the well-to-do are characterized by a relatively high percentage of three generation stem-families and the poor by a disproportionately large number of denuded families. Similar data from other peasant societies relating to the social organization of peasant production have

1. Field-work in West Malaysia was conducted between April 1979 and April 1980 with a grant from the Sociology of Development Research Centre, The University of Bielefeld (FRG).

been interpreted as indicative of a 'traditional village economy' in which 'social and moral arrangements [...] typically operated to assure a minimum income to inhabitants' (Scott 1976:5). This 'moral economy of the peasant' has been seen as based in either the moral quality of kinship or the characteristics of the 'pre-capitalist village'. In studies of the Malaysian peasantry both have been invoked in explaining the occurrence of apparently income-sharing practices (cf. Fujimoto 1980) while the role of kinship in regulating access to land 'in its aspect of mutual aid or "reciprocity"' (Horii 1972:60) has received special attention.

In many Southeast Asian societies the cognatic character of the kinship system has accentuated the perception of intra-village relations as being based on sharing, if only because within a few generations the rapid spread of bilateral links tends to extend the kinship ideology of help without calculation to most if not all residents. At the village level, Malay kinship is frequently cited by anthropologists and in Gelung Rambai by villagers themselves as an ordering principle which crucially impinges on the processes of production, consumption and distribution. Curiously enough, however, most academic attention has been given to those systems of exchange operating between kin at the synchronic level as they pertain to labour, notably the sharing of work opportunities via tenancies and harvesting arrangements (see Massard, this volume). Far less attention has been given to the actual process of transmission of resources between generations and the ties which are thus generated between households. This is all the more surprising in that there is a pervasive notion that the conjugal, nuclear family is the structurally significant unit in the society given the absence of descent groups, so that one might have expected this aspect of the interconnection between households to have been more fully explored. Overall then there seems to be some assumption that bilateral reckoning permits the extension of kin ties and in like manner bilateral devolution leads to the dispersal, not the concentration of resources. Another factor which has to be taken into account in a study of access to village land and labour, is the fact that the Kedah village in no way functions as a corporate community. This means that the patterns of exchange and sharing referred to take place between households rather than within any larger entity.

One is thus faced with the significance of kinship as it affects the household being manifest at two distinct levels of exchange. In a synchronic dimension kinship involving the 'axiom of amity' apparently supports the uncalculated sharing of material and emotional resources between households of related kin. Diachronically it regulates the transmission of resources between the generations which is to be far more immediately and directly understood through the workings of the so-called family development cycle than by reference to the jurally formulated laws of inheritance (which are frequently undermined by the former).

The family development cycle and the constraints it imposes on peasant production where the household is the basic unit of production and consumption was first discussed extensively by Chayanov (1966). Focusing upon the demographic variable, he attempted to show how the growth and decline of peasant farm sizes was dictated by the internally-generated labour supply and self-defined consumption needs specific to each particular stage of the cycle.

In this paper I examine those sharing practices between village households which are commonly expressed by reference to kinship, and relate them to the processes of household formation and distribution of household types in the village. For analytical purposes two types of sharing have to be distinguished, that involving immediate or short-term exchanges between kin-related as well as other households, and the longer-term intergenerational transfer of land and labour occurring within a cluster of kin-related households. To use Marshall Sahlins' (1974) terminology, balanced or asymmetrical reciprocity characterizes the first whereas generalized reciprocity with its specifically moral emphasis is confined to the network of intergenerational exchanges. Nevertheless, contrary to the assumptions of Chayanov (1966) this latter pattern of transfer does not, despite its moral character, necessarily lead to the emergence of essentially homogeneous units where any differences in consumption and production patterns are accountable solely in terms of differences in family size. Rather, as I shall try to show, these differences in household size and composition are conditioned by differential access to land and labour which in turn is determined by the process of intergenerational transmission. In other words, patterns of usufructuary access to land and labour are less subject to prescribed formulas of sharing than to the exigencies of peasant production and reproduction. Thus the way in which households are formed and provided with means to subsistence and production by the parental unit in this Malay village, does not necessarily allow for the adequate or egalitarian provision of productive resources to all, but rather allows for individual accumulation and differentiation between kin-related households.

Intergenerational transfer

Most studies of intergenerational transfer confine themselves to an analysis of the allocation of land rights as regulated by the inheritance system, which in the Malay case means either the Islamic Law of Inheritance or *adat*. In practice, however, this type of land transfer is rarely effected by legal act in spite of the appearance of a legally determined machinery of inheritance. It does not, as a rule, begin with the death of an owner but with the sequential 'coming of age' of the potential heirs. Customary practice (*adat*) prescribes that regardless of sex each child should be equally provided with the means of subsistence to support a new family of procreation. The process of transmission is thus intimately associated with the domestic development cycle in which, during the course of growth and fission, land and labour are transferred from one generation to the next. What perhaps requires emphasis, though, is the fact that this process is social rather than biological. The actual development of the cycle cannot be reduced to the autonomous free-play of demographic forces. Marriage, divorce, adoption and so forth, are social phenomena to which people have differential access. It is this perspective which is most useful in an analysis of issues raised by the Chayanovian problematic, that is, the significance of the domestic development cycle where the family is also the unit of production.

According to the Malay folk model of the development cycle, a newly-married couple live with the wealthier parental family and contribute their labour to this unit. The surplus generated by them is then theoretically returned when they move out to set up on their own, at which time they are granted a house and the usufruct of a certain amount of land which they can work as a separate unit of production. With this economic base, the new household must next try to expand upon it during the nuclear phase of the cycle, and this seems to happen especially when the woman is finished with child-bearing and can devote more time to agricultural work. It is also at this time that the children become economically productive and can contribute to both house- and field-work. More land should now be opened for cultivation, bought, or, as tends to happen nowadays, be rented in. Only if this expansion takes place can the couple ensure subsequent reproduction by providing marriage partners for their children and land for them to work upon. If they do not succeed, they lose the children's labour to the families into which they marry. Eventually one child is left, who contributes to the parents' surplus accumulation through labour beyond the two years or so which the other siblings usually spent at their parental home following their marriage. Because this child frequently cares for the parents in their old age, he or she also usually receives more land in usufruct than the others, and for a far longer period. Any surplus generated in this phase is officially controlled by the parent as household head but de facto it is managed by the child, who can consume it or invest it in the purchase of productive fields or opening up of new land to cultivation.

In the course of its developmental process household composition undergoes a series of possible transformations, according to our ideal model from nuclear to stem, where the parents live with a married child, his or her spouse and their children, to nuclear and so on. Table 1 shows the actual household composition for 114 of the 133 households in Kampong Gelung Rambai and reveals interesting variations according to wealth and in the occurrence of denuded households. These consist of old people living alone, as a couple, or with a grandchild. According to our model these people should be comfortably ensconced in the bosom of the young family created around their youngest child, but in practice they are not. The existence of these denuded households and their association with the 'poor' suggest that there are different paths within the household development cycle. It is not merely that the phases do not necessarily unfold in a set order, but that we need to talk of different patterns which correspond closely to differences in wealth.

Table 1. Household composition in Kampong Gelung Rambai, 1979

Relative wealth of household	Nuclear family	Stem family	Denuded family	Total
Well-to-do	64%	36%	0%	14
Middle	85%	13%	2%	55
Poor	64%	7%	29%	45
Total				114

The ideology of *adat* specifies an equal division of property between siblings, and the Islamic Law of Inheritance also maintains the principle of equality except that it favours males according to a 2:1 ratio. Theoretically, the process of property devolution should therefore not lead to social differentiation between kin, but the usufructuary access to the means of production which is maintained in defiance of the jural norms significantly alters the situation.

Case 1

Jusuh and Saad are brothers, both living in the village, yet the younger of them, Jusuh, is a middle peasant and has married into the established Tok Idris family, while Saad is one of the poorest peasants in the village. How has this come about? Their parents operated 3.5 *relong* of rice land. Before his marriage Saad opened 2.5 *relong* of land while still living with his parents, but upon going to the Land Office to register it in his name found that the *Penghulu* had already put in a claim. Thereupon Saad became a tenant of the latter, though it was some years before he had to pay rent. However, even before this land became fully productive Saad had to supplement his income by agricultural and other forms of wage labour, especially when, following his marriage and birth of the children, there were more mouths to feed. On the other hand, Jusuh continued to live with his parents and eventually, in his mother's old age, cultivated all the family's land. With this as a start, he was able to open up a further 7 *relong* which now constitute his personal secure economic base.

Case 2

The estate of Lebai Darus, long deceased, is still not divided. Five *relong* were given (not officially transferred) to his eldest son, and two or more to each of the three daughters and the other son. The youngest son remained in the house of Lebai Darus until his father's death, managing the remaining property in the latter's name; he invested part of the surplus in a rice huller, which is still the only one in the village. He is today one of the wealthiest villagers. Upon the death of the father, he appropriated the fields which two of his sisters had been operating for decades.

These two examples illustrate well the significance of the stem-structure in organizing usufructuary access to the means of production and a secure subsistence base for further accumulation. However, they also suggest that to interpret the informal tenurial arrangements often found between kin as a 'sharing of poverty' is problematic.

Marriage and childbirth is another moment where deviations from the ideal norm of the development cycle can occur. I have not been able to identify any fixed patterns to finding a marriage partner, though there are two striking types of marriage preference. The first is for marriage between parallel cousins which is a recognized religious ideal and frequently recorded in the literature. The rationale for this type of marriage was formulated by a village informant as 'this way, the property can be kept in the family'.

There is also a striking tendency for the wealthy villagers to marry complete outsiders who are often poor. The pattern seems to arise as follows: the daughter of a wealthy family is married off while young, often at fifteen, to a cousin or perhaps a wealthy family from another village. Many of these unions end in failure with the daughter returning home after one or two months residence with her in-laws. As a divorcee living at home the value of the *mas kawin* (bride price) she can command is greatly reduced. In these circumstances the family tends to welcome the offer of a poor young man who scrapes together a modest sum and agrees to reside with them after the marriage and to work the family farm.

A divorced heiress is thus quickly remarried, but for a young woman without property, divorce or widowhood tends to result in a very different future. She may return to her parents' household where she will be assured of a living. She will, however, remain in a dependent position without the opportunity to save money or accumulate any land to pass on to her children. If she does eventually remarry, then her children are often left with the grandparents. In either case, on marriage her children will join the household of their parents-in-law and feel little obligation to provide for their mother's needs in old age. The example of Biyah (Case 4) strikingly illustrates this pattern.

These cases of divorce and widowhood thus show important deviations from our (normative) model of the domestic development cycle. The significance of this should not be underestimated, as in Kedah the divorce rate between 1951 and 1956 was 61.4% (Tsubouchi 1976:31) although there are indications that in recent years this rate has declined. Divorce not only affects women's own future opportunities but the 'starting conditions' of their children as well. The children of divorced parents and orphans are often brought up by grandparents which explains why the grandparent–grandchild tie is such a significant one in rural Malay society where in the not too distant past a high rate of divorce went together with high mortality rates. These children often enjoy the usufruct of part of the estate of their grandparents. Islamic law, however, only grants inheritance rights to the first descending generation leaving these children without any property upon the death of their grandparents.

Case 3

> Mat, in his mid-twenties, lives with his wife and young daughter in the household of his father-in-law, a well-to-do peasant whose farm he helps cultivate. Mat himself however owns no land and has applied to FELDA, the government land resettlement agency, for a place in one of their schemes. This rather precarious phase in the development cycle, of dependence on his father-in-law was, however, not entirely unforeseen. Upon the divorce of his parents he was brought up by his paternal grandfather who was a wealthy peasant. It was he who provided Mat with the dowry for his marriage and the land he was operating. Upon the grandfather's death, however, Mat's father who had subsequently remarried became the sole heir to the land, leaving his son with no access to any resources whatsoever.

Poverty and access to labour

Altogether there are thirteen denuded households in the village. Seven of them are headed by women, six originated outside the village, and twelve are classified as poor. All thirteen heads have been married and have children who now form nuclear units of their own within or without the village. As mentioned above, the overall poverty of these households is closely related to their domestic development cycle, or more specifically, to a breakdown in the traditional ideal pattern of that cycle. Nevertheless, the question remains, why are these ageing people not integrated into a stem-family domestic structure?

Case 4

> Biyah, aged sixty-seven, lives with a granddaughter of thirty-five and a thirteen-year-old grandson. Biyah does not come from Gelung Rambai itself but moved to the village when she married Haji Hassan. After she had one son she was divorced. This son, Yaacob, is now one of the middle peasants in the village and farms 8 *relong* of rice fields. This includes 2.5 *relong* belonging to his mother; he has used this land for 39 years in return for supporting her financially. Why does Tok Biyah not live with her son, especially when he has not divested himself of the responsibility of support for her in her old age? The key reason is the weak position of an elderly person who has not provided a significant amount of material resources to the younger generation. Although Tok Biyah lets her son use 2.5 *relong*, the bulk of his land is inherited from his father's side.

It is clear from this case that poverty can be directly associated with the path followed in the domestic development cycle. There is thus a sharp distinction between the elderly rich and elderly poor: the former tend to live in stem families and the latter in denuded families, the crucial factor being their differential access to domestic family labour and consumption. The elderly rich profit from the domestic labour of their in-laws as well as from any increased consumption directly resulting from higher production, while the elderly poor are dependent on themselves alone or on younger children. Due to the fact that they possess little land they are not in a position to control the labour (both agricultural and domestic) of their children. Thus, in contrast to the well-to-do, they form independent residential units, usually with a single child or grandchild, even when their married children are living in the same village and giving support.

The network of intra-generational exchange

I now turn to a wide set of Malay exchange practices enjoined by kinship which tend to be lumped together under the rubric of 'income sharing' or 'mutual aid'. These include various tenurial and labour arrangements such as sharecropping or labour exchange (*derau*), almsgiving (*sedekah*), mutual help (*tolong-menolong*), and others. Village data indicate that between kin tenurial arrangements other than intergenerational transmission are characterized by a principle of balanced reciprocity. Furthermore, the behaviour expected of kin in such arrangements as, for example, in the fixing of rents (see Mohd. Shadli Abdullah 1978:144 ff) or labour-sharing practices, is not distinguishable from that for non-kin.

Labour-exchange practices include the work groups known locally as *kumpulan derau* formed for the transplanting and harvesting of rice. This type of co-operative labour has often been taken to exemplify the pervasiveness of mutual-aid principles in the rice economy. Co-operation and aid is certainly involved, but we should also be aware that *derau* operates on the principle of strictly balanced reciprocity or, as the villagers say, '*buat sepagi bayar sepagi*' — to receive a morning's work is to give a morning's work. The principle of equivalence is strictly observed, so that the *derau* for pulling seedlings (*cabut semai*) are kept distinct from those for transplanting (*tanam*). The former is calculated at a piece-work rate, one bundle of seedlings being gathered in return for each that has been provided, whereas for transplanting the unit of work is a morning's labour. As a rule a farmer calls upon the number of people he estimates necessary to transplant a field within a given time. The system is in fact quite flexible: any individual might contribute one or more units of labour depending on his or her own requirements. The contract is always between individual households and not with the *berderau* group as such, and when through illness or some other commitment a debt cannot be paid within the season in question it is carried over to the next year.

Those with large farms as well as the landless engage in *derau*. For the former the advantage is a work group big enough to complete transplanting quickly, while the landless can accumulate rights in other people's time. They can then 'sell' the work units owed to them to 'patron' farmers with whom they have longstanding contracts (*kontrek*) to provide labour.[2] Finally, it is important to note that the same principle of balanced reciprocity and even the term *derau* itself are carried over into other areas of co-operation. Sugar, milk, eggs, cigarettes, and rice are contributed to events such as wedding feasts with the obligation that an exact return in kind be made on a future occasion.

Conclusion

I have argued that the language of sharing frequently blurs the distinction between, on the one hand, the land and labour exchanges associated with the course of the domestic development cycle which further bind together households related by kinship, and on the other, the network of labour and land exchanges between households which may or may not be kin-related. In the former, exchanges are structured by the long-term process of intergenerational transmission of resources which at the same time balances out the asymmetries between productive capacity and consumption needs in the course of an individual's life cycle. In the latter the exchanges are primarily influenced by the exigencies of current production and reproduction needs.

However, while one might observe this balancing mechanism operating at the individual level, it is also connected with very different social changes. In particular, I would like to stress the way control over family labour is both an expression of and a contributory factor to the process of social differentiation in the rural economy. The poor 'lose' their children and thus their ability to increase resources, whereas the wealthy can profitably 'bind' them by means of their resources in property. Property thus seems not only to be valued for its own direct economic significance but also for its possible exchange against labour services in a local economy still characterized by a scarcity of labour. One thus has a situation contrary to the Chayanovian proposition that access to resources depends mainly on control over familial labour and that this control is intimately connected with the demographic composition of the household. What we see in Kampong Gelung Rambai is that control over familial labour depends on actual control over land and other economic resources, thereby generating progressive social differentiation within the village.

---

2. Apart from their role in concentrating labour inputs within a given period of time the *derau* are social occasions relieving the tedium of work and providing an opportunity for fun and gossip, especially in work breaks when titbits were traditionally served by the 'host'.

Bibliography

AA   = American Anthropologist
BKI   = Bijdragen tot de Taal-, Land- en Volkenkunde
JMBRAS = Journal of the Malayan Branch of the Royal Anthropological Society

AMRSP
  n.d.   *The sugar workers of Negros.* Manila: Association of Major Religious Superiors in the Philippines (1975).
Appell, George N.
  1965   *The nature of social groupings among the Rungus Dusun of Sabah, Malaysia.* [Ph.D. thesis, Australian National University, Canberra.]
  1967   'Observational procedure for identifying kindred; Social isolates among the Rungus of Borneo', *South Western Journal of Anthropology* 23:192–207.
  1976   'The cognitive tactics of anthropological inquiry; Comments on King's approach to the study of the kindred', in: G. N. Appell (ed.) 1976, pp. 146–51.
  1978   'The Rungus Dusun', in: V. T. King (ed.) 1978, pp. 143–71.
Appell, George N. (ed.)
  1976   *The societies of Borneo; Explorations in the theory of cognatic social structure.* Washington, D.C.: American Anthropological Association. [Special Publication 6.]
Austin, J. L.
  1962   *How to do things with words.* Oxford: Clarendon Press.
Baal, J. van
  1977   *Geschiedenis en groei van de theorie der culturele anthropologie.* Leiden: Koninklijk Instituut voor Taal-, Land- en Volkenkunde, Bureau Indonesische Studiën.
Bachtiar Rifai
  1958   *Bentuk milik tanah dan tingkat kemakmuran; Penjelidikan pedesaan di daerah Pati, Djawa Tengah.* [Ph.D. thesis, Department of Agriculture, Universitas Indonesia, Bogor.]
Banks, David J.
  1972   'Changing kinship in north Malaya', *AA* 74:1254–75.
  1974   'Malay kinship terms and Morgan's Malayan terminology; The complexity of simplicity', *BKI* 130:44–68.
  1976   'Islam and inheritance in Malaya; Culture conflict or Islamic revolution?', *American Ethnologist* 3:573–86.
Banton, M. (ed.)
  1966   *The social anthropology of complex societies.* London: Tavistock. [ASA Monographs 4.]
Barnes, John A.
  1980   'Kinship studies; Some impressions of the current state of play', *Man (N.S.)* 15: 293–303.

Barton, R. F.
1949   *The Kalingas; Their institutions and custom law.* Chicago: University of Chicago Press.
1969   *Ifugao law.* Berkeley: University of California Press. [1st edition 1919.]
Benda-Beckmann, Keebet von
1981   'Forum shopping and shopping forums; Dispute processing in a Minangkabau village in West Sumatra', *Journal of Legal Pluralism* 19:117–59.
Benda-Beckmann, Keebet von, and Franz von Benda-Beckmann
1978   'Residence in a Minangkabau nagari', *Indonesia Circle* 15:6–17.
Berthe, L.
1965   'Aînés et cadets; L'Alliance et la hiérarchie chez les Baduj (Java occidental)', *L'Homme* 5 (3):189–223.
1970   'Parenté, pouvoir et mode de production; Éléments pour une typologie des sociétés agricoles de l'Indonésie', in: J. Pouillon and P. Maranda (eds), *Échanges et communications; Mélanges offerts à Claude Lévi-Strauss*, pp. 707–38. La Haye/Paris: Mouton.
Bertling, C. Tj.
1936   'Huwverbod op grond van verwantschapsposities in Middel-Java', *Indisch Tijdschrift van het Recht* 143:119–34.
Bloch, Maurice
1973   'The long term and the short term; The economic and political significance of the morality of kinship', in: Jack Goody (ed.), *The character of kinship*, pp. 75–87. London: Cambridge University Press.
1975   'Property and the end of affinity', in: Maurice Bloch (ed.), *Marxist analyses and social anthropology*, pp. 203–28. London: Malaby Press. [ASA Studies 2.]
1981   'Hierarchy and equality in Merina kinship', *Ethnos* 1–2:50–8.
Boissevain, Jeremy
1968   'The place of non-groups in the social sciences', *Man* (N.S.) 3:542–56.
Boon, James A.
1977   *The anthropological romance of Bali; 1597–1972.* Cambridge: Cambridge University Press. [Cambridge Studies in Cultural Systems 1.]
Bourdieu, P.
1977   *Outline of a theory of practice.* Cambridge: Cambridge University Press.
Burns, P. L.
1982   'Capitalism and the Malay states', in: Hamza Alavi *et al.* (eds), *Capitalism and colonial production*, pp. 159–78. London: Croom Helm.
Carsten, Janet
1987   'Analogues or opposites; Household and community in Pulau Langkawi, Malaysia', in: Charles Macdonald *et al.* (eds), *De la hutte au palais; Sociétés 'à maison' en Asie du Sud-Est insulaire*, pp. 153–6. Paris: CNRS.
Chayanov, A. V.
1966   *The theory of peasant economy* (ed. by D. Thorner, R. E. F. Smith and B. Kerblay). Homewood, Ill.: Richard D. Irwin for the American Economic Association.
Collingwood, R. G.
1945   *The idea of nature.* Oxford: Clarendon Press.
Conklin, Harold C.
1964   'Ethnogenealogical method', in: Ward H. Goodenough (ed.), *Explorations in cultural anthropology; Essays in honor of George Peter Murdock*, pp. 25–55. New York: McGraw-Hill.

Crain, Jay B.
    1970   *The Lun Dayeh of Sabah, East Malaysia; Aspects of marriage and social exchange.*
            [Ph.D. thesis, Cornell University, Ithaca.]
    1978   'The Lun Dayeh', in: V. T. King (ed.) 1978, pp. 123–42.
Davenport, William
    1959   'Nonunilinear descent and descent groups', AA 61:557–72.
Deegan, James L.
    1973   *Change among the Lun Bawang, a Borneo people.* [Ph.D. thesis, University of
            Washington.]
Dewey, Alice
    1962   *Peasant marketing in Java.* New York: The Free Press of Glencoe.
Dhofier, Z.
    1980   'Kinship and marriage among the Javanese Kyai', *Indonesia (Cornell)* 29:47–58.
Djamour, Judith
    1959   *Malay kinship and marriage in Singapore.* London: The Athlone Press. [London
            School of Economics Monographs on Social Anthropology 21.]
Douglas, Mary
    1969   'Is matriliny doomed in Africa?', in: M. Douglas and P. M. Kaberry (eds), *Man
            in Africa*, pp. 121–35. London: Tavistock.
Du Bois, Cora
    1960   *The people of Alor; A social-psychological study of an East Indian island.* Cam-
            bridge, Mass.: Harvard University Press. [1st edition 1944.]
Durkheim, Émile
    1964   *The division of labor in society.* New York: The Free Press of Glencoe. [1st French
            edition 1893.]
Eggan, Fred
    1967   'Some aspects of bilateral kinship systems in the northern Philippines', in: M. D.
            Zamora (ed.), *Studies in Philippine anthropology*, pp. 186–203. Quezon City:
            Alemar Phoenix.
Embree, John F.
    1950   'Thailand – a loosely structured social system', AA 52:181–93.
Emerson, Donald K.
    1984   '"Southeast Asia": What's in a name?', *Journal of Southeast Asian Studies* 15:
            1–21.
Evans-Pritchard, E. E.
    1937   *Witchcraft, oracles and magic among the Azande.* Oxford: Clarendon Press.
    1940   *The Nuer; A description of the modes of livelihood and political institutions of a
            Nilotic people.* Oxford: Clarendon Press.
    1956   *Nuer religion.* Oxford: Clarendon Press.
    1963   *The comparative method in social anthropology.* London: The Athlone Press. [L. T.
            Hobhouse Memorial Trust Lecture 33.]
Evers, Hans-Dieter (ed.)
    1980   *Sociology of South-East Asia; Readings on social change.* Kuala Lumpur: Oxford
            University Press
Fett, I.
    1983   'Women's land in Negeri Sembilan', in: L. Manderson (ed.), *Women's work and
            women's roles*, pp. 73–96. Canberra: Australia National University, Develop-
            ment Studies Centre. [Monograph 32.]

Firth, Raymond
    1957   'A note on descent groups in Polynesia', *Man* 57:4–8.
    1963   'Bilateral descent groups; An operational viewpoint', in: I. Shapira (ed.), *Studies in kinship and marriage*, pp. 22–7. London: Royal Anthropological Institute. [Occasional Paper 16.]
    1964   'Social organization and social change', in: *Essays on social organization and values*, pp. 30–58. London: The Athlone Press. [London School of Economics Monographs on Social Anthropology 17.]
Firth, Rosemary
    1966   *Housekeeping among Malay peasants*. London: The Athlone Press. [London School of Economics Monographs on Social Anthropology 7.] [1st edition 1943.]
Fleischer, Eberhard F.
    1881   *Was sucht man denn bei der Brust?* Köln: Lutscher.
Fortes, Meyer
    1970a   *Kinship and the social order*. London: Routledge and Kegan Paul
    1970b   'Kinship and the axiom of amity', in: *Kinship and the social order*, pp. 219–49. London: Routledge and Kegan Paul.
Fox, J. J.
    1986   'The ordering of generations; Change and continuity in Old Javanese kinship', in: D. G. Marr and A. C. Milner (eds), *Southeast Asia in the 9th to 14th centuries*, pp. 315–26. Singapore: Institute of South-East Asian Studies.
Fox, R.
    1967   *Kinship and marriage; An anthropological perspective*. Harmondsworth: Penguin.
Franke, R. W.
    1971   The Javanese Kangen family. [Unpubl. manuscript.]
Fraser, Thomas M.
    1960   *Rusembilan; A Malay fishing village in southern Thailand*. Ithaca: Cornell University Press.
Freedman, Maurice
    1970   'Introduction', in: Maurice Freedman (ed.), *Family and kinship in Chinese society*, pp. 5–17. Stanford: Stanford University Press.
Freeman, J. Derek
    1960   'The Iban of western Borneo', in: G. P. Murdock (ed.) 1960, pp. 65–87.
    1961   'On the concept of the kindred', *Journal of the Royal Anthropological Institute* 91: 192–220.
    1970   *Report on the Iban*. London: The Athlone Press. [London School of Economics Monographs on Social Anthropology 41.] [1st edition 1955.]
    1981   *Some reflections on the nature of Iban society*. Canberra: Department of Anthropology, Research School of Pacific Studies, Australian National University. [Occasional Paper of the Department of Anthropology.]
Fried, Morton
    1967   *The evolution of political society; An essay in political anthropology*. New York· Random House.
Fujimoto, A.
    1980   *Land tenure, rice production and income sharing among Malay peasants; A study of four villages*. [Ph.D. thesis, Flinders University of South Australia, Bedford Park.]

Gabel, N. O.
1970 'Interdigitalizing methodologies in the evaluation of Chomsky's competence and performance', *Seattle Studies in Medical Statistics* 5:27–56.

Geddes, William R.
1954 *The land Dyaks of Sarawak*. London: H.M.S.O. [Colonial Research Studies 14.]

Geertz, Clifford
1959a 'Form and variation in Balinese village structure', *AA* 61:991–1012.
1959b 'The Javanese village', in: G. W. Skinner (ed.), *Local, ethnic, and national loyalties in village Indonesia; A symposium*, pp. 34–41. New Haven: Yale University Southeast Asia Studies. [Cultural Report Series.]
1961 Review of 'Bali; studies in life, thought and ritual', *BKI* 117:498–502.
1962 'Studies in peasant life; Community and society,' in: Bernard Siegel (ed.), *Biennial Review of Anthropology 1961*, pp. 1–41. Stanford: Stanford University Press.
1963 *Agricultural involution; The processes of ecological change in Indonesia*. Berkeley: University of California Press.
1965 *The social history of an Indonesian town*. Cambridge, Mass.: MIT Press.
1973 'Thick description; Toward an interpretive theory of culture', in: *The interpretation of cultures*, pp. 3–30. New York: Basic Books.

Geertz, Hildred
1961 *The Javanese family; A study of kinship and socialization*. New York: The Free Press of Glencoe.

Geertz, Hildred and Clifford Geertz
1975 *Kinship in Bali*. Chicago: University of Chicago Press.

Gellner, E.
1970 'Concepts and society,' in: B. R. Wilson (ed.), *Rationality*, pp. 18–49. Oxford: Basil Blackwell.

Gibbs Jr., J. L.
1965 'Social organization', in: Sol Tax (ed.), *Horizons of anthropology*, pp. 160–70. London: Allen and Unwin.

Gibson, Thomas
1986 *Sacrifice and sharing in the Philippine highlands; Religion and society among the Buhid of Mindoro*. London: The Athlone Press.

Godelier, Maurice
1973 *Horizon; Trajets marxistes en anthropologie*. Paris: Maspéro.

Gonda, J.
1952 *Sanskrit in Indonesia*. Nagpur: International Academy of Indian Culture.
1970 *Visnuism and Sivaism; A comparison*. London: The Athlone Press.

Gonzales, M. A.
1965 'The Ilongo kinship system and terminology', *Philippine Sociological Review* 13: 23–31.

Goodenough, Ward H.
1955 'A problem in Malayo-Polynesian social organization', *AA* 57:71–83.
1961 Review of G. P. Murdock (ed.), 'Social structure in Southeast Asia', *AA* 63: 1341–6.

Goodman, N.
1978 *Ways of worldmaking*. Hassocks, Sussex: Harvester Press.

Goody, Jack R.
   1965   Review of G. P. Murdock (ed.), 'Social structure in Southeast Asia', *Man* 65:
          61–2.
Goody, Jack, Joan Thirsk and E. P. Thompson
   1976   *Family and inheritance; Rural society in Western Europe, 1200–1800*. Cambridge:
          Cambridge University Press.
Gourou, P.
   1936   *Les paysans du delta tonkinois*. Paris: Éditions d'art et d'histoire.
Gudeman, S. and M. Penn
   1982   'Models, meaning and reflexivity', in: D. J. Parkin (ed.), *Semantic anthropology*,
          pp. 89–106. London: Academic Press. [ASA Monograph 22.]
Gullick, J. M.
   1951   'The Negri Sembilan economy of the 1890s', *JMBRAS* 24 (1):38–55.
   1958   *Indigenous political systems of western Malaya*. London: The Athlone Press.
          [London School of Economics Monographs on Social Anthropology 17.]
Haar, Bernard ter
   1923   'Losse aantekeningen over adatrecht', *Adatrechtbundel* 22:219–21.
   1962   *Adat law in Indonesia*. Djakarta: Bhratara. [1st Dutch edition 1940.]
Hammel, E. A.
   1968   *Alternative social structures and ritual relations in the Balkans*. Englewood Cliffs,
          N.J.: Prentice-Hall. [Anthropology of Modern Societies Series.]
Harrison, Robert
   1971   *An analysis of the variation among Ranau Dusun communities of Sabah, Malaysia*.
          [Ph.D. thesis, Columbia University, New York.]
Hart, D. V.
   1977   *Compadrinazgo; Ritual kinship in the Philippines*. DeKalb: Northern Illinois Uni-
          versity Press.
Hirokoshi, Hiroko
   1976   *A traditional leader in a time of change; The 'Kyai' and 'Ulama' in West Java*. [Ph.D.
          thesis, University of Illinois at Urbana-Champaign.]
Hirsch, E.
   1967   *Validity in interpretation*. New Haven: Yale University Press.
Hobart, Mark
   1974   'Are aristocrats pigs? Some Balinese uses of animal symbolism', *Indonesia Circle*
          5:18–20.
   1977   Review of H. and C. Geertz, 'Kinship in Bali', *Bulletin of the School of Oriental
          and African Studies* 40:195–7.
   1979   *A Balinese village and its field of social relations*. [Ph.D. thesis, University of
          London.]
   1983   'Through western eyes; or, How my Balinese neighbour became a duck', *Indone-
          sia Circle* 22:33–47.
   1985a 'Is god evil?', in: D. J. Parkin (ed.), *The anthropology of evil*, pp. 165–93. Oxford:
          Basil Blackwell.
   1985b 'Texte est un con', in: R. H. Barnes, D. de Coppet and D. J. Parkin (eds),
          Contexts and levels; Essays on hierarchy, pp. 33–53. Oxford: JASO. [JASO
          Occasional Paper 4.]
Holleman, F.
   1919   'Gegevens over Kediri', *Adatrechtbundel* 18:139–67.
   1921   'Nadere gegevens over Kediri', *Adatrechtbundel* 19:208–21.

Hollnsteiner, M. R.
  1963   *The dynamics of power in a Philippine municipality.* Quezon City: University of the Philippines.

Hooker, M. B.
  1972   *Adat law in modern Malaya.* Kuala Lumpur: Oxford University Press.

Horii, Kenzo
  1972   'The land tenure system of Malay padi farmers; A case study of Kampong Sungei Bujor in the state of Kedah', *The Developing Economies* 10:45–73.

Howe, L. E. A.
  1980   *Pujing; An investigation into the foundations of Balinese culture.* [Ph.D. thesis, Edinburgh University.]

Hsien, V. and A. Weiss
  1954   'Volkommenheit und die Zwischenbrustwärze-entfernung', *Leipziger Beiträge zur Anthropometrie* 13:173–210.

Hudson, A. B.
  1967   *Padju Epat; The ethnography and social structure of a Ma'anjan Dajak group in Southeastern Borneo.* [Ph.D. thesis, Cornell University, Ithaca.]
  1972   *Paju Epat; The Ma'anyan of Indonesian Borneo.* New York: Holt, Rinehart and Winston. [Case Studies in Cultural Anthropology.]

Hudson, A. B. and Judith M. Hudson
  1978   'The Ma'anyan of Paju Epat', in: V. T. King (ed.) 1978, pp. 215–32.

Hüsken, Frans
  1979   'Landlords, sharecroppers and agricultural labourers; Changing labour relations in rural Java', *Journal of Contemporary Asia* 9:140–51.
  1988   *Een dorp op Java; Sociale differentiatie in een boerengemeenschap, 1850–1980.* Overveen: Acasea.
  1989   'Cycles of commercialization and accumulation in a Central Javanese village', in: G. Hart *et al.* (eds), *Agrarian transformations; Local processes and the state in Southeast Asia*, pp. 303–31. Berkeley: University of California Press.

Inden, R.
  1976   *Marriage and rank in Bengali culture.* Berkeley: University of California Press.

Inden, R. and R. W. Nicholas
  1977   *Kinship in Bengali culture.* Chicago: Chicago University Press.

Iskandar, T.
  1970   *Kamus Dewan.* Kuala Lumpur: Dewan Bahasa dan Pustaka, Kementerian Pelajaran.

Jaspan, M. A.
  1964   *From patriliny to matriliny; Structural change among the Redjang of Southwest Sumatra.* [Ph.D. thesis, Australian National University, Canberra.]

Jay, Robert R.
  1969   *Javanese villagers; Social relations in rural Modjokuto.* Cambridge, Mass.: MIT Press.

Jocano, F. L.
  1983   *The Hiligaynons; An ethnography of family and community life in Western Bisayas region.* Quezon City: University of the Philippines.

Jomo Sundaram
  1977   *Class formation in Malaysia.* [Ph.D. thesis, Harvard University, Boston.]

Josselin de Jong, J. P. B. de
  1977 'The Malay archipelago as a field of ethnological study', in: P. E. de Josselin de
        Jong (ed.), *Structural anthropology in the Netherlands*, pp. 166–82. The Hague:
        Nijhoff. [KITLV, Translation Series 17.] [1st Dutch edition 1935.]

Josselin de Jong, P. E. de
  1952 *Minangkabau and Negri Sembilan; Socio-political structure in Indonesia.* The
        Hague: Nijhoff.
  1960 'Islam versus adat in Negri Sembilan (Malaya)', *BKI* 116:158–203.
  1985 'The relevance of Minangkabau studies for anthropological theory', in: L. L.
        Thomas and F. von Benda-Beckmann (eds) 1985, pp. 19–29.

Kahar bin Bador, A.
  1970 *Political authority and leadership in Malay society in Perak, Malaysia.* Tokyo: Insti-
        tute of Developing Economies. [V.R.F. Series 5.]

Kahn, Joel S.
  1980 *Minangkabau social formations; Indonesian peasants and the world-economy.* Cam-
        bridge: Cambridge University Press. [Cambridge Studies in Social Anthropo-
        logy 30.]

Kato, T.
  1982 *Matriliny and migration; Evolving Minangkabau traditions in Indonesia.* Ithaca:
        Cornell University Press.

Kaufman, Howard Keva
  1960 *Bangkhuad; A community study in Thailand.* Locust Valley, N.Y.: Augustin.
        [Monographs of the Association for Asian Studies 10.]

Kemp, Jeremy H.
  1976 *Social organization of a hamlet in Phitsanulok Province, North-Central Thailand.*
        [Ph.D. thesis, University of London.]
  1978 'Cognatic descent and the generation of social stratification in Southeast Asia',
        BKI 134:63–83.
  1982 'Kinship and locality in Hua Kok', *Journal of the Siam Society* 70:100–13.
  1983 'Kinship and the management of personal relations; Kin terminologies and the
        "axiom of amity"', *BKI* 139:81–98.
  1984 'The manipulation of personal relationships; From kinship to patron-clientage',
        in: Han ten Brummelhuis and Jeremy H. Kemp (eds), *Strategies and struc-
        tures in Thai society*, pp. 55–69. Amsterdam: Universiteit van Amsterdam,
        Antropologisch-Sociologisch Centrum. [ZZOA Publikaties 31.]

Keyes, Charles F.
  1975 'Kin groups in a Thai-Lao community', in: G. William Skinner and A. Thomas
        Kirsch (eds), *Change and persistence in Thai society*, pp. 274–97. Ithaca: Cornell
        University Press.

King, Victor T.
  1974 'Maloh social structure', in: J. Rousseau (ed.), *The peoples of Central Borneo*,
        pp. 203–27. Kuching: Sarawak Museum. [Sarawak Museum Journal, Special
        Issue.]
  1976 'Conceptual and analytical problems in the study of the kindred', in: G. N.
        Appell (ed.) 1976, pp. 121–45.

King, Victor T. (ed.)
  1978 *Essays on Borneo societies.* London: Oxford University Press. [Hull Monographs
        on South-East Asia 7.]

Koentjaraningrat, R. M.
1957   A preliminary description of the Javanese kinship system. New Haven: Yale University Southeast Asia Studies. [Cultural Report Series.]
1960   'The Javanese of South Central Java', in: G. P. Murdock (ed.) 1960, pp. 88–115.
1961   Some social-anthropological observations on gotong rojong practices in two villages of Central Java. Ithaca: Cornell University, Modern Indonesia Project. [Monograph Series.]
1967   'Tjelapar; A village in Java', in: R. M. Koentjaraningrat (ed.), Villages in Indonesia, pp. 244–80. Ithaca: Cornell University Press.
1968   'Javanese data on the unresolved problems of the kindred', Ethnology 7:53–8.
1975   Anthropology in Indonesia. The Hague: Nijhoff. [KITLV, Bibliographical Series 8.]
Kratoska, Paul H.
1982   'Rice cultivation and the ethnic division of labor in British Malaya', Comparative Studies in Society and History 24:280–314.
Kroeber, A. L.
1948   Anthropology. New York: Harcourt/Brace.
Kuchiba, Masuo and Yoshihiro Tsubouchi
1968   'Cooperation patterns in a Malay village', Asian Survey 8:836–41.
Kuhn, T. S.
1977   The essential tension. Chicago: Chicago University Press.
Kuper, A.
1982   'Lineage theory; A critical retrospect', Annual Review of Anthropology 11:71–95.
Lansing, John Stephen
1974   Evil in the morning of the world; Phenomenological approaches to a Balinese community. Ann Arbor: University of Michigan Center for South and Southeast Asian Studies. [Michigan Papers on South and Southeast Asia 6.]
Larson, G. J.
1980   'Karma as a "sociology of knowledge" or "social psychology" of process/praxis', in: W. D. O'Flaherty (ed.) 1980, pp. 303–16.
Leach, Edmund R.
1950   Social science research in Sarawak. London: H.M.S.O.
1958   'Concerning Trobriand clans and the kinship category "tabu"', in: Jack Goody (ed.), The developmental cycle in domestic groups, pp. 120–45. Cambridge: Cambridge University Press. [Cambridge Papers in Social Anthropology 1.]
1960   'The Sinhalese of the dry zone of northern Ceylon', in: G. P. Murdock (ed.) 1960, pp. 116–26.
1961   Pul Eliya; A village in Ceylon. Cambridge: Cambridge University Press.
1962   'On certain unconsidered aspects of double descent systems', Man 62:130–4.
1970   Political systems of Highland Burma. London: The Athlone Press. [London School of Economics Monographs on Social Anthropology 44.] [1st edition 1954.]
Lee, George
1973   'Commodity production and reproduction amongst the Malayan peasantry', Journal of Contemporary Asia 3:441–56.
Leur, J. C. van
1955   Indonesian trade and society; Essays in Asian social and economic history. The Hague: Van Hoeve. [1st Dutch edition 1934.]

Lévi-Strauss, Claude
  1969 *The elementary structures of kinship.* Boston: Beacon Press. [1st French edition 1949.]
Lienhardt, Godfrey
  1961 *Divinity and experience.* Oxford: Clarendon Press.
Lim Teck Ghee
  1977 *Peasants and their agricultural economy in colonial Malaya, 1874–1941.* Kuala Lumpur: Oxford University Press.
Little, M. and E. S. Moe
  1977 'Puberty and the end of infinity', *Bulletin de Logique Occidental et Cahiers Herméneutiques* 3:1–25.
Long, B. J.
  1980 'The concepts of human action and rebirth in the Mahabharata', in: W. D. O'Flaherty (ed.) 1980, pp. 38–60.
Maine, Sir Henry
  1917 *Ancient law.* London: Everyman's Library. [1st edition 1861.]
Massard, Josiane
  1981 *Rapport à l'environment et réseaux d'échange dans un village malais.* [Ph.D. thesis, École des Hautes Études en Sciences Sociales, Paris.]
  1983 'Le don d'enfants dans la société malaise', *L'Homme* 23:101–14.
McCoy, A. W.
  1982 'A queen dies slowly; The rise and decline of Iloilo City', in: A. W. McCoy and Ed. C. de Jesus (eds), *Philippine social history; Global trade and local transformation*, pp. 297–358. Quezon City: Ateneo de Manila University Press. [Asian Studies Association of Australia, Southeast Asia Publications Series 7.]
Meillassoux, C.
  1981 *Maidens, meal and money; Capitalism and the domestic community.* Cambridge: Cambridge University Press.
Metcalf, Peter
  1976a 'Berawan mausoleums', *Sarawak Museum Journal* 24:121–36.
  1976b 'Who are the Berawan? Ethnic classification and the distribution of secondary treatment of the dead in central-north Borneo', *Oceania* 47:35–105.
Miles, Douglas
  1970 'The Ngadju Dayaks of Central Kalimantan with special reference to the Upper Mentaya', *Behavior Science Notes* 5:291–319.
  1971 'Ngadju kinship and social change on the Upper Mentaya', in: L. R. Hiatt and C. Jayawardena (eds), *Anthropology in Oceania*, pp. 36–51. Sydney: Angus and Robertson.
Mintz, Sydney
  1966 'Canamelar; The subculture of a rural sugar plantation proletariat', in: J. Steward (ed.), *The people of Puerto Rico*, pp. 314–41. DeKalb: University of Illinois Press.
Mitchell, William L.
  1963 'Theoretical problems in the concept of the kindred', *AA* 65:343–54.
Mohamad Shadli Abdullah
  1978 The relationship of the kinship system to land tenure; A case study of Kg. G.R. [M.A. thesis, Universiti Sains Malaysia, Penang.]

Morris, H. S.
  1953   *Report on a Melanau sago producing community in Sarawak.* London: H.M.S.O. [Colonial Research Studies 9.]
  1976   'A problem of land tenure', in: G. N. Appell (ed.) 1976, pp. 110–20.
  1978   'The coastal Melanau', in: V. T. King (ed.) 1978, pp. 37–58.
Moubray, George Alexander de Chazal de
  1931   *Matriarchy in the Malay Peninsula and neighbouring countries.* London: Routledge.
Murdock, George P.
  1949   *Social structure.* New York: Macmillan.
  1960   'Cognatic forms of social organization', in: G. P. Murdock (ed.) 1960, pp. 1–14.
  1964   'The kindred', AA 66:129–31.
Murdock, George P. (ed.)
  1960   *Social structure in Southeast Asia.* Chicago: Quadrangle Books. [Viking Publications in Anthropology 29.]
Murphy, R.
  1983   'The struggle for scholarly recognition; The development of the closure concept in sociology', *Theory and Society* 12:603–30.
Nagata, Judith A.
  1976   'Kinship and social mobility among the Malays', *Man (N.S.)* 11:400–9.
Needham, Rodney
  1966   'Age, category, and descent', BKI 122:1–35.
  1971   'Remarks on the analysis of kinship and marriage', in: Rodney Needham (ed.) 1971, pp. 1–34. London: Tavistock.
  1975   'Polythetic classification; Convergence and consequences', *Man (N.S.)* 10:349–69.
  1976   'Skulls and causality', *Man (N.S.)* 11:71–88.
  1979   *Symbolic classification.* Santa Monica: Goodyear.
Needham, Rodney (ed.)
  1971   *Rethinking kinship and marriage.* London: Tavistock. [ASA Monograph 11.]
Norhalim bin Haji Ibrahim
  1976   Social change and continuity in the matrilineal society of Rembau, Negeri Sembilan. [M.A. thesis, University of Hull.]
O'Flaherty, W. D. (ed.)
  1980   *Karma and rebirth in classical Indian tradition.* Berkeley: University of California Press.
Ossenbrugge, F. D. E. van
  1918   'De oorsprong van het Javaansche begrip montja-pat in verband met primitieve classificaties', *Verslagen en mededeelingen der Koninklijke Akademie van Wetenschappen, Afdeling Letterkunde* 5(3):6–44.
Palmier, Leslie H.
  1960   *Social status and power in Java.* London: The Athlone Press. [London School of Economics Monographs on Social Anthropology 20.]
Pandam Guritno
  1958   *Masjarakat Marangan; Sebuah laporan sosiografi ketjamatan Prambanan, daerah istimewa Jogjakarta.* Jogjakarta: Universitas Gadjah Mada.
Parkin, F.
  1979   *Marxism and class theory; A bourgeois critique.* London: Tavistock.

Parr, C. W. C. and W. H. Mackray
   1910 'Rembau, one of the nine states; Its history, constitution and customs', *Journal of the Straits Branch, Royal Asiatic Society* 56:1–157.
Peranio, Roger D.
   1977 *The structure of Bisaya society; A ranked cognatic social system.* [Ph.D. thesis, Columbia University, New York.]
Pertabalan
   1975 *Pertabalan kebawah duli Yang Maha Sultan Haji Ahmad Shah [...].* Kuantan, Pahang: Pahang Properties.
Phillips, N.
   1981 *Sijobang sung narrative poetry of West Sumatra.* Cambridge: Cambridge University Press. [Cambridge Studies in Oral and Literate Cultures 1.]
Potter, Jack M.
   1976 *Thai peasant social structure.* Chicago: University of Chicago Press.
Potter, K.
   1980 'The karma theory and its interpretation in some Indian philosophical systems', in: W. D. O'Flaherty (ed.) 1980, pp. 241–67.
Prindiville, J. C. J.
   n.d. Food, form and forum; Minangkabau women as culinary communicators. [Unpubl. manuscript.]
Quine, W. V. O.
   1953 'Two dogmas of empiricism', in: *From a logical point of view*, pp. 20–46. London: Harvard University Press.
   1960 *Word and object.* Cambridge, Mass.: MIT Press.
Radcliffe-Brown, A. R.
   1950 'Introduction', in: A. R. Radcliffe-Brown and C. D. Forde (eds), *African systems of kinship and marriage*, pp. 1–85. London: Oxford University Press.
   1952 *Structure and function in primitive society.* London: Cohen and West.
Rassers, W. H.
   1959 *Panji, the culture hero; A structural study of religion in Java.* The Hague: Nijhoff. [KITLV, Translation Series 3.] [1st Dutch edition 1922.]
Redfield, Robert
   1960 *The little community and peasant society and culture.* Chicago: University of Chicago Press. [Phoenix Books.]
Rein-Dreque, O. U. I.
   1976 'Pourquoi croire le I.B.G.?', *Montréal Medicine* 17:1011–34.
Riley, James N.
   1972 *Family organization and population dynamics in a Central Thai village.* [Ph.D. thesis, University of North Carolina, Chapel Hill.]
Rousseau, Jérome
   1974 *The social organization of the Baluy Kayan.* [Ph.D. thesis, University of Cambridge.]
   1978 'The Kayan', in: V. T. King (ed.) 1978, pp. 78–91.
   1979 'Kayan stratification', *Man (N.S.)* 14:215–36.
Rutten, Rosanne
   1982 *Women workers of hacienda Milagros; Wage labor and household subsistence on a Philippine sugarcane plantation.* Amsterdam: Universiteit van Amsterdam, Antropologisch-Sociologisch Centrum. [ZZOA Publikaties 30.]

Sahlins, Marshall
  1963 Remarks on 'Social structure in Southeast Asia', *Journal of the Polynesian Society* 78:39–50.
  1974 *Stone age economics.* London: Tavistock.
Sather, Clifford A.
  1967 'Social rank and marriage payments in an immigrant Moro community in Malaysia', *Ethnology* 6:97–102.
  1971 *Kinship and domestic relations among the Bajau Laut of northern Sabah.* [Ph.D. thesis, Harvard University, Cambridge, Mass.]
  1976 'Kinship and contiguity; Variation in social alignments among the Semporna Bajau Laut', in: G. N. Appell (ed.) 1976, pp. 40–65.
  1978 'The Bajau Laut', in: V. T. King (ed.) 1978, pp. 172–92.
Schneider, David
  1968 *American kinship; A cultural account.* New Jersey: Prentice-Hall
  1972 'What is kinship all about?', in: Priscilla Reining (ed.), *Kinship studies in the Morgan centennial year*, pp. 32–63. Washington, D.C.: The Anthropological Society of Washington.
Schneider, David M. and Kathleen Gough
  1961 *Matrilineal kinship.* Berkeley: University of California Press.
Schneider, William
  1974 *Social organization of the Selako Dayaks of Borneo.* [Ph.D. thesis, University of North Carolina, Chapel Hill.]
  1978 'The Selako Dayak', in: V. T. King (ed.) 1978, pp. 59–77.
Schulte Nordholt, N. G.
  1981 *Opbouw in opdracht of ontwikkeling in overleg?* [Ph.D. thesis, Vrije Universiteit, Amsterdam.]
Scott, James C.
  1976 *The moral economy of the peasant; Rebellion and subsistence in Southeast Asia.* New Haven: Yale University Press.
Searle, J. R.
  1971 'What is a speech act?', in: J. R. Searle (ed.), *The philosophy of language*, pp. 39–53. Oxford: Oxford University Press.
Sharp, Lauriston and Lucien M. Hanks
  1978 *Bang Chan; Social history of a rural community in Thailand.* Ithaca: Cornell University Press.
Sharp, Lauriston, Hazel M. Hauck, Kamol Janlekha and Robert B. Textor
  1953 *Siamese rice village; A preliminary study of Bangchan 1948–1949.* Bangkok: Cornell Research Center.
Sibley, W. E.
  1957 'Work partner choice in a Philippine village', *Silliman Journal* 4:196–206.
Sjafri Sairin
  1982 *The Javanese Trah; Kin-based social organization.* Yogyakarta: Gadjah Mada University Press.
Skinner, G. W.
  1964 'Marketing and social structure in rural China, part 1', *Journal of Asian Studies* 24:3–43.
Stevenson, H. N. C.
  1968 *The economics of the Central Chin tribes.* Farnborough, Hants.: Gregg Press. [1st edition 1943.]

Stivens, Maila
    1984 'Women, kinship and capitalist development', in: Kate Young, Carol Wolkowitz
          and Roslyn McCullogh (eds), *Of marriage and the market; Women's subordination
          in international perspective*, pp. 178–92. London: Routledge and Kegan Paul.
    1985 *Sexual politics in Rembau; Gender, matriliny and agrarian change in Negeri Sembi-
          lan, Malaysia.* Canterbury: Centre of South-East Asian Studies, University of
          Kent. [Occasional Paper 5.]
Swift, Michael G.
    1965 *Malay peasant society in Jelebu.* London: The Athlone Press. [London School of
          Economics Monographs on Social Anthropology 29.]
Tambiah, Stanley J.
    1973 'From varna to caste through mixed unions', in: J. R. Goody (ed.), *The character
          of kinship*, pp. 191–229. Cambridge: Cambridge University Press.
Tanner, Nancy
    1974 'Matrifocality in Indonesia and Africa and among black Americans', in: M.
          Rosaldo and L. Lamphere (eds), *Women, culture and society*, pp. 129–56. Palo
          Alto: Stanford University Press.
    1982 'The nuclear family in Minangkabau matriliny; Mirror of disputes', *BKI* 138:
          129–51.
Taylor, E. N.
    1929 'The customary law of Rembau', *JMBRAS* 7:14–55.
    1948 'Inheritance in Negri Sembilan', *JMBRAS* 21:41–130.
Thomas, Lynn L. and Franz von Benda-Beckmann (eds)
    1985 *Change and continuity in Minangkabau; Local, regional, and historical perspectives
          on West Sumatra.* Athens, Ohio: Ohio University Center for International
          Studies. [Monographs in International Studies, Southeast Asia Series 71.]
Tönnies, Ferdinand
    1963 *Community and society.* New York: Harper Torchbooks. [1st German edition
          1887.]
Tsubouchi, Yoshihiro
    1976 'Islam and divorce among Malay peasants', in: Shinichi Ichimura (ed.), *South-
          east Asia; Nature, society and development*, pp. 24–43. Honolulu: The University
          Press of Hawaii.
Ukun Suryaman
    n.d. *Tempat pemakaian istilah klasifikasi kekerabatan pada orang Djawa dan Sunda
          dalam susunan masjarakat.* Jogjakarta: Penerbitan Universitas.
Vitebsky, P. G.
    1982 *Dialogues with the dead; The experience of mortality and its discussion among the
          Sora of Central India.* [Ph.D. thesis, University of London.]
Vollenhoven, C. van
    1918–1933 *Het adatrecht van Nederlandsch-Indië.* Leiden: Brill. [3 vols.]
Weber, M.
    1922 *Wirtschaft und Gesellschaft.* Tübingen: Mohr.
Whittier, H. L.
    1973 *Social organization and symbols of social differentiation; An ethnographic study of
          the Kenyah Dayak of East Kalimantan (Borneo).* [Ph.D. thesis, Michigan State
          University, Ann Arbor.]
    1978 'The Kenyah', in: V. T. King (ed.) 1978, pp. 92–122.

Wiersma, J.
   1982   *Loonacties van hacienda arbeiders; Strijd voor betere arbeidsvoorwaarden in een 'upland' suikerdistrict in Negros Occidental, Filippijnen, 1972–1980.* Amsterdam: Vakgroep Zuid- en Zuidoost-Azië, Universiteit van Amsterdam. [Working Paper 15.]
Wilder, William D.
   1982   *Communication, social structure and development in rural Malaysia; A study of kampung Kuala Bera.* London: The Athlone Press. [London School of Economics Monographs on Social Anthropology 56.]
Wilkinson, R. J.
   1932   *A Malay–English dictionary (romanized).* Mytilene: Salavopoulos and Kinderlis.
Williams, Thomas Rhys
   1965   *The Dusun; A North Borneo society.* New York: Holt, Rinehart and Winston. [Case Studies in Cultural Anthropology.]
Wilson, Peter J.
   1967   *A Malay village and Malaysia; Social values and rural development.* New Haven: HRAF Press.
Wittgenstein, L.
   1969   *The blue and brown books; Preliminary studies from the 'Philosophical investigations'.* Oxford: Basil Blackwell.
Wolf, Eric R.
   1966   'Kinship, friendship, and patron–client relations in complex societies', in: Michael Banton (ed.), *The social anthropology of complex societies,* pp. 1–22. London: Tavistock. [ASA Monographs 4.]
Wolters, Willem G.
   1983   *Politics, patronage and class conflict in Central Luzon.* The Hague: Institute of Social Studies. [Research Report Series 14.]
Wong, David S. Y.
   1975   *Tenure and land dealings in the Malay states.* Singapore: Singapore University Press.
Yanagisako, S.
   1979   'Family and household; The analysis of domestic groups', *Annual Review of Anthropology* 8:161–205.
Zderzaki, C. Y. C.
   1969   *Rowek miedzy persiami w perspektywie porownanwczej.* Cracow: University of Cracow. [University of Cracow Occasional Studies in Anthropometry 7.]

Index